Reading Chaucer

An Interlinear Translation of Selections in
The Norton Anthology of English Literature

EIGHTH EDITION

Translated by Larry D. Benson
HARVARD UNIVERSITY

Compiled by

Alfred David
EMERITUS, INDIANA UNIVERSITY

James Simpson
HARVARD UNIVERSITY

W · W · NORTON & COMPANY • *New York* • *London*

ISBN 0-393-92914-0

W. W. Norton & Company, Inc., 500 Fifth Avenue, New York, N.Y. 10110
www.wwnorton.com

W. W. Norton & Company Ltd., Castle House, 75/76 Wells Street, London WIT 3QT

Contents

A Guide to Chaucer's Language

by ALFRED DAVID *and* JAMES SIMPSON

Before we can enjoy texts of any kind, we need to be able to understand their prose meaning. For many periods of writing in English that is unproblematic. In the case of texts written either long ago or far away, the form of English might, however, be unfamiliar, and so requires a certain attention. This brief guide offers some simple ways into rapid understanding of the form of English in which Chaucer wrote. An interlinear translation of the Chaucerian texts in this anthology follows the guide. This translation might help you get some bearings on the basic sense of Chaucer's poetry, but do bear these points in mind: (i) that the sense of Chaucer's original language is not at all difficult to grasp; and (ii) that you will enjoy Chaucer's poetry much more through sustained contact with the original. The translations, then, are not offered as an alternative to, so much as a way into the original texts.

Chaucer wrote about six hundred years ago, in one dialect of the type of English known as Middle English. Middle English comprises the many geographically and temporally differing forms of English written between around 1100 and 1500; Chaucer (1343–1400) wrote in the dialect characteristic of both London and the east Midlands of England. The following suggestions are arranged into a graded series of steps designed to facilitate a rapid grasp of Chaucer's language. The steps follow in this order: listening; unfamiliar vocabulary; unfamiliar grammatical forms.

Listening

You might begin by hearing Chaucer's verse recited (at, for example, <wwnorton.com/nael/noa/audio.htm>). You might recite some lines yourself, in imitation of the audio recordings. The quickest way to real possession of any text is to impress it on your inner ear by reading aloud, or by learning a section by heart; you thereby gain familiarity with its meter and rhythms. If you wanted to learn more about the sounds of Middle English, you could visit the Harvard Chaucer website, at <courses.fas.harvard.edu/~chaucer/teachslf/less-2.htm>. By far the simplest way to reproduce the sounds of Middle English is, however, to imitate a reading by a practiced reader. You might even learn a few lines off by heart. For the principles of Chaucerian meter, see the Introduction to The Middle Ages ("Old and Middle English Prosody").

1

Listening familiarity actually resolves many problems of prose meaning, since words that seem unfamiliar quickly become recognizable once heard rather than merely seen. Even with that familiarity some difficulties of comprehension will remain. They are of two kinds: unfamiliar vocabulary; and unfamiliar grammatical endings ("inflections") on words.

Unfamiliar Vocabulary

The following classes of Chaucerian vocabulary require some attention:

(i)   words with the same meaning as their modern equivalents but whose forms are slightly different from the modern spellings;

(ii)   words whose form might be familiar but whose sense has changed over time; and

(iii) words that have simply dropped out of usage in the intervening six hundred years.

(i) Words whose Chaucerian and modern meanings are pretty much the same, despite different spellings, are easily mastered. Simply listen and look at the word, and try to hear or see its modern equivalent. In the *Miller's Tale* reading at <wwnorton.com/nael/noa/audio.htm>, for example, the word "wrastling" at line 550 is clearly our word "wrestling."

(ii) Words whose form looks familiar but whose sense has changed are known as "false friends": they look familiar but hide different meanings. The common Chaucerian word "nice," for example, means "silly, foolish." You have to be on the lookout for these (a warning signal might be that application of the modern sense provides an odd overall meaning of a line). One quickly gathers a small collection of frequently occurring examples of such words.

(iii) Words that have dropped out of usage are easy to spot, since a modern speaker simply doesn't understand them. Some of these words might have recognizable cousins in other European languages (especially French) you might know, in which case you will be able to recognize them. Otherwise they need to be learned. There aren't so many of them in Chaucer's dialect, however, precisely because that dialect was the basis for what became a national and international standard. A few hours reading Chaucer will produce a collection of repeated and easily absorbed examples.

Unfamiliar Grammatical Forms

Middle English indicates the grammatical function of words not only by word order (as in Modern English), but also by the endings on words (i.e., "inflections"). Modern English also does this (e.g., in the different endings on verbs), but Middle English does it to a greater extent, and on a slightly wider range of parts of speech. The following discussion of inflections is divided into parts of speech. The parts of speech in English are as follows: nouns, pronouns, adjectives, verbs, adverbs, conjunctions, prepositions, and interjections. The following presentation is restricted to those parts of speech with significant inflections.

1. NOUNS

The plural and possessive of nouns end in *es*, formed by adding *s* or *es* to the singular: *knight, knightes; root, rootes*. A final consonant is frequently doubled before *es*: *bed, beddes*. A common alternative plural is *–en*, as in *yën*, from *yë*, *eye*. The Prioress has "ÿen greye as glas" (*General Prologue*, 152), "eyes as gray as glass." Plurals in *–en* survive in a few modern English words, e.g., *oxen*.

2. PRONOUNS

The chief comparisons with Modern English are as follows:

Modern English	East Midlands Middle English
I	*I, ich* (*ik* is a northern form)
you (singular)	*thou* (subjective); *thee* (objective)
her	*hir(e), her(e)*
its	*his*
you (plural)	*ye* (subjective); *you* (objective)
they	*they*
their	*hir* (*their* is a Northern form)
them	*hem* (*them* is a Northern form)

In formal speech, the second person plural is often used for the singular. The possessive adjectives *my, thy* take *n* before a word beginning with a vowel or *h*: *thyn yë, myn host*.

The singular second person, *thou* and *thee*, were commonly used between friends, intimates, and commoners (as French *tu* and German *du* are still so used today in distinction with the plural second person *vous* and *sie*). Middle and Early Modern English still had this social distinction. Thus the Host respectfully invites the Monk to follow the Knight's tale (*Miller's Prologue*, 10): "Now telleth ye, sire Monk, if that ye conne." But after the drunken Miller interrupts and foils the Host's effort to call on the tellers in order of rank, the Host bitterly concedes: "Tel on, a devele way / Thou art a fool; thy wit is overcome" (26–27). In the tale itself, the clerk and the carpenter's wife address each other with the familiar "thou" and "thee." In the *Nun's Priest's Tale*, on the other hand, the noble rooster and his favorite hen address each other in the formal plural: " 'Herte dere, / What aileth you to grone in this manere? / Ye been a verray slepere, fy for shame!'/ And he answerde and saide thus, 'Madame, / I praye you that ye take it nat agrief' " (69–73).

The possessive form of the neuter is still identical with the masculine *his*. Thus, according to the marginal gloss *its*, "April" (*General Prologue*, 1) is not being personified, nor is the sun which "Hath in the ram his halve cours yronne" (*General Prologue*, 5).

The subject form of the second person plural is *ye* as in Chaucer's apology to his audience, "My wit is short, ye may wel understonde" (*General Prologue*, 748), or the Host's address to the pilgrims: "Ye goon to Canterbury" (*General Prologue*, 771).

The possessive form of the third person plural is *hir* in Chaucer's dialect, as when he tells how he joined the company of pilgrims at the Tabard: "I was of hir felaweshipe anoon" (*General Prologue*, 32). The northern dialect of Robert Henryson already had the modern form, as in *The Cock and the Fox*: "in their kindes natural" (p. 457, line 3).

The object form of the third person plural in Chaucer is *hem*, as in the pilgrims seeking St. Thomas "that hem hath holpen whan that they were seke" (*General Prologue*, 18) or as Chaucer had "spoken with hem everichoon" (*General Prologue*, 31).

3. ADJECTIVES

Adjectives ending in a consonant add final *e* when they stand before the noun they modify and after another modifying word such as *the, this, that*, or nouns or pronouns in the possessive: *a good hors*, but *the (this, my, the kinges) goode hors*. They also generally add *e* when standing before and modifying a plural noun, a noun in the vocative, or any proper noun: *goode men, oh goode man, faire Venus*.

Adjectives are compared by adding *er(e)* for the comparative, *est(e)* for the superlative. Sometimes the stem vowel is shortened or altered in the process: *sweete, swettere, swettest; long, lenger, lengest*.

There is no problem understanding the forms of adjectives. Whether or not they add final -e may affect the meter by adding a syllable, but final -e on any word may also be elided. Compare the following: "A good Wif was ther of biside Bathe" (*General Prologue*, 447). "This goode wif wente on an haliday" (*Miller's Tale*, 201).

The stem vowel in the comparative and superlative forms of some adjectives is shortened. This is indicated in the text by changing double -ee (e.g., "greet strengthe" (*General Prologue*, 84), to single -e in the comparative and superlative (e.g., "grettere end" (*General Prologue*, 197), "hir gretteste ooth" (*General Prologue*, 120).

4. ADVERBS

Adverbs are formed from adjectives by adding *e, ly*, or *liche*; the adjective *fair* thus yields *faire, fairly, fairliche*.

The forms of adverbs, like those of adjectives, present few problems. The ending of the first degree of some adverbs in -e may be the same as that of some cases of the adjective, but the adverbial sense is usually quite clear in the sentence. The elegance of the Prioress's French is emphasized by three adverbs, "And Frenssh she spak ful faire and fetisly" (*General Prologue*, 124). Chaucer uses two adverbs in apologizing to his audience for the obligation he has to repeat word for word the speech of every pilgrim, "Al speke he never so rudeliche and large" (*General Prologue*, 736).

5. VERBS

With minor inflectional differences, the verb system of Middle English is the same as that of Modern English. The easiest way to absorb the verb system is simply by frequent reading.

The basic form of a verb is its infinitive form, i.e., its form without limitation in time (cf. the infinitive "to run" as distinct from a finite form of that verb, such as "he ran"). In Chaucer's dialect the infinitive form ends in *–en* or often *–e*.

If a verb strikes you as difficult to understand, you can find your way into it by analyzing, or parsing, it under the following heads: person, number, tense, voice, and mood.

Person can either be first, second, or third (I, you, he/she/it). Number can be either singular or plural (I/we; you/you; he, she, it/they). Tense indicates the time (e.g., pluperfect, past, present, future) in which an action occurred. A "pluperfect" tense indicates that an event took place before another event in the past (e.g. "I had swept before I polished"). The simple past tense in Middle English is sometimes called the preterite tense. Voice can either be active or passive ("I love" / "I am loved"). Mood indicates the status of a verb with regard to fact: a verb can designate an actual event (indicative mood: "I am a king"), a command (imperative mood: "Be a king!"), or a hypothesis (subjunctive mood: "Were I a king").

Middle English verbs, like Modern English verbs, are either "weak" or "strong." Weak verbs form their preterite tense (i.e., simple past tense) and past participle with a *t* or *d* suffix (i.e., ending). Weak verbs preserve the same vowel in the stem (i.e., principal syllable), throughout all tenses and moods. Strong verbs, by contrast, do not use the *t* or *d* suffix, but vary their stem vowel in the preterite and past participle: *take, took, taken; begin, began, begun; find, found, found.* This is not at all difficult to absorb, since it is identical to the system in Modern English.

	Present Indicative	Preterite Indicative
I	*love, heere*	*loved(e), herde*
	take, ginne	*took, gan*
thou	*lovest, heerest*	*lovedest, herdest*
	takest, ginnest	*tooke, gonne*
he, she, it	*loveth, heereth*	*loved(e), herde*
	taketh, ginneth	*took, gan*
we	*love(n), heere(n)*	*loved(e) (en), herde(n)*
	take(n), ginne(n)	*tooke(n), gonne(n)*
ye	*loveth, heereth*	*loved(e) (en), herde(n)*
	taketh, ginneth	*tooke(n), gonne(n)*
they	*love(n), heere(n)*	*loved(e) (en), herde(n)*
	take(n), ginne(n)	*tooke(n), gonne(n)*

The imperative singular of most weak verbs is *e*: *(thou) love*, but of some weak verbs and all strong verbs, the imperative singular is without termination: *(thou) heer, taak, gin.* The imperative plural of all verbs is either *e* or *eth*: *(ye) love(th), heere(th), take(th), ginne(th).*

The infinitive of verbs is *e* or *en*: *love(n), heere(n), take(n), ginne(n).*

The past participle of weak verbs is the same as the preterite without inflectional ending: *loved, herd.* In strong verbs the ending is either *e* or *en*: *take(n), gonne(n).* The prefix *y* often appears on past participles: *yloved, yherd, ytake(n).*

Take any passage of Chaucer and analyze the forms of the verb; you will very quickly become familiar with the standard forms. Take, for example, the beginning of the *Miller's Prologue*:

Line 1: *"hadde . . . ytold"*: third person, singular, pluperfect tense of strong verb, active voice, indicative mood. The pluperfect tense is formed by using preterite of "have" and past participle.

Line 2: *"nas"*: a contraction of *"ne was,"* third person, singular, preterite tense of verb "to be," active voice, indicative mood.

Line 3: *"said"*: third person, singular, preterite tense, active voice, indicative mood.

Line 4: *"to drawen"*: infinitive form of the verb.

Line 6: *"lough"*: third person, singular, preterite tense, active voice, indicative mood.

Line 6: *"swoor"*: third person, singular, preterite tense of strong verb, active voice, indicative mood.

Line 7: *"gooth"*: a syncopated, or abbreviated form of "go-eth;" third person, singular, present tense, active voice, indicative mood.

Line 7: *"unbokeled is"*: third person, singular, present tense, passive voice, indicative mood. The passive is formed by the past participle and the verb to be.

THE CANTERBURY TALES

The General Prologue[1]

Whan that Aprill with his shoures sote
When April with its sweet-smelling showers
The droghte of Marche hath perced to the rote,
Has pierced the drought of March to the root,
And bathed every veyne in swich licour,
And bathed every vein (of the plants) in such liquid
Of which vertu engendred is the flour;
By which power the flower is created;
5   Whan Zephirus eek with his swete breeth
When the West Wind also with its sweet breath,
Inspired hath in every holt and heeth
In every wood and field has breathed life into
The tendre croppes, and the yonge sonne
The tender new leaves, and the young sun
Hath in the Ram his halfe cours y-ronne;
Has run half its course in Aries,
And smale fowles maken melodye,
And small fowls make melody,
10   That slepen al the night with open yë—
Those that sleep all the night with open eyes
So priketh hem Nature in hir corages—

1. Unlike the normalized spelling of the Chaucer selections in the *Anthology* itself, the Middle English text here, taken from the Norton Critical Edition of *The Canterbury Tales*, edited by V. A. Kolve and Glending Olson, reproduces the actual spelling of manuscripts before spelling became more or less standardized. Individual scribes employed their own spelling practices in which a scribe might spell the same word differently at different times. For example, in the General Prologue, "I saw" is here spelled "I seigh" (line 193) and "I saugh" (line 766); in the *Anthology* it is spelled "I sawgh" in both places.

(So Nature incites them in their hearts),
Than longen folk to goon on pilgrimages,
Then folk long to go on pilgrimages,
And palmeres for to seken straunge strondes,
And professional pilgrims to seek foreign shores,
To ferne halwes, couthe in sondry londes;
To distant shrines, known in various lands;
15 And specially, from every shires ende
And specially from every shire's end
Of Engelond to Caunterbury they wende,
Of England to Canterbury they travel,
The holy blisful martir for to seke,
To seek the holy blessed martyr,
That hem hath holpen, whan that they were seke.
Who helped them when they were sick.
   Bifel that, in that seson on a day,
   It happened that in that season on one day,
20 In Southwerk at the Tabard as I lay
In Southwark at the Tabard Inn as I lay
Redy to wenden on my pilgrimage
Ready to go on my pilgrimage
To Caunterbury with ful devout corage,
To Canterbury with a very devout spirit,
At night was come into that hostelrye
At night had come into that hostelry
Wel nyne and twenty in a companye
Well nine and twenty in a company
25 Of sondry folk, by aventure y-falle
Of various sorts of people, by chance fallen
In felawshipe, and pilgrims were they alle,
In fellowship, and they were all pilgrims,
That toward Caunterbury wolden ryde.
Who intended to ride toward Canterbury.
The chambres and the stables weren wyde,
The bedrooms and the stables were spacious,
And wel we weren esed atte beste.
And we were well accommodated in the best way.
30 And shortly, whan the sonne was to reste,
And in brief, when the sun was (gone) to rest,
So hadde I spoken with hem everichon
I had so spoken with everyone of them
That I was of hir felawshipe anon,
That I was of their fellowship straightway,
And made forward erly for to ryse,
And made agreement to rise early,
To take oure wey, ther as I yow devyse.
To take our way where I (will) tell you.
35   But natheles, whyl I have tyme and space,
      But nonetheless, while I have time and opportunity,
Er that I ferther in this tale pace,
Before I proceed further in this tale,
Me thinketh it acordaunt to resoun
It seems to me in accord with reason

To telle yow al the condicioun
To tell you all the circumstances
Of ech of hem, so as it semed me,
Of each of them, as it seemed to me,
40 And whiche they weren, and of what degree,
And who they were, and of what social rank,
And eek in what array that they were inne;
And also what clothing that they were in;
And at a knight than wol I first beginne.
And at a knight then will I first begin.
    A Knight ther was, and that a worthy man,
    A KNIGHT there was, and that (one was) a worthy man,
That fro the tyme that he first bigan
Who from the time that he first began
45 To ryden out, he loved chivalrye,
To ride out, he loved chivalry,
Trouthe and honour, fredom and curteisye.
Fidelity and good reputation, generosity and courtesy.
Ful worthy was he in his lordes werre,
He was very worthy in his lord's war,
And therto hadde he riden, no man ferre,
And for that he had ridden, no man farther,
As wel in Cristendom as hethenesse,
As well in Christendom as in heathen lands,
50 And evere honoured for his worthinesse.
And (was) ever honored for his worthiness;
    At Alisaundre he was whan it was wonne;
    He was at Alexandria when it was won.
Ful ofte tyme he hadde the bord bigonne
He had sat very many times in the place of honor,
Aboven alle naciouns in Pruce.
Above (knights of) all nations in Prussia;
In Lettow hadde he reysed and in Ruce,
He had campaigned in Lithuania and in Russia,
55 No Cristen man so ofte of his degree.
No Christian man of his rank so often.
In Gernade at the sege eek hadde he be
Also he had been in Granada at the siege
Of Algezir, and riden in Belmarye.
Of Algeciras, and had ridden in Morocco.
At Lyeys was he and at Satalye,
He was at Ayash and at Atalia,
Whan they were wonne; and in the Grete See
When they were won, and in the Mediterranean
60 At many a noble arivee hadde he be.
He had been at many a noble landing.
    At mortal batailles hadde he been fiftene,
    He had been at fifteen mortal battles,
And foughten for oure feith at Tramissene
And fought for our faith at Tlemcen
In listes thryes, and ay slayn his foo.
Three times in formal duels, and each time slain his foe.
    This ilke worthy knight hadde been also

This same worthy knight had also been

65 Somtyme with the lord of Palatye,
At one time with the lord of Balat
Ageyn another hethen in Turkye;
Against another heathen in Turkey;
And everemore he hadde a sovereyn prys.
And evermore he had an outstanding reputation
And though that he were worthy, he was wys,
And although he was brave, he was prudent,
And of his port as meke as is a mayde.
And of his deportment as meek as is a maid.

70 He nevere yet no vileinye ne sayde
He never yet said any rude word
In al his lyf, unto no maner wight.
In all his life unto any sort of person.
He was a verray, parfit, gentil knight.
He was a truly perfect, noble knight.
But for to tellen yow of his array,
But to tell you of his clothing,
His hors were gode, but he was nat gay.
His horses were good, but he was not gaily dressed.

75 Of fustian he wered a gipoun
He wore a tunic of coarse cloth
Al bismotered with his habergeoun,
All stained (with rust) by his coat of mail,
For he was late y-come from his viage,
For he was recently come (back) from his expedition,
And wente for to doon his pilgrimage.
And went to do his pilgrimage.

With him ther was his sone, a young Squyer,
With him there was his son, a young SQUIRE,

80 A lovyere, and a lusty bacheler,
A lover and a lively bachelor,
With lokkes crulle, as they were leyd in presse.
With locks curled as if they had been laid in a curler.
Of twenty yeer of age he was, I gesse.
He was twenty years of age, I guess.
Of his stature he was of evene lengthe,
Of his stature he was of moderate height,
And wonderly delivere, and of greet strengthe.
And wonderfully agile, and of great strength.

85 And he hadde been somtyme in chivachye
And he had been for a time on a cavalry expedition
In Flaundres, in Artoys, and Picardye,
In Flanders, in Artois, and Picardy,
And born him wel, as of so litel space,
And conducted himself well, for so little a space of time,
In hope to stonden in his lady grace.
In hope to stand in his lady's good graces.

Embrouded was he, as it were a mede
He was embroidered, as if it were a mead

90 Al ful of fresshe floures, whyte and rede.
All full of fresh flowers, white and red.

Singinge he was, or floytinge, al the day;
Singing he was, or fluting, all the day;
He was as fresh as is the month of May.
He was as fresh as is the month of May.
Short was his gowne, with sleves longe and wyde.
His gown was short, with long and wide sleeves.
Wel coude he sitte on hors, and faire ryde.
He well knew how to sit on horse and handsomely ride.
95   He coude songes make and wel endyte,
He knew how to make songs and well compose (the words),
Juste and eek daunce, and wel purtreye and wryte.
Joust and also dance, and well draw and write.
So hote he lovede that by nightertale
He loved so passionately that at nighttime
He sleep namore than dooth a nightingale.
He slept no more than does a nightingale.
Curteys he was, lowly, and servisable,
Courteous he was, humble, and willing to serve,
100 And carf biforn his fader at the table.
And carved before his father at the table.
    A Yeman hadde he, and servaunts namo
    He (the Knight) had A YEOMAN and no more servants
At that tyme, for him, liste ryde so;
At that time, for it pleased him so to travel,
And he was clad in cote and hood of grene.
And he (the yeoman) was clad in coat and hood of green.
A sheef of pecok arwes brighte and kene
A sheaf of peacock arrows, bright and keen,
105 Under his belt he bar ful thriftily.
He carried under his belt very properly.
Wel coude he dresse his takel yemanly:
He well knew how to care for his equipment as a yeoman should:
His arwes drouped noght with fetheres lowe,
His arrows did not fall short because of drooping feathers,
And in his hand he bar a mighty bowe.
And in his hand he carried a mighty bow.
A not-heed hadde he, with a broun visage.
He had a close-cropped head, with a brown face.
110 Of wodecraft wel coude he al the usage.
He well knew all the practice of woodcraft.
Upon his arm he bar a gay bracer,
He wore an elegant archer's wrist-guard upon his arm,
And by his syde a swerd and a bokeler,
And by his side a sword and a small shield,
And on that other syde a gay daggere,
And on that other side an elegant dagger
Harneised wel, and sharp as point of spere;
Well ornamented and sharp as the point of a spear;
115 A Cristofre on his brest of silver shene.
A Christopher-medal of bright silver on his breast.
An horn he bar, the bawdrik was of grene;
He carried a horn, the shoulder strap was green;
A forster was he, soothly, as I gesse.

He was a forester, truly, as I guess.
   Ther was also a Nonne, a Prioresse,
   There was also a Nun, a PRIORESS,
That of hir smyling was ful simple and coy—
Who was very simple and modest in her smiling;
120 Hir gretteste ooth was but by Seynte Loy—
Her greatest oath was but by Saint Loy;
And she was cleped madame Eglentyne.
And she was called Madam Eglantine.
Ful wel she song the service divyne,
She sang the divine service very well,
Entuned in hir nose ful semely;
Intoned in her nose in a very polite manner;
And Frensh she spak ful faire and fetisly,
And she spoke French very well and elegantly,
125 After the scole of Stratford atte Bowe,
In the manner of Stratford at the Bow,
For Frensh of Paris was to hire unknowe.
For French of Paris was to her unknown.
At mete wel y-taught was she with alle:
At meals she was well taught indeed;
She leet no morsel from hir lippes falle,
She let no morsel fall from her lips,
Ne wette hir fingres in hir sauce depe.
Nor wet her fingers deep in her sauce;
130 Wel coude she carie a morsel, and wel kepe
She well knew how to carry a morsel (to her mouth) and take good care
That no drope ne fille upon hire brest.
That no drop fell upon her breast.
In curteisye was set ful muchel hir lest.
Her greatest pleasure was in good manners.
Hir over-lippe wyped she so clene,
She wiped her upper lip so clean
That in hir coppe was no ferthing sene
That in her cup there was seen no tiny bit
135 Of grece, whan she dronken hadde hir draughte.
Of grease, when she had drunk her drink.
Ful semely after hir mete she raughte,
She reached for her food in a very seemly manner.
And sikerly she was of greet disport,
And surely she was of excellent deportment,
And ful plesaunt, and amiable of port,
And very pleasant, and amiable in demeanor,
And peyned hire to countrefete chere
And she took pains to imitate the manners
140 Of court, and to been estatlich of manere,
Of court, and to be dignified in behavior,
And to ben holden digne of reverence.
And to be considered worthy of reverence.
But, for to speken of hire conscience,
But to speak of her moral sense,
She was so charitable and so pitous,
She was so charitable and so compassionate

She wolde wepe, if that she sawe a mous
She would weep, if she saw a mouse
145 Caught in a trappe, if it were deed or bledde.
Caught in a trap, if it were dead or bled.
Of smale houndes hadde she, that she fedde
She had some small hounds that she fed
With rosted flesh, or milk and wastel-breed.
With roasted meat, or milk and fine white bread.
But sore wepte she if oon of hem were deed,
But sorely she wept if one of them were dead,
Or if men smoot it with a yerde smerte;
Or if someone smote it smartly with a stick;
150 And al was conscience and tendre herte.
And all was feeling and tender heart.
Ful semely hir wimpel pinched was,
Her wimple was pleated in a very seemly manner,
Hir nose tretys, hir eyen greye as glas,
Her nose well formed, her eyes gray as glass,
Hir mouth ful smal, and therto softe and reed.
Her mouth very small, and moreover soft and red.
But sikerly she hadde a fair forheed—
But surely she had a fair forehead;
155 It was almost a spanne brood, I trowe—
It was almost nine inches broad, I believe;
For hardily she was nat undergrowe.
For, certainly, she was not undergrown.
Ful fetis was hir cloke, as I was war.
Her cloak was very well made, as I was aware.
Of smal coral aboute hire arm she bar
About her arm she bore of small coral
A peire of bedes, gauded al with grene;
A set of beads, adorned with large green beads,
160 And theron heng a broche of gold ful shene,
And thereon hung a brooch of very bright gold,
On which ther was first write a crowned A,
On which there was first written an A with a crown,
And after, Amor vincit omnia.
And after "Love conquers all."
    Another Nonne with hire hadde she,
    She had another NUN with her,
That was hir chapeleyne, and Preestes three.
Who was her secretary, and three priests.
165   A Monk ther was, a fair for the maistrye,
    There was a MONK, an extremely fine one,
An outrydere that lovede venerye:
*An outrider (a monk with business outside the monastery), who loved
    hunting,*
A manly man, to been an abbot able.
A virile man, qualified to be an abbot.
Ful many a deyntee hors hadde he in stable,
He had very many fine horses in his stable,
And whan he rood, men mighte his brydel here
And when he rode, one could hear his bridle

170 Ginglen in a whistling wind als clere
  Jingle in a whistling wind as clear
  And eek as loude as dooth the chapel belle,
  And also as loud as does the chapel belle
  Ther as this lord was kepere of the celle.
  Where this lord was prior of the subordinate monastery.
  The reule of Seint Maure or of Seint Beneit,
  The rule of Saint Maurus or of Saint Benedict,
  By cause that it was old and somdel streit,
  Because it was old and somewhat strict,
175 This ilke monk leet olde thinges pace,
  This same Monk let old things pass away,
  And held after the newe world the space.
  And followed the broader customs of modern times.
  He yaf nat of that text a pulled hen,
  He gave not a plucked hen for that text
  That seith that hunters ben nat holy men,
  That says that hunters are not holy men,
  Ne that a monk, whan he is reccheless,
  Nor that a monk, when he is heedless of rules,
180 Is lykned til a fish that is waterlees
  Is like a fish that is out of water—
  (This is to seyn, a monk out of his cloistre);
  This is to say, a monk out of his cloister.
  But thilke text held he nat worth an oistre.
  But he considered that same text not worth an oyster;
  And I seyde his opinioun was good:
  And I said his opinion was good.
  What sholde he studie, and make himselven wood,
  Why should he study and make himself crazy,
185 Upon a book in cloistre alwey to poure,
  Always to pore upon a book in the cloister,
  Or swinken with his handes and laboure
  Or work with his hands, and labor,
  As Austin bit? How shal the world be served?
  As Augustine commands? How shall the world be served?
  Lat Austin have his swink to him reserved!
  Let Augustine have his work reserved to him!
  Therfore he was a pricasour aright:
  Therefore he was indeed a vigorous horseman:
190 Grehoundes he hadde, as swifte as fowel in flight;
  He had greyhounds as swift as fowl in flight;
  Of priking and of hunting for the hare
  Of tracking and of hunting for the hare
  Was al his lust, for no cost wolde he spare.
  Was all his pleasure, by no means would he refrain from it.
  I seigh his sleves purfiled at the hond
  I saw his sleeves lined at the hand
  With grys, and that the fyneste of a lond;
  With squirrel fur, and that the finest in the land;
195 And, for to festne his hood under his chin,
  And to fasten his hood under his chin,
  He hadde of gold y-wroght a ful curious pin:

He had a very skillfully made pin of gold;
A love-knotte in the gretter ende ther was.
There was an elaborate knot in the larger end.
His heed was balled, that shoon as any glas,
His head was bald, which shone like any glass,
And eek his face, as he had been anoint.
And his face did too, as if he had been rubbed with oil.
200   He was a lord ful fat and in good point:
He was a very plump lord and in good condition;
His eyen stepe, and rollinge in his heed,
His eyes were prominent, and rolling in his head,
That stemed as a forneys of a leed;
Which gleamed like a furnace under a cauldron;
His bootes souple, his hors in greet estat—
His boots supple, his horse in excellent condition.
Now certeinly he was a fair prelat.
Now certainly he was a handsome ecclesiastical dignitary;
205   He was nat pale as a forpyned goost;
He was not pale as a tormented spirit.
A fat swan loved he best of any roost.
A fat swan loved he best of any roast.
His palfrey was as broun as is a berye.
His saddle horse was as brown as is a berry.
   A Frere ther was, a wantowne and a merye,
   There was a FRIAR, a pleasure-loving and merry one,
A limitour, a ful solempne man.
A limiter (with an assigned territory), a very solemn man.
210   In alle the ordres foure is noon that can
In all the four orders of friars is no one that knows
So muchel of daliaunce and fair langage.
So much of sociability and elegant speech.
He hadde maad ful many a mariage
He had made very many a marriage
Of yonge wommen, at his owne cost.
Of young women at his own cost.
Unto his ordre he was a noble post.
He was a noble supporter of his order.
215   Ful wel biloved and famulier was he
Very well beloved and familiar was he
With frankeleyns over al in his contree,
With landowners every where in his country,
And with worthy wommen of the toun;
And with worthy women of the town;
For he hadde power of confessioun,
For he had power of confession,
As seyde himself, more than a curat,
As he said himself, more than a parish priest,
220   For of his ordre he was licentiat.
For he was licensed by his order.
Ful swetely herde he confessioun,
He heard confession very sweetly,
And plesaunt was his absolucioun;
And his absolution was pleasant:

He was an esy man to yeve penaunce
He was a lenient man in giving penance,
Ther as he wiste to have a good pitaunce.
Where he knew he would have a good gift.
225   For unto a povre ordre for to yive
For to give to a poor order (of friars)
Is signe that a man is wel y-shrive—
Is a sign that a man is well confessed;
For if he yaf, he dorste make avaunt,
For if he gave, he (the friar) dared to assert,
He wiste that a man was repentaunt.
He knew that a man was repentant;
For many a man so hard is of his herte,
For many a man is so hard in his heart,
230   He may nat wepe althogh hym sore smerte:
He can not weep, although he painfully suffers.
Therfore, in stede of wepinge and preyeres,
Therefore instead of weeping and prayers
Men moot yeve silver to the povre freres.
One may give silver to the poor friars.
    His tipet was ay farsed ful of knyves
    His hood was always stuffed full of knives
And pinnes, for to yeven faire wyves.
And pins, to give to fair wives.
235   And certeinly he hadde a murye note;
And certainly he had a merry voice:
Wel coude he singe and pleyen on a rote;
He well knew how to sing and play on a rote (string instrument);
Of yeddinges he bar outrely the prys.
He absolutely took the prize for reciting ballads.
His nekke whyt was as the flour-de-lys;
His neck was white as a lily flower;
Therto he strong was as a champioun.
Furthermore he was strong as a champion fighter.
240   He knew the tavernes wel in every toun,
He knew the taverns well in every town
And everich hostiler and tappestere
And every innkeeper and barmaid
Bet than a lazar or a beggestere,
Better than a leper or a beggar-woman,
For unto swich a worthy man as he
For unto such a worthy man as he
Acorded nat, as by his facultee,
It was not suitable, in view of his official position,
245   To have with seke lazars aqueyntaunce:
To have acquaintance with sick lepers.
It is nat honest, it may nat avaunce
It is not respectable; it can not be profitable,
For to delen with no swich poraille,
To deal with any such poor people,
But al with riche and selleres of vitaille.
But all with rich people and sellers of victuals.
And over al, ther as profit sholde aryse,

And every where, where profit should arise,
250 Curteys he was, and lowely of servyse.
He was courteous and graciously humble;
Ther nas no man nowher so vertuous.
There was no man anywhere so capable (of such work).
He was the beste beggere in his hous,
He was the best beggar in his house;
And yaf a certeyn ferme for the graunt:
And he gave a certain fee for his grant (of begging rights);
Noon of his bretheren cam ther in his haunt.
None of his brethren came there in his territory;
255 For thogh a widwe hadde noght a sho,
For though a widow had not a shoe,
So plesaunt was his *In principio,*
So pleasant was his "In the beginning,"
Yet wolde he have a ferthing, er he wente.
Yet he would have a farthing, before he went away.
His purchas was wel bettre than his rente.
His total profit was much more than his proper income.
And rage he coude, as it were right a whelpe;
And he knew how to frolic, as if he were indeed a pup.
260 In love-dayes ther coude he muchel helpe,
He knew how to be much help on days for resolving disputes,
For there he was nat lyk a cloisterer,
For there he was not like a cloistered monk
With a thredbare cope, as is a povre scoler.
With a threadbare cope, like a poor scholar,
But he was lyk a maister or a pope:
But he was like a master of arts or a pope.
Of double worsted was his semi-cope,
Of wide (expensive) cloth was his short cloak,
265 That rounded as a belle out of the presse.
Which was round as a bell fresh from the casting mold.
Somwhat he lipsed, for his wantownesse,
Somewhat he lisped, for his affectation,
To make his English swete upon his tonge;
To make his English sweet upon his tongue;
And in his harping, whan that he hadde songe,
And in his harping, when he had sung,
His eyen twinkled in his heed aright
His eyes twinkled in his head exactly
270 As doon the sterres in the frosty night.
As do the stars in the frosty night.
This worthy limitour was cleped Huberd.
This worthy friar was called Huberd.
  A Marchant was ther with a forked berd,
  There was a MERCHANT with a forked beard,
In mottelee, and hye on horse he sat;
Wearing parti-colored cloth, and proudly he sat on his horse;
Upon his heed a Flaundrish bever hat,
Upon his head (he wore a) Flemish beaver hat,
275 His bootes clasped faire and fetisly.
His boots were buckled handsomely and elegantly.

His resons he spak ful solempnely,
His opinions he spoke very solemnly,
Souninge alway th'encrees of his winning.
Concerning always the increase of his profits.
He wolde the see were kept for any thing
He wanted the sea to be guarded at all costs
Bitwixe Middleburgh and Orewelle.
Between Middelburgh (Holland) and Orwell (England).
280   Wel coude he in eschaunge sheeldes selle.
He well knew how to deal in foreign currencies.
This worthy man ful wel his wit bisette:
This worthy man employed his wit very well:
Ther wiste no wight that he was in dette,
There was no one who knew that he was in debt,
So estatly was he of his governaunce,
He was so dignified in managing his affairs
With his bargaynes and with his chevisaunce.
With his buying and selling and with his financial deals.
285   For sothe he was a worthy man with alle,
Truly, he was a worthy man indeed,
But sooth to seyn, I noot how men him calle.
But, to say the truth, I do not know what men call him.
     A Clerk ther was of Oxenford also,
     There was also a CLERK (scholar) from Oxford,
That unto logik hadde longe y-go.
Who long before had begun the study of logic.
As leene was his hors as is a rake,
His horse was as lean as is a rake,
290   And he was nat right fat, I undertake,
And he was not very fat, I affirm,
But loked holwe, and therto soberly.
But looked emaciated, and moreover abstemious.
Ful thredbar was his overest courtepy,
His short overcoat was very threadbare,
For he hadde geten him yet no benefyce,
For he had not yet obtained an ecclesiastical living,
Ne was so worldly for to have offyce;
Nor was he worldly enough to take secular employment.
295   For him was levere have at his beddes heed
For he would rather have at the head of his bed
Twenty bokes, clad in blak or reed,
Twenty books, bound in black or red,
Of Aristotle and his philosophye,
Of Aristotle and his philosophy
Than robes riche, or fithele, or gay sautrye.
Than rich robes, or a fiddle, or an elegant psaltery.
But al be that he was a philosophre,
But even though he was a philosopher,
300   Yet hadde he but litel gold in cofre;
Nevertheless he had but little gold in his strongbox;
But al that he mighte of his freendes hente,
But all that he could get from his friends,
On bokes and on lerninge he it spente,

He spent on books and on learning,
And bisily gan for the soules preye
And diligently did pray for the souls
Of hem that yaf him wherwith to scoleye.
Of those who gave him the wherewithal to attend the schools.
305 Of studie took he most cure and most hede.
He took most care and paid most heed to study.
Noght o word spak he more than was nede,
He spoke not one word more than was needed,
And that was seyd in forme and reverence,
And that was said with due formality and respect,
And short and quik, and ful of hy sentence.
And short and lively and full of elevated content;
Souninge in moral vertu was his speche,
His speech was consonant with moral virtue,
310 And gladly wolde he lerne, and gladly teche.
And gladly would he learn and gladly teach.
   A Sergeant of the Lawe, war and wys,
   A SERGEANT OF THE LAW (high-ranking attorney), prudent and
     wise,
That often hadde been at the Parvys,
Who often had been at the Porch of St. Paul's (where lawyers gather)
Ther was also, ful riche of excellence.
Was also there, very rich in superior qualities.
Discreet he was and of greet reverence:
He was judicious and of great dignity—
315 He semed swich, his wordes weren so wyse.
He seemed such, his words were so wise.
Justyce he was ful often in assyse,
He was very often a judge in the court of assizes,
By patente and by pleyn commissioun;
By royal appointment and with full jurisdiction.
For his science and for his heigh renoun,
For his knowledge and for his excellent reputation,
Of fees and robes hadde he many oon.
He had many grants of yearly income.
320 So greet a purchasour was nowher noon:
There was nowhere so great a land-buyer:
Al was fee simple to him in effect;
In fact, all was unrestricted possession to him;
His purchasing mighte nat been infect.
His purchasing could not be invalidated.
Nowher so bisy a man as he ther nas;
There was nowhere so busy a man as he,
And yet he semed bisier than he was.
And yet he seemed busier than he was.
325 In termes hadde he caas and domes alle,
He had in Year Books all the cases and decisions
That from the tyme of King William were falle.
That from the time of king William have occurred.
Therto he coude endyte, and make a thing;
Furthermore, he knew how to compose and draw up a legal document,
Ther coude no wight pinche at his wryting,

So that no one could find a flaw in his writing;
And every statut coude he pleyn by rote.
And he knew every statute completely by heart.
330 He rood but hoomly in a medlee cote,
He rode but simply in a parti-colored coat,
Girt with a ceint of silk, with barres smale;
Girded with a belt of silk, with small stripes;
Of his array telle I no lenger tale.
I tell no longer tale of his clothing.
    A Frankeleyn was in his companye.
    A FRANKLIN was in his company.
Whyt was his berd as is the dayesye;
His beard was white as a daisy;
335 Of his complexioun he was sangwyn.
As to his temperament, he was dominated by the humor blood.
Wel loved he by the morwe a sop in wyn.
He well loved a bit of bread dipped in wine in the morning;
To liven in delyt was evere his wone,
His custom was always to live in delight,
For he was Epicurus owene sone,
For he was Epicurus' own son,
That heeld opinioun that pleyn delyt
Who held the opinion that pure pleasure
340 Was verray felicitee parfyt.
Was truly perfect happiness.
An housholdere, and that a greet, was he;
He was a householder, and a great one at that;
Seint Julian he was in his contree.
He was Saint Julian (patron of hospitality) in his country.
His breed, his ale, was alweys after oon;
His bread, his ale, was always of the same (good) quality;
A bettre envyned man was nevere noon.
Never was there any man better stocked with wine.
345 Withoute bake mete was nevere his hous,
His house was never without baked pies
Of fish and flesh, and that so plentevous
Of fish and meat, and that so plentiful
It snewed in his hous of mete and drinke.
That in his house it snowed with food and drink;
Of alle deyntees that men coude thinke,
Of all the dainties that men could imagine,
After the sondry sesons of the yeer,
In accord with the various seasons of the year,
350 So chaunged he his mete and his soper.
So he varied his midday meal and his supper.
Ful many a fat partrich hadde he in mewe,
He had very many fat partridges in pens,
And many a breem and many a luce in stewe.
And many a bream and many a pike in his fish pond.
Wo was his cook, but if his sauce were
Woe was his cook unless his sauce was
Poynaunt and sharp, and redy al his gere.
Hotly spiced and sharp, and ready all his cooking equipment.

355 His table dormant in his halle alway
In his hall his dining table always
Stood redy covered al the longe day.
Stood covered (with table cloth) and ready all the long day.
At sessiouns ther was he lord and sire;
He presided as lord and sire at court sessions;
Ful ofte tyme he was knight of the shire.
He was a member of parliament many times.
An anlas and a gipser al of silk
A dagger and a purse all of silk
360 Heng at his girdel, whyt as morne milk.
Hung at his belt, white as morning milk.
A shirreve hadde he been, and a countour;
He had been a sheriff, and an auditor of taxes.
Was nowher such a worthy vavasour.
There was nowhere such a worthy landowner.
　　An Haberdassher and a Carpenter,
*　A HABERDASHER and a CARPENTER,*
A Webbe, a Dyere, and a Tapicer,
A WEAVER, a DYER, and a TAPESTRY-MAKER—
365 Were with us eek, clothed in o liveree
Were also with us, clothed in one livery
Of a solempne and greet fraternitee.
Of a solemn and a great parish guild.
Ful fresh and newe hir gere apyked was;
Their equipment was adorned all freshly and new;
Hir knyves were chaped noght with bras,
Their knives were not mounted with brass
But al with silver; wroght ful clene and weel
But entirely with silver, wrought very neatly and well,
370 Hire girdles and hire pouches everydeel.
Their belts and their purses every bit.
Wel semed ech of hem a fair burgeys
Each of them well seemed a solid citizen
To sitten in a yeldhalle on a deys.
To sit on a dais in a city hall.
Everich, for the wisdom that he can,
Every one of them, for the wisdom that he knows,
Was shaply for to been an alderman.
Was suitable to be an alderman.
375 For catel hadde they ynogh and rente,
For they had enough possessions and income,
And eek hir wyves wolde it wel assente;
And also their wives would well assent to it;
And elles certein were they to blame.
And otherwise certainly they would be to blame.
It is ful fair to been y-clept "Madame,"
It is very fine to be called "my lady,"
And goon to vigilyës al bifore,
And go to feasts on holiday eves heading the procession,
380 And have a mantel royalliche y-bore.
And have a gown with a train royally carried.
　　A Cook they hadde with hem for the nones,

A COOK *they had with them for the occasion*
To boille the chiknes with the mary-bones
To boil the chickens with the marrow bones,
And poudre-marchant tart and galingale.
And tart poudre-marchant and galingale (spices).
Wel coude he knowe a draughte of London ale.
He well knew how to judge a draft of London ale.
385   He coude roste, and sethe, and broille, and frye,
He knew how to roast, and boil, and broil, and fry,
Maken mortreux, and wel bake a pye.
Make stews, and well bake a pie.
But greet harm was it, as it thoughte me,
But it was a great harm, as it seemed to me,
That on his shine a mormal hadde he.
That he had an open sore on his shin.
For blankmanger, that made he with the beste.
As for white pudding, he made that of the best quality.
390   A Shipman was ther, woninge fer by weste:
A SHIPMAN was there, dwelling far in the west;
For aught I woot, he was of Dertemouthe.
For all I know, he was from Dartmouth.
He rood upon a rouncy, as he couthe,
He rode upon a cart horse, insofar as he knew how,
In a gowne of falding to the knee.
In a gown of woolen cloth (that reached) to the knee.
A daggere hanginge on a laas hadde he
He had a dagger hanging on a cord
395   Aboute his nekke, under his arm adoun.
About his neck, down under his arm.
The hote somer hadde maad his hewe al broun;
The hot summer had made his hue all brown;
And certeinly he was a good felawe.
And certainly he was a boon companion.
Ful many a draughte of wyn had he y-drawe
He had drawn very many a draft of wine
Fro Burdeux-ward, whyl that the chapman sleep.
While coming from Bordeaux, while the merchant slept.
400   Of nyce conscience took he no keep:
He had no concern for a scrupulous conscience.
If that he faught, and hadde the hyer hond,
If he fought and had the upper hand,
By water he sente hem hoom to every lond.
He sent them home by water to every land (they walked the plank).
But of his craft, to rekene wel his tydes,
But of his skill to reckon well his tides,
His stremes and his daungers him bisydes,
His currents, and his perils near at hand,
405   His herberwe and his mone, his lodemenage,
His harbors, and positions of his moon, his navigation,
Ther nas noon swich from Hulle to Cartage.
There was none other such from Hull to Cartagena (Spain).
Hardy he was, and wys to undertake;
He was bold and prudent in his undertakings;

With many a tempest hadde his berd been shake.
His beard had been shaken by many a tempest.
He knew wel alle the havenes, as they were,
He knew all the harbors, how they were,
From Gootlond to the cape of Finistere,
From Gotland to the Cape of Finisterre,
And every cryke in Britayne and in Spayne;
And every inlet in Brittany and in Spain.
His barge y-cleped was the Maudelayne.
His ship was called the Magdalene.
  With us ther was a Doctour of Phisyk;
  With us there was a DOCTOR OF MEDICINE
In al this world ne was ther noon him lyk
In all this world there was no one like him,
To speke of phisik and of surgerye,
To speak of medicine and of surgery,
For he was grounded in astronomye.
For he was instructed in astronomy.
He kepte his pacient a ful greet deel
He took care of his patient very many times
In houres, by his magik naturel.
In (astronomically suitable) hours by (use of) his natural science.
Wel coude he fortunen the ascendent
He well knew how to calculate the planetary position
Of his images for his pacient.
Of his astronomical talismans for his patient.
He knew the cause of everich maladye,
He knew the cause of every malady,
Were it of hoot or cold, or moiste, or drye,
Were it of hot, or cold, or moist, or dry elements,
And where engendred, and of what humour;
And where they were engendered, and by what bodily fluid.
He was a verrey parfit practisour.
He was a truly, perfect practitioner:
The cause y-knowe, and of his harm the roote,
The cause known, and the source of its harm,
Anon he yaf the seke man his boote.
Straightway he gave the sick man his remedy.
  Ful redy hadde he his apothecaries
  He had his apothecaries all ready
To sende him drogges and his letuaries,
To send him drugs and his electuaries,
For ech of hem made other for to winne;
For each of them made the other to profit—
Hir frendschipe nas nat newe to biginne.
Their friendship was not recently begun.
Wel knew he the olde Esculapius,
He well knew the old Aesculapius,
And Deiscorides, and eek Rufus,
And Dioscorides, and also Rufus,
Old Ypocras, Haly, and Galien,
Old Hippocrates, Haly, and Galen,
Serapion, Razis, and Avicen,

410

415

420

425

430

Serapion, Rhazes, and Avicenna,
435 Averrois, Damascien, and Constantyn,
Averroes, John the Damascan, and Constantine,
Bernard, and Gatesden, and Gilbertyn.
Bernard, and Gaddesden, and Gilbertus.
Of his diete mesurable was he,
He was moderate in his diet,
For it was of no superfluitee
For it was of no excess,
But of greet norissing and digestible.
But greatly nourishing and digestible.
440 His studie was but litel on the Bible.
His study was but little on the Bible.
In sangwin and in pers he clad was al,
He was clad all in red and in blue,
Lyned with taffata and with sendal;
Lined with taffeta and with silk.
And yet he was but esy of dispence.
And yet he was moderate in spending;
He kepte that he wan in pestilence,
He kept what he earned in (times of) plague.
445 For gold in phisik is a cordial;
Since in medicine gold is a restorative for the heart,
Therefore he lovede gold in special.
Therefore he loved gold in particular.
     A good Wyf was ther of bisyde Bathe,
     There was a good WIFE OF beside BATH,
But she was somdel deef, and that was scathe.
But she was somewhat deaf, and that was a pity.
Of clooth-making she hadde swiche an haunt,
She had such a skill in cloth-making
450 She passed hem of Ypres and of Gaunt.
She surpassed them of Ypres and of Ghent.
In al the parisshe wyf ne was ther noon
In all the parish there was no wife
That to the offringe bifore hir sholde goon;
Who should go to the Offering before her;
And if ther dide, certeyn so wrooth was she,
And if there did, certainly she was so angry
That she was out of alle charitee.
That she was out of all charity (love for her neighbor).
455 Hir coverchiefs ful fyne were of ground;
Her kerchiefs were very fine in texture;
I dorste swere they weyeden ten pound
I dare swear they weighed ten pound
That on a Sonday weren upon hir heed.
That on a Sunday were upon her head.
Hir hosen weren of fyn scarlet reed,
Her stockings were of fine scarlet red,
Ful streite y-teyd, and shoos ful moiste and newe.
Very closely laced, and shoes very supple and new.
460 Bold was hir face, and fair, and reed of hewe.
Bold was her face, and fair, and red of hue.

She was a worthy womman al hir lyve:
She was a worthy woman all her life:
Housbondes at chirche dore she hadde fyve,
She had (married) five husbands at the church door
Withouten other companye in youthe—
Not counting other company in youth—
But therof nedeth nat to speke as nouthe—
But there is no need to speak of that right now.

465 And thryes hadde she been at Jerusalem.
And she had been three times at Jerusalem;
She hadde passed many a straunge streem:
She had passed many a foreign sea;
At Rome she hadde been, and at Boloigne,
She had been at Rome, and at Boulogne,
In Galice at Seint Jame, and at Coloigne;
In Galicia at Saint-James (of Compostella), and at Cologne.
She coude muchel of wandringe by the weye.
She knew much about wandering by the way.

470 Gat-tothed was she, soothly for to seye.
She had teeth widely set apart, truly to say.
Upon an amblere esily she sat,
She sat easily upon a pacing horse,
Y-wimpled wel, and on hir heed an hat
Wearing a large wimple, and on her head a hat
As brood as is a bokeler or a targe;
As broad as a buckler or a shield;
A foot-mantel aboute hir hipes large,
An overskirt about her large hips,

475 And on hir feet a paire of spores sharpe.
And on her feet a pair of sharp spurs.
In felawschipe wel coude she laughe and carpe.
In fellowship she well knew how to laugh and chatter.
Of remedyes of love she knew per chaunce,
She knew, as it happened, about remedies for love
For she coude of that art the olde daunce.
For she knew the old dance (tricks of the trade) of that art.

   A good man was ther of religioun,
   A good man was there of religion,
480 And was a povre Persoun of a toun,
And (he) was a poor PARSON OF A TOWN,
But riche he was of holy thoght and werk.
But he was rich in holy thought and work.
He was also a lerned man, a clerk,
He was also a learned man, a scholar,
That Cristes gospel trewely wolde preche;
Who would preach Christ's gospel truly;
His parisshens devoutly wolde he teche.
He would devoutly teach his parishioners.

485 Benigne he was, and wonder diligent,
He was gracious, and wonderfully diligent,
And in adversitee ful pacient,
And very patient in adversity,
And swich he was y-preved ofte sythes.

And such he was proven many times.
Ful looth were him to cursen for his tithes,
He was very reluctant to excommunicate for (nonpayment of) his tithes,
But rather wolde he yeven, out of doute,
But rather would he give, there is no doubt,
490 Unto his povre parisshens aboute
Unto his poor parishioners about
Of his offring, and eek of his substaunce.
Some of his offering (received at mass) and also some of his income.
He coude in litel thing han suffisaunce.
He knew how to have sufficiency in few possessions.
Wyd was his parisshe, and houses fer asonder,
His parish was wide, and houses far apart,
But he ne lafte nat, for reyn ne thonder,
But he did not omit, for rain nor thunder,
495 In siknes nor in meschief, to visyte
In sickness or in trouble to visit
The ferreste in his parisshe, muche and lyte,
Those living farthest away in his parish, high-ranking and low,
Upon his feet, and in his hand a staf.
Going by foot, and in his hand a staff.
This noble ensample to his sheep he yaf,
He gave this noble example to his sheep,
That first he wroghte, and afterward he taughte.
That first he wrought, and afterward he taught.
500 Out of the gospel he tho wordes caughte,
He took those words out of the gospel,
And this figure he added eek therto,
And this metaphor he added also to that,
That if gold ruste, what shal iren do?
That if gold rust, what must iron do?
For if a preest be foul, on whom we truste,
For if a priest, on whom we trust, should be foul
No wonder is a lewed man to ruste;
It is no wonder for a layman to go bad;
505 And shame it is, if a preest take keep,
And it is a shame, if a priest is concerned:
A shiten shepherde and a clene sheep.
A shit-stained shepherd and a clean sheep.
Wel oghte a preest ensample for to yive,
Well ought a priest to give an example,
By his clennesse, how that his sheep sholde live.
By his purity, how his sheep should live.
He sette nat his benefice to hyre,
He did not rent out his benefice (ecclesiastical living)
510 And leet his sheep encombred in the myre,
And leave his sheep encumbered in the mire
And ran to London unto Seynte Poules
And run to London unto Saint Paul's
To seken him a chaunterie for soules,
To seek an appointment as a chantry priest (praying for a patron)
Or with a bretherhed to been withholde,
Or to be hired (as a chaplain) by a guild;

But dwelte at hoom, and kepte wel his folde,
But dwelt at home, and kept well his sheep fold (parish),
515   So that the wolf ne made it nat miscarie;
So that the wolf did not make it go wrong;
He was a shepherde and noght a mercenarie.
He was a shepherd and not a hireling.
And though he holy were, and vertuous,
And though he was holy and virtuous,
He was to sinful men nat despitous,
He was not scornful to sinful men,
Ne of his speche daungerous ne digne,
Nor domineering nor haughty in his speech,
520   But in his teching discreet and benigne.
But in his teaching courteous and kind.
To drawen folk to heven by fairnesse,
To draw folk to heaven by gentleness,
By good ensample, this was his bisinesse;
By good example, this was his business.
But it were any persone obstinat,
Unless it were an obstinate person,
What so he were, of heigh or lough estat,
Whoever he was, of high or low rank,
525   Him wolde he snibben sharply for the nones.
He would rebuke him sharply at that time.
A bettre preest I trowe that nowher noon is.
I believe that nowhere is there a better priest.
He wayted after no pompe and reverence,
He expected no pomp and ceremony,
Ne maked him a spyced conscience,
Nor made himself an overly fastidious conscience,
But Cristes lore, and his apostles twelve,
But Christ's teaching and His twelve apostles
530   He taughte, and first he folwed it himselve.
He taught; but first he followed it himself.
    With him ther was a Plowman, was his brother,
    With him there was a PLOWMAN, who was his brother,
That hadde y-lad of dong ful many a fother.
Who had hauled very many a cartload of dung;
A trewe swinkere and a good was he,
He was a true and good worker,
Livinge in pees and parfit charitee.
Living in peace and perfect love.
535   God loved he best with al his hole herte
He loved God best with all his whole heart
At alle tymes, thogh him gamed or smerte,
At all times, whether it pleased or pained him,
And thanne his neighebour right as himselve.
And then (he loved) his neighbor exactly as himself.
He wolde thresshe, and therto dyke and delve,
He would thresh, and moreover make ditches and dig,
For Cristes sake, for every povre wight,
For Christ's sake, for every poor person,
540   Withouten hyre, if it lay in his might.

Without payment, if it lay in his power.
His tythes payed he ful faire and wel,
He paid his tithes completely and well,
Bothe of his propre swink and his catel.
Both of his own labor and of his possessions.
In a tabard he rood upon a mere.
He rode in a tabard (sleeveless jacket) upon a mare.
    Ther was also a Reve and a Millere,
    There was also a REEVE, and a MILLER,
545 A Somnour and a Pardoner also,
A SUMMONER, and a PARDONER also,
A Maunciple, and myself—ther were namo.
A MANCIPLE, and myself—there were no more.
    The Millere was a stout carl for the nones;
    The MILLER was a stout fellow indeed;
Ful big he was of brawn, and eek of bones—
He was very strong of muscle, and also of bones.
That proved wel, for over al ther he cam,
That was well proven, for wherever he came,
550 At wrastling he wolde have alwey the ram.
At wrestling he would always take the the prize.
He was short-sholdred, brood, a thikke knarre:
He was stoutly built, broad, a large-framed fellow;
Ther nas no dore that he nolde heve of harre,
There was no door that he would not heave off its hinges,
Or breke it at a renning with his heed.
Or break it by running at it with his head.
His berd as any sowe or fox was reed,
His beard was red as any sow or fox,
555 And therto brood, as though it were a spade.
And moreover broad, as though it were a spade.
Upon the cop right of his nose he hade
Upon the exact top of his nose he had
A werte, and theron stood a tuft of herys,
A wart, and thereon stood a tuft of hairs,
Reed as the bristles of a sowes erys;
Red as the bristles of a sow's ears;
His nosethirles blake were and wyde.
His nostrils were black and wide.
560 A swerd and a bokeler bar he by his syde.
He wore a sword and a buckler by his side.
His mouth as greet was as a greet forneys;
His mouth was as large as a large furnace.
He was a janglere and a goliardeys,
He was a loudmouth and a buffoon,
And that was most of sinne and harlotryes.
And that was mostly of sin and deeds of harlotry.
Wel coude he stelen corn, and tollen thryes,
He well knew how to steal corn and take payment three times;
565 And yet he hadde a thombe of gold, pardee.
And yet he had a thumb of gold, indeed.
A whyt cote and a blew hood wered he.
He wore a white coat and a blue hood.

A baggepype wel coude he blowe and sowne,
He well knew how to blow and play a bag-pipe,
And therwithal he broghte us out of towne.
And with that he brought us out of town.
   A gentil Maunciple was ther of a temple,
There was a fine MANCIPLE of a temple (law school),
570 Of which achatours mighte take exemple
Of whom buyers of provisions might take example
For to be wyse in bying of vitaille,
For how to be wise in buying of victuals;
For whether that he payde, or took by taille,
For whether he paid (cash) or took (goods) on credit,
Algate he wayted so in his achat
Always he watched so (carefully for his opportunity) in his purchases
That he was ay biforn and in good stat.
That he was always ahead and in good state.
575   Now is nat that of God a ful fair grace,
Now is not that a very fair grace of God
That swich a lewed mannes wit shal pace
That such an unlearned man's wit shall surpass
The wisdom of an heep of lerned men?
The wisdom of a heap of learned men?
Of maistres hadde he mo than thryes ten
He had more than three times ten masters,
That weren of lawe expert and curious,
Who were expert and skillful in law,
580 Of which ther were a doseyn in that hous
Of whom there were a dozen in that house
Worthy to been stiwardes of rente and lond
Worthy to be stewards of rent and land
Of any lord that is in Engelond,
Of any lord that is in England,
To make him live by his propre good
To make him live by his own wealth
In honour, dettelees, but he were wood,
In honor and debtless (unless he were crazy),
585 Or live as scarsly as him list desire,
Or live as economically as it pleased him to desire;
And able for to helpen al a shire
And (they would be) able to help all a shire
In any cas that mighte falle or happe;
In any emergency that might occur or happen.
And yit this maunciple sette hir aller cappe.
And yet this Manciple fooled them all.
   The Reve was a sclendre colerik man.
The REEVE was a slender choleric man.
590 His berd was shave as ny as ever he can;
His beard was shaved as close as ever he can;
His heer was by his eres ful round y-shorn,
His hair was closely cropped by his ears;
His top was dokked lyk a preest biforn.
The top of his head in front was cut short like a priest's.
Ful longe were his legges, and ful lene,

His legs were very long and very lean,
Ylyk a staf; ther was no calf y-sene.
Like a stick; there was no calf to be seen.
595 Wel coude he kepe a gerner and a binne—
He well knew how to keep a granary and a storage bin;
Ther was noon auditour coude on him winne.
There was no auditor who could earn anything (by catching him).
Wel wiste he by the droghte and by the reyn
He well knew by the drought and by the rain
The yeldinge of his seed and of his greyn.
(What would be) the yield of his seed and of his grain.
His lordes sheep, his neet, his dayerye,
His lord's sheep, his cattle, his herd of dairy cows,
600 His swyn, his hors, his stoor, and his pultrye,
His swine, his horses, his livestock, and his poultry
Was hoolly in this reves governinge,
Was wholly in this Reeve's control,
And by his covenaunt yaf the rekeninge,
And in accord with his contract he gave the reckoning,
Sin that his lord was twenty yeer of age.
Since his lord was twenty years of age.
Ther coude no man bringe him in arrerage.
There was no man who could find him in arrears.
605 Ther nas baillif, ne herde, ne other hyne,
There was no farm manager, nor herdsman, nor other servant,
That he ne knew his sleighte and his covyne;
Whose trickery and treachery he did not know;
They were adrad of him as of the deeth.
They were afraid of him as of the plague.
His woning was ful fair upon an heeth;
His dwelling was very nicely situated upon an heath;
With grene trees shadwed was his place.
His place was shaded by green trees.
610 He coude bettre than his lord purchace.
He could buy property better than his lord could.
Ful riche he was astored prively;
He was secretly very richly provided.
His lord wel coude he plesen subtilly,
He well knew how to please his lord subtly,
To yeve and lene him of his owne good,
By giving and lending him some of his lord's own possessions,
And have a thank, and yet a cote and hood.
And have thanks, and also a coat and hood (as a reward).
615 In youthe he hadde lerned a good mister:
In youth he had learned a good craft:
He was a wel good wrighte, a carpenter.
He was a very good craftsman, a carpenter.
This reve sat upon a ful good stot
This Reeve sat upon a very good horse
That was al pomely grey and highte Scot.
That was all dapple gray and was called Scot.
A long surcote of pers upon he hade,
He had on a long outer coat of dark blue,

620 And by his syde he bar a rusty blade.
And by his side he wore a rusty sword.
Of Northfolk was this reve of which I tell,
Of Norfolk was this Reeve of whom I tell,
Bisyde a toun men clepen Baldeswelle.
Near to a town men call Bawdeswell.
Tukked he was as is a frere aboute;
He had his coat hitched up and belted, like a friar,
And evere he rood the hindreste of oure route.
And ever he rode as the last of our company.
625   A Somonour was ther with us in that place,
There was a SUMMONER with us in that place,
That hadde a fyr-reed cherubinnes face,
Who had a fire-red cherubim's face,
For sawcefleem he was, with eyen narwe.
For it was pimpled and discolored, with swollen eyelids.
As hoot he was and lecherous as a sparwe,
He was as hot and lecherous as a sparrow,
With scalled browes blake, and piled berd;
With black, scabby brows and a beard with hair fallen out.
630 Of his visage children were aferd.
Children were afraid of his face.
Ther nas quiksilver, litarge, ne brimstoon,
There was no mercury, lead monoxide, nor sulphur,
Boras, ceruce, ne oille of tartre noon,
Borax, white lead, nor any cream of tartar,
Ne oynement that wolde clense and byte,
Nor ointment that would cleanse and burn,
That him mighte helpen of his whelkes whyte,
That could cure him of his white pustules,
635 Nor of the knobbes sittinge on his chekes.
Nor of the knobs sitting on his cheeks.
Wel loved he garleek, oynons, and eek lekes,
He well loved garlic, onions, and also leeks,
And for to drinken strong wyn, reed as blood.
And to drink strong wine, red as blood;
Thanne wolde he speke, and crye as he were wood;
Then he would speak and cry out as if he were crazy.
And whan that he wel dronken hadde the wyn,
And when he had drunk deeply of the wine,
640 Thanne wolde he speke no word but Latyn.
Then he would speak no word but Latin.
A fewe termes hadde he, two or three,
He had a few legal terms, two or three,
That he had lerned out of som decree—
That he had learned out of some text of ecclesiastical law—
No wonder is, he herde it al the day;
That is no wonder, he heard it all the day;
And eek ye knowen wel how that a jay
And also you know well how a jay
645 Can clepen "Watte" as well as can the Pope.
Can call out "Walter" as well as the pope can.
But whoso coude in other thing him grope,

But whoever knew how to examine him in other matters,
Thanne hadde he spent al his philosophye;
(Would find that) he had used up all his learning;
Ay "Questio quid iuris" wolde he crye.
Always "The question is, what point of the law applies?" he would cry.
   He was a gentil harlot and a kinde;
   He was a fine rascal and a kind one;
650 A bettre felawe sholde men noght finde:
One could not find a better fellow.
He wolde suffre, for a quart of wyn,
For a quart of wine he would allow
A good felawe to have his concubyn
A good fellow to have his concubine
A twelf-month, and excuse him atte fulle;
For twelve months, and excuse him completely;
Ful prively a finch eek coude he pulle.
Secretly he also knew how to pull off a clever trick.
655 And if he fond owher a good felawe,
And if he found anywhere a good fellow,
He wolde techen him to have non awe
He would teach him to have no awe
In swich cas of the erchedeknes curs,
Of the archdeacon's curse (of excommunication) in such a case,
But-if a mannes soule were in his purs,
Unless a man's soul were in his purse;
For in his purs he sholde y-punisshed be.
For in his purse he would be punished.
660 "Purs is the erchedeknes helle," seyde he.
"Purse is the archdeacon's hell," he said.
   But wel I woot he lyed right in dede:
   But well I know he lied right certainly;
Of cursing oghte ech gilty man him drede—
Each guilty man ought to be afraid of excommunication,
For curs wol slee, right as assoilling saveth—
For excommunication will slay just as forgiveness saves,
And also war him of a *significavit.*
And let him also beware of a Significavit (order for imprisonment).
665   In daunger hadde he at his owene gyse
   In his control he had as he pleased
The yonge girles of the diocyse,
The young people of the diocese,
And knew hir counseil, and was al hir reed.
And knew their secrets, and was the adviser of them all.
A gerland hadde he set upon his heed,
He had set a garland upon his heed,
As greet as it were for an ale-stake;
As large as if it were for the sign of a tavern
670 A bokeler hadde he maad him of a cake.
He had made himself a shield of a cake.
   With him ther rood a gentil Pardoner
   With him there rode a fine PARDONER
Of Rouncival, his freend and his compeer,
Of Rouncivale, his friend and his companion,

That streight was comen fro the court of Rome.
Who had come straight from the court of Rome.
Ful loude he song, "Com hider, love, to me."
Very loud he sang "Come hither, love, to me!"
675 This Somnour bar to him a stif burdoun,
This Summoner harmonized with him in a strong bass;
Was nevere trompe of half so greet a soun.
There was never a trumpet of half so great a sound.
   This pardoner hadde heer as yelow as wex,
   This Pardoner had hair as yellow as wax,
But smothe it heng, as dooth a strike of flex;
But smooth it hung as does a clump of flax;
By ounces henge his lokkes that he hadde,
By small strands hung such locks as he had,
680 And therwith he his shuldres overspradde;
And he spread them over his shoulders;
But thinne it lay, by colpons oon and oon;
But thin it lay, by strands one by one.
But hood, for jolitee, wered he noon,
But to make an attractive appearance, he wore no hood,
For it was trussed up in his walet.
For it was trussed up in his knapsack.
Him thoughte he rood al of the newe jet;
It seemed to him that he rode in the very latest style;
685 Dischevele, save his cappe, he rood al bare.
With hair unbound, save for his cap, he rode all bare-headed.
Swiche glaringe eyen hadde he as an hare.
He had glaring eyes such as has a hare.
A vernicle hadde he sowed on his cappe.
He had sewn a Veronica upon his cap.
His walet biforn him in his lappe,
Before him in his lap, (he had) his knapsack,
Bretful of pardoun comen from Rome al hoot.
Brimful of pardons come all fresh from Rome.
690 A voys he hadde as smal as hath a goot. ∿ broad
He had a voice as small as a goat has.
No berd hadde he, ne nevere sholde have,
He had no beard, nor never would have;
As smothe it was as it were late shave:
It (his face) was as smooth as if it were recently shaven.
I trowe he were a gelding or a mare.
I believe he was a eunuch or a homosexual.
But of his craft, fro Berwik into Ware,
But as to his craft, from Berwick to Ware
695 Ne was ther swich another pardoner.
There was no other pardoner like him.
For in his male he hadde a pilwe-beer,
For in his pouch he had a pillow-case,
Which that he seyde was Oure Lady veyl.
Which he said was Our Lady's veil;
He seyde he hadde a gobet of the seyl
He said he had a piece of the sail
That seynt Peter hadde, whan that he wente

That Saint Peter had, when he went
700 Upon the see, til Jesu Christ him hente.
Upon the sea, until Jesus Christ took him.
He hadde a croys of latoun, ful of stones,
He had a cross of latten (brass-like alloy) covered with stones,
And in a glas he hadde pigges bones.
And in a glass container he had pigs' bones.
But with thise relikes, whan that he fond
But with these relics, when he found
A povre person dwellinge upon lond,
A poor parson dwelling in the countryside,
705 Upon a day he gat him more moneye
In one day he got himself more money
Than that the person gat in monthes tweye.
Than the parson got in two months;
And thus, with feyned flaterye and japes,
And thus, with feigned flattery and tricks,
He made the person and the peple his apes.
He made fools of the parson and the people.
But trewely to tellen, atte laste,
But truly to tell at the last,
710 He was in chirche a noble ecclesiaste.
He was in church a noble ecclesiast.
Wel coude he rede a lessoun or a storie,
He well knew how to read a lesson or a story,
But alderbest he song an offertorie;
But best of all he sang an Offertory;
For wel he wiste, whan that song was songe,
For he knew well, when that song was sung,
He moste preche, and wel affyle his tonge
He must preach and well smooth his speech
715 To winne silver, as he ful wel coude—
To win silver, as he very well knew how;
Therefore he song the murierly and loude.
Therefore he sang the more merrily and loud.
   Now have I told you soothly, in a clause,
   Now have I told you truly, briefly,
Th'estaat, th'array, the nombre, and eek the cause
The rank, the dress, the number, and also the cause
Why that assembled was this compaignye
Why this company was assembled
720 In Southwerk, at this gentil hostelrye,
In Southwark at this fine hostelry
That highte the Tabard, faste by the Belle.
That is called the Tabard, close by the Bell.
But now is tyme to yow for to telle
But now it is time to tell to you
How that we baren us that ilke night,
How we conducted ourselves that same night,
Whan we were in that hostelrye alight;
When we had arrived in that hostelry;
725 And after wol I telle of our viage,
And after that I will tell of our journey

And al the remenaunt of oure pilgrimage.
And all the rest of our pilgrimage.
But first I pray yow, of youre curteisye,
But first I pray yow, of your courtesy,
That ye n'arette it nat my vileinye,
That you do not attribute it to my rudeness,
Thogh that I pleynly speke in this matere,
Though I speak plainly in this matter,
730 To tell yow hir wordes and hir chere,
To tell you their words and their behavior,
Ne thogh I speke hir wordes properly.
Nor though I speak their words accurately.
For this ye knowen al so wel as I:
For this you know as well as I:
Whoso shal telle a tale after a man,
Whoever must repeat a story after someone,
He moot reherce as ny as evere he can
He must repeat as closely as ever he knows how
735 Everich a word, if it be in his charge,
Every single word, if it be in his power,
Al speke he never so rudeliche and large;
Although he may speak ever so rudely and freely,
Or elles he moot telle his tale untrewe,
Or else he must tell his tale inaccurately,
Or feyne thing, or finde wordes newe.
Or make up things, or find new words.
He may nat spare, althogh he were his brother;
He may not refrain from (telling the truth), although he were his brother;
740 He moot as wel seye o word as another.
He must as well say one word as another.
Crist spak himself ful brode in Holy Writ,
Christ himself spoke very plainly in holy writ,
And wel ye woot, no vileinye is it.
And you know well it is no rudeness.
Eek Plato seith, whoso can him rede,
Also Plato says, whosoever knows how to read him,
The wordes mote be cosin to the dede.
The words must be closely related to the deed.
745 Also I prey yow to foryeve it me,
Also I pray you to forgive it to me,
Al have I nat set folk in hir degree
Although I have not set folk in order of their rank
Here in this tale, as that they sholde stonde;
Here in this tale, as they should stand.
My wit is short, ye may wel understonde.
My wit is short, you can well understand.
Greet chere made oure Hoste us everichon,
Our Host made great hospitality to everyone of us,
750 And to the soper sette he us anon;
And to the supper he set us straightway.
He served us with vitaille at the beste.
He served us with victuals of the best sort;

Strong was the wyn, and wel to drinke us leste.
The wine was strong, and it well pleased us to drink.
A semely man oure hoste was withalle
OUR HOST was an impressive man indeed
For to been a marshal in an halle;
(Qualified) to be a master of ceremonies in a hall.
755 A large man he was with eyen stepe—
He was a large man with prominent eyes—
A fairer burgeys was ther noon in Chepe.
There was no better business man in Cheapside—
Bold of his speche, and wys, and wel y-taught,
Bold of his speech, and wise, and well mannered,
And of manhod him lakkede right naught.
And he lacked nothing at all of the qualities proper to a man.
Eek therto he was right a mery man,
Also moreover he was a right merry man;
760 And after soper pleyen he bigan,
And after supper he began to be merry,
And spak of mirthe amonges othere thinges—
And spoke of mirth among other things,
Whan that we hadde maad oure rekeninges—
When we had paid our bills,
And seyde thus: "Now, lordinges, trewely,
And said thus: "Now, gentlemen, truly,
Ye been to me right welcome hertely.
You are right heartily welcome to me;
765 For by my trouthe, if that I shal nat lye,
For by my word, if I shall not lie (I must say),
I saugh nat this yeer so mery a compaignye
I saw not this year so merry a company
Atones in this herberwe as is now.
At one time in this lodging as is (here) now.
Fayn wolde I doon yow mirthe, wiste I how,
I would gladly make you happy, if I knew how.
And of a mirthe I am right now bithoght,
And I have just now thought of an amusement,
770 To doon yow ese, and it shal coste noght.
To give you pleasure, and it shall cost nothing.
   Ye goon to Caunterbury—God yow spede;
   "You go to Canterbury—God give you success,
The blisful martir quyte yow your mede.
May the blessed martyr give you your reward!
And wel I woot, as ye goon by the weye,
And well I know, as you go by the way,
Ye shapen yow to talen and to pleye;
You intend to tell tales and to amuse yourselves;
775 For trewely, confort ne mirthe is noon
For truly, it is no comfort nor mirth
To ryde by the weye doumb as a stoon;
To ride by the way dumb as a stone;
And therfore wol I maken yow disport,
And therefore I will make a game for you,
As I seyde erst, and doon yow som confort.

As I said before, and provide you some pleasure.
And if yow lyketh alle, by oon assent,
And if pleases you all unanimously
780 Now for to stonden at my jugement,
To be subject to my judgment,
And for to werken as I shal yow seye,
And to do as I shall tell you,
To-morwe, whan ye ryden by the weye—
Tomorrow, when you ride by the way,
Now by my fader soule that is deed—
Now, by the soul of my father who is dead,
But ye be merye, I wol yeve yow myn heed.
Unless you be merry, I will give you my head!
785 Hold up youre hondes, withouten more speche."
Hold up your hands, without more speech."
   Oure counseil was nat longe for to seche;
   Our decision was not long to seek out.
Us thoughte it was noght worth to make it wys,
It seemed to us it was not worthwhile to deliberate on it,
And graunted him withouten more avys,
And (we) granted his request without more discussion,
And bad him seye his voirdit as him leste.
And asked him to say his decision as it pleased him.
790   "Lordinges," quod he, "now herkneth for the beste,
   "Gentlemen," said he, "now listen for the best course of action;
But tak it nought, I prey yow, in desdeyn.
But, I pray yow, do not take it in disdain (scorn it).
This is the poynt, to speken short and pleyn:
This is the point, to speak briefly and clearly,
That ech of yow, to shorte with oure weye,
That each of yow, to make our way seem short by this means,
In this viage shal telle tales tweye,
Must tell two tales in this journey
795 To Caunterbury-ward, I mene it so,
On the way to Canterbury, that is what I mean,
And homward he shal tellen othere two,
And on the homeward trip he shall tell two others,
Of aventures that whylom han bifalle.
About adventures that in old times have happened.
And which of yow that bereth him best of alle,
And whoever of you who does best of all—
That is to seyn, that telleth in this cas
That is to say, who tells in this case
800 Tales of best sentence and most solas,
Tales of best moral meaning and most pleasure—
Shal have a soper at oure aller cost
Shall have a supper at the cost of us all
Here in this place, sittinge by this post,
Here in this place, sitting by this post,
Whan that we come agayn fro Caunterbury.
When we come back from Canterbury.
And for to make yow the more mery,
And to make you the more merry,

805 I wol myselven goodly with yow ryde,
I will myself gladly ride with you,
Right at myn owne cost, and be youre gyde.
Entirely at my own cost, and be your guide;
And whoso wole my jugement withseye   a
And whosoever will not accept my judgment
Shal paye al that we spenden by the weye.
Shall pay all that we spend by the way.
And if ye vouchesauf that it be so,
And if you grant that it be so,
810 Tel me anon, withouten wordes mo,
Tell me straightway, without more words,
And I wol erly shape me therfore."
And I will get ready early for this."
   This thing was graunted, and oure othes swore
   This thing was granted, and our oaths sworn
With ful glad herte, and preyden him also
With very glad hearts, and (we) prayed him also
That he wolde vouchesauf for to do so,
That he would consent to do so,
815 And that he wolde been oure governour
And that he would be our governor,
And of oure tales juge and reportour,
And judge and score keeper of our tales,
And sette a soper at a certeyn prys;
And set a supper at a certain price,
And we wol reuled been at his devys
And we will be ruled as he wishes
In heigh and lowe; and thus, by oon assent,
In every respect; and thus unanimously
820 We been acorded to his jugement.
We are accorded to his judgment.
And therupon the wyn was fet anon;
And thereupon the wine was fetched immediately;
We dronken, and to reste wente echon,
We drank, and each one went to rest,
Withouten any lenger taryinge.
Without any longer tarrying.
   Amorwe, whan that day bigan to springe,
   In the morning, when day began to spring,
825 Up roos oure Host and was oure aller cok,
Our Host arose, and was the rooster of us all (awakened us).
And gadrede us togidre, in a flok;
And gathered us together in a flock,
And forth we riden, a litel more than pas,
And forth we rode at little more than a walk
Unto the watering of Seint Thomas,
Unto the Watering of Saint Thomas;
And there oure Host bigan his hors areste,
And there our Host stopped his horse
830 And seyde, "Lordinges, herkneth, if yow leste.
And said, "Gentlemen, listen, if you please.
   Ye woot youre forward, and I it yow recorde.

You know your agreement, and I remind you of it.
If even-song and morwe-song acorde,
If what you said last night agrees with what you say this morning,
Lat se now who shal telle the firste tale.
Let's see now who shall tell the first tale.
As evere mote I drinke wyn or ale,
As ever I may drink wine or ale,
835 Whoso be rebel to my jugement
Whosoever may be rebel to my judgment
Shal paye for al that by the weye is spent.
Shall pay for all that is spent by the way.
Now draweth cut, er that we ferrer twinne;
Now draw straws, before we depart further (from London);
He which that hath the shortest shal biginne.
He who has the shortest shall begin.
    Sire Knight," quod he, "my maister and my lord,
    Sir Knight," said he, "my master and my lord,
840 Now draweth cut for that is myn acord.
Now draw a straw, for that is my decision.
Cometh neer," quod he, "my lady Prioresse;
Come nearer," he said, "my lady Prioress.
And ye, sire Clerk, lat be youre shamfastnesse,
And you, sir Clerk, let be your modesty,
Ne studieth noght. Ley hond to, every man!"
And study not; lay hand to (draw a straw), every man!"
    Anon to drawen every wight bigan,
    Every person began straightway to draw,
845 And shortly for to tellen as it was,
And shortly to tell as it was,
Were it by aventure, or sort, or cas,
Were it by chance, or destiny, or luck,
The sothe is this, the cut fil to the Knight,
The truth is this: the draw fell to the Knight,
Of which ful blythe and glad was every wight;
For which everyone was very happy and glad,
And telle he moste his tale, as was resoun,
And he must tell his tale, as was reasonable,
850 By forward and by composicioun,
By our previous promise and by formal agreement,
As ye han herd. What nedeth wordes mo?
As you have heard; what more words are needed?
And whan this gode man saugh it was so,
And when this good man saw that it was so,
As he that wys was and obedient
Like one who was wise and obedient
To kepe his forward by his free assent,
To keep his agreement by his free assent,
855 He seyde: "Sin I shal biginne the game,
He said, "Since I must begin the game,
What, welcome be the cut, a Goddes name!
What! Welcome be the draw, in God's name!
Now lat us ryde, and herkneth what I seye."
Now let us ride, and listen to what I say."

And with that word we riden forth oure weye;
And with that word we rode forth on our way,
And he bigan with right a mery chere
And he began with a truly merry demeanor
860 His tale anon, and seyde as ye may heere.
To tell his tale straightway, and said as you may hear.

The Miller's Prologue and Tale

The Prologue

Whan that the Knight had thus his tale y-told,
When the Knight had thus told his tale,
In al the route nas ther yong ne old
In all the company there was no one young nor old
That he ne seyde it was a noble storie,
Who did not say it was a noble story
And worthy for to drawen to memorie,
And worthy to draw into memory,
5 And namely the gentils everichoon.
And especially the gentlefolk every one.
     Oure Hoste lough and swoor, "So moot I goon,
     Our Host laughed and swore, "As I may move about (I swear),
This gooth aright; unbokeled is the male.
This goes well; the bag is opened.
Lat see now who shal telle another tale,
Let's see now who shall tell another tale;
For trewely, the game is wel bigonne.
For truly the game is well begun.
10 Now telleth ye, sir Monk, if that ye conne,
Now tell you, sir Monk, if you can,
Sumwhat to quyte with the Knightes tale."
Something to equal the Knight's tale."
     The Miller, that fordronken was al pale,
     The Miller, who for drunkenness was all pale,
So that unnethe upon his hors he sat,
So that he hardly sat upon his horse,
He nolde avalen neither hood ne hat,
He would not doff neither hood nor hat,
15 Ne abyde no man for his curteisye,
Nor give preference to any man out of courtesy,
But in Pilates vois he gan to crye,
But in Pilate's voice he began to cry,
And swoor, "By armes and by blood and bones,
And swore, "By (Christ's) arms, and by blood and bones,
I can a noble tale for the nones,
I know a noble tale for this occasion,
With which I wol now quyte the Knightes tale."
With which I will now requite the Knight's tale."
20   Oure Hoste saugh that he was dronke of ale,
     Our Host saw that he was drunk on ale,
And seyde, "Abyd, Robin, my leve brother,

And said, "Wait, Robin, my dear brother;
Som bettre man shal telle us first another:
Some better man shall first tell us another.
Abyd, and lat us werken thriftily."
Wait, and let us act properly."
   "By Goddes soul," quod he, "that wol nat I;
*   "By God's soul," said he, "that will not I;*
25 For I wol speke or elles go my wey."
For I will speak or else go my way."
   Oure Hoste answerde, "Tel on, a devel wey!
*   Our Host answered, "Tell on, in the devil's name!*
Thou art a fool, thy wit is overcome."
Thou art a fool; thy wit is overcome."
   "Now herkneth," quod the Miller, "alle and some!
*   "Now listen," said the Miller, "everyone!*
But first I make a protestacioun
But first I make a protestation
30 That I am dronke, I knowe it by my soun.
That I am drunk; I know it by my sound.
And therfore, if that I misspeke or seye,
And therefore if that I misspeak or say (amiss),
Wyte it the ale of Southwerk, I yow preye;
Blame it on ale of Southwerk, I you pray.
For I wol telle a legende and a lyf
For I will tell a legend and a life
Bothe of a carpenter and of his wyf,
Both of a carpenter and of his wife,
hoo 35 How that a clerk hath set the wrightes cappe."
How a clerk has set the carpenter's cap (fooled him)."
   The Reve answerde and seyde, "Stint thy clappe!
*   The Reeve answered and said, "Hold your tongue!*
Lat be thy lewed dronken harlotrye.
Let be thy ignorant drunken ribaldry.
It is a sinne and eek a greet folye
It is a sin and also a great folly
To apeiren any man, or him diffame,
To slander any man, or defame him,
40 And eek to bringen wyves in swich fame.
And also to bring wives in such ill fame.
Thou mayst ynogh of othere thinges seyn."
Thou canst say enough about other things."
   This dronken Miller spak ful sone ageyn,
*   This drunken Miller spoke very quickly in reply*
And seyde, "Leve brother Osewold,
And said, "Dear brother Oswald,
Who hath no wyf, he is no cokewold.
He who has no wife, he is no cuckold.
45 But I sey nat therfore that thou art oon;
But I say not therefore that thou art one;
Ther been ful gode wyves many oon,
There are very good wives, many a one,
And ever a thousand gode ayeyns oon badde.
And ever a thousand good against one bad.

That knowestow wel thyself, but if thou madde.
Thou knowest that well thyself, unless thou art mad.
Why artow angry with my tale now?
Why art thou angry with my tale now?
50 I have a wyf, pardee, as well as thou,
I have a wife, by God, as well as thou;
Yet nolde I, for the oxen in my plogh,
Yet I would not, for the oxen in my plow,
Take upon me more than ynogh,
Take upon me more than enough (trouble),
As demen of myself that I were oon;
As to believe of myself that I were one (a cuckold);
I wol beleve wel that I am noon.
I will believe well that I am not one.
55 An housbond shal nat been inquisitif
A husband must not be inquisitive
Of Goddes privetee, nor of his wyf.
Of God's secrets, nor of his wife.
So he may finde Goddes foyson there,
So long as he can find God's plenty there,
Of the remenant nedeth nat enquere."
Of the rest he needs not enquire."
    What sholde I more seyn, but this Millere
    What more should I say, but this Miller
60 He nolde his wordes for no man forbere,
He would not refrain from speaking for any man,
But tolde his cherles tale in his manere.
But told his churl's tale in his manner.
M'athynketh that I shal reherce it here.
I regret that I must repeat it here.
And therfore every gentil wight I preye,
And therefore every respectable person I pray,
For Goddes love, demeth nat that I seye
For God's love, think not that I speak
65 Of evel entente, but that I moot reherce
Out of evil intention, but because I must repeat
Hir tales alle, be they bettre or werse,
All their tales, be they better or worse,
Or elles falsen som of my matere.
Or else (I must) falsify some of my material.
And therfore, whoso list it nat y-here,
And therefore, whoever does not want to hear it,
Turne over the leef, and chese another tale;
Turn over the leaf and choose another tale;
70 For he shal finde ynowe, grete and smale,
For he shall find enough, of every sort,
Of storial thing that toucheth gentillesse,
Of historical matter that concerns nobility,
And eek moralitee and holinesse.
And also morality and holiness.
Blameth nat me if that ye chese amis.
Blame not me if you choose amiss.
The Millere is a cherl, ye knowe wel this;

The Miller is a churl; you know this well.
75 So was the Reve eek and othere mo,
So was the Reeve also and many others,
And harlotrye they tolden bothe two.
And ribaldry they told, both of the two.
Avyseth yow and putte me out of blame;
Think about this, and don't blame me;
And eek men shal nat maken ernest of game.
And also people should not take a joke too seriously.

The Tale

Whylom ther was dwellinge at Oxenford
There was once dwelling at Oxford
80 A riche gnof, that gestes heeld to bord,
A rich churl, who took in boarders,
And of his craft he was a carpenter.
And of his craft he was a carpenter.
With him ther was dwellinge a povre scoler,
With him there was dwelling a poor scholar,
Hadde lerned art, but al his fantasye
Who had learned the arts curriculum, but all his desire
Was turned for to lerne astrologye,
Was turned to learning astrology,
85 And coude a certeyn of conclusiouns
And he knew a certain (number of) of astronomical operations,
To demen by interrogaciouns,
To determine by scientific calculations,
If that men asked him in certein houres
If men asked him, in specific (astronomical) hours
Whan that men sholde have droghte or elles shoures,
When men should have drought or else showers,
Or if men asked him what sholde bifalle
Or if people asked him what should happen
90 Of every thing, I may nat rekene hem alle.
Concerning every thing; I can not reckon them all.
    This clerk was cleped hende Nicholas.
    This clerk was called clever Nicholas.
Of derne love he coude and of solas;
Of secret love he knew and of its satisfaction;
And therto he was sleigh and ful privee,
And moreover he was sly and very discreet,
And lyk a mayden meke for to see.
And like a maiden meek in appearance.
95 A chambre hadde he in that hostelrye
A room had he in that hostelry
Allone, withouten any companye,
Alone, without any company,
Ful fetisly y-dight with herbes swote;
Very elegantly strewn with sweet-smelling herbs;
And he himself as swete as is the rote
And he himself as sweet as is the root
Of licorys, or any cetewale.

Of licorice or any zedoary (a ginger-like herb).

100 His Almageste and bokes grete and smale,
His Almagest, and books large and small,
His astrelabie, longinge for his art,
His astrolabe, belonging to his art (of astronomy),
His augrim-stones layen faire apart
His counting stones (for his abacus) lie neatly apart,
On shelves couched at his beddes heed;
Arranged on shelves at his bed's head;
His presse y-covered with a falding reed.
His linen press covered with a red woolen cloth;

105 And al above ther lay a gay sautrye,
And all above there lay a fine psaltery,
On which he made a-nightes melodye
On which at night he made melody
So swetely, that al the chambre rong,
So sweetly that all the room rang;
And *Angelus ad virginem* he song,
And "The Angel to the Virgin" he sang;
And after that he song the kinges note;
And after that he sang the King's Tune.

110 Ful often blessed was his mery throte.
Very often his merry throat was blessed.
And thus this swete clerk his tyme spente
And thus this sweet clerk spent his time
After his freendes finding and his rente.
Living on his friends' support and his (own) income.

This carpenter hadde wedded newe a wyf
This carpenter had recently wedded a wife,
Which that he lovede more than his lyf;
Whom he loved more than his life;

115 Of eightetene yeer she was of age.
She was eighteen years of age.
Jalous he was, and heeld hire narwe in cage,
Jealous he was, and held her narrowly in confinement,
For she was wilde and yong, and he was old
For she was wild and young, and he was old
And demed himself ben lyk a cokewold.
And believed himself likely to be a cuckold.
He knew nat Catoun, for his wit was rude,
He knew not Cato, for his wit was rude,

120 That bad man sholde wedde his similitude.
Who advised that man should wed his equal.
Men sholde wedden after hire estaat,
Men should wed according to their status in life,
For youthe and elde is often at debaat.
For youth and old age are often in conflict.
But sith that he was fallen in the snare,
But since he was fallen in the snare,
He moste endure, as other folk, his care.
He must endure, like other folk, his troubles.

125 Fair was this yonge wyf, and therwithal
Fair was this young wife, and moreover

As any wesele hir body gent and smal.
As any weasel was her body graceful and slender.
A ceynt she werede barred al of silk;
A belt she wore, with decorative strips all of silk,
A barmclooth eek as whyt as morne milk
An apron also, as white as morning milk
Upon hir lendes, ful of many a gore.
Upon her loins, full of many a flounce.
130   Whyt was hir smok, and broyden al bifore
White was her smock, and embroidered all in front
And eek bihinde, on hir coler aboute,
And also behind, around her collar,
Of col-blak silk, withinne and eek withoute.
With coal-black silk, within and also without.
The tapes of hir whyte voluper
The ribbons of her white cap
Were of the same suyte of hir coler;
Were of the same color as her collar;
135   Hir filet brood of silk and set ful hye.
Her headband broad of silk, and set very high.
And sikerly she hadde a likerous yë.
And surely she had a wanton eye;
Ful smale y-pulled were hire browes two,
Her two eyebrows were plucked very thin,
And tho were bent, and blake as any sloo.
And those were bent and black as any sloe.
She was ful more blisful on to see
She was much more blissful to look upon
140   Than is the newe pere-jonette tree;
Than is the new early-ripe pear tree,
And softer than the wolle is of a wether.
And softer than the wool is of a sheep.
And by hir girdel heeng a purs of lether
And by her girdle hung a purse of leather,
Tasseled with silk, and perled with latoun.
Tasseled with silk and ornamented with latten "pearls."
In al this world, to seken up and doun,
In all this world, to seek up and down,
145   There nis no man so wys that coude thenche
There is no man so wise that he could imagine
So gay a popelote, or swich a wenche.
So lovely a little doll or such a wench.
Ful brighter was the shyning of hir hewe
Much brighter was the shining of her complexion
Than in the Tour the noble y-forged newe.
Than the newly minted noble in the Tower.
But of hir song, it was as loude and yerne
But of her song, it was as loud and lively
150   As any swalwe sittinge on a berne.
As any swallow sitting on a barn.
Therto she coude skippe and make game,
Moreover she could skip and play,
As any kide or calf folwinge his dame.

Like any kid or calf following its mother.
Hir mouth was swete as bragot or the meeth,
Her mouth was sweet as ale and honey or mead,
Or hord of apples leyd in hey or heeth.
Or a hoard of apples laid in hay or heather.

155 Winsinge she was, as is a joly colt,
Skittish she was, as is a spirited colt,
Long as a mast, and upright as a bolt.
Tall as a mast, and straight as an arrow.
A brooch she baar upon hir lowe coler,
A brooch she wore upon her low collar,
As brood as is the bos of a bocler;
As broad as is the boss of a shield.
Hir shoes were laced on hir legges hye.
Her shoes were laced high on her legs.

160 She was a prymerole, a piggesnye,
She was a primrose, a pig's eye (a flower),
For any lord to leggen in his bedde,
For any lord to lay in his bed,
Or yet for any good yeman to wedde.
Or yet for any good yeoman to wed.
    Now sire, and eft sire, so bifel the cas,
    Now, sir, and again, sir, it so happened
That on a day this hende Nicholas
That one day this clever Nicholas

165 Fil with this yonge wyf to rage and pleye,
Happened with this young wife to flirt and play,
Whyl that hir housbond was at Osney,
While her husband was at Osney,
As clerkes ben ful subtile and ful queynte.
For clerks are very subtle and very clever;
And prively he caughte hire by the queynte,
And intimately he caught her by her crotch,
And seyde, "Ywis, but if ich have my wille,
And said, "Indeed, unless I have my will,

170 For derne love of thee, lemman, I spille,"
For secret love of thee, sweetheart, I die."
And heeld hire harde by the haunche-bones,
And held her hard by the thigh,
And seyde, "Lemman, love me al atones,
And said, "Sweetheart, love me immediately
Or I wol dyen, also God me save!"
Or I will die, so save me God!"
And she sprong as a colt doth in the trave,
And she sprang as a colt does when restrained,

175 And with hir heed she wryed faste awey,
And with her head she twisted fast away,
And seyde, "I wol nat kisse thee, by my fey.
And said, "I will not kiss thee, by my faith!
Why, lat be," quod she, "lat be, Nicholas,
Why, let me be!" said she. "Let me be, Nicholas,
Or I wol crye 'out, harrow' and 'allas.'
Or I will cry 'out, help' and 'alas'!

Do wey your handes for your curteisye!"
Take away your hands, for your courtesy!"
180   This Nicholas gan mercy for to crye,
        This Nicholas began to cry for mercy,
And spak so faire, and profred him so faste,
And spoke so fair, and pressed his suit so fast,
That she hir love him graunted atte laste,
That she granted him her love at the last,
And swoor hir ooth, by Seint Thomas of Kent,
And swore her oath, by Saint Thomas of Kent,
That she wol been at his comandement,
That she will be at his commandment,
185   Whan that she may hir leyser wel espye.
        When she may well espy her opportunity.
"Myn housbond is so ful of jalousye,
"My husband is so full of jealousy
That but ye wayte wel and been privee,
That unless you wait patiently and are secretive,
I woot right wel I nam but deed," quod she.
I know right well I am as good as dead," said she.
"Ye moste been ful derne, as in this cas."
"You must been very secret in this matter."
190   "Nay, therof care thee noght," quod Nicholas.
        "No, care thee not about that," said Nicholas.
"A clerk had litherly biset his whyle,
"A clerk had badly wasted his time (studying),
But if he coude a carpenter bigyle."
If he could not outwit a carpenter."
And thus they been acorded and y-sworn
And thus they are agreed and sworn
To wayte a tyme, as I have told biforn.
To wait for a time, as I have told before.
195   Whan Nicholas had doon thus everydeel,
        When Nicholas had done thus every bit
And thakked hire aboute the lendes weel,
And well patted her about the loins,
He kiste hire swete, and taketh his sautrye,
He kissed her sweetly and takes his psaltery,
And pleyeth faste, and maketh melodye.
And plays fast, and makes melody.
        Thanne fil it thus, that to the parish chirche,
        Then it thus happened, that to the parish church,
200   Cristes owene werkes for to wirche,
        Christ's own works to do,
This gode wyf wente on an haliday;
This good wife went on a holiday.
Hir forheed shoon as bright as any day,
Her forehead shone as bright as any day,
So was it wasshen whan she leet hir werk.
It was so washed when she left her work.
        Now was ther of that chirche a parish clerk,
        Now was there of that church a parish clerk,
205   The which that was y-cleped Absolon.

Who was called Absolon.
Crul was his heer, and as the gold it shoon,
Curly was his hair, and as the gold it shone,
And strouted as a fanne large and brode;
And stretched out like a fan large and broad;
Ful streight and evene lay his joly shode.
Very straight and even lay his elegant parted hair.
His rode was reed, his eyen greye as goos;
His complexion was ruddy, his eyes gray as a goose.

210   With Powles window corven on his shoos,
With St. Paul's window carved on his shoes,
In hoses rede he wente fetisly.
In red hose he went elegantly.
Y-clad he was ful smal and properly,
Clad he was very trimly and properly
Al in a kirtel of a light waget—
All in a tunic of a light blue;
Ful faire and thikke been the poyntes set—
Very fair and thick are the laces set.

215   And therupon he hadde a gay surplys
And over that he had a gay surplice
As whyt as is the blosme upon the rys.
As white as is the blossom upon the branch.
A mery child he was, so God me save.
A merry lad he was, so save me God.
Wel coude he laten blood and clippe and shave,
Well could he draw blood, and cut hair and shave,
And make a chartre of lond or acquitaunce.
And make a charter of land or a legal release.

220   In twenty manere coude he trippe and daunce
In twenty different ways could he trip and dance
After the scole of Oxenforde tho,
After the school of Oxford as it was then,
And with his legges casten to and fro,
And with his legs kick to and fro,
And pleyen songes on a small rubible,
And play songs on a small fiddle,
Therto he song som tyme a loud quinible;
To which he some times sang a loud high treble;

225   And as wel coude he pleye on a giterne.
And he could play as well on a guitar.
In al the toun nas brewhous ne taverne
In all the town there was no brew house nor tavern
That he ne visited with his solas,
That he did not visit with his entertainment,
Ther any gaylard tappestere was.
Where any merry barmaid was.
But sooth to seyn, he was somdel squaymous
But to say the truth, he was somewhat squeamish

230   Of farting, and of speche daungerous.
About farting, and fastidious in his speech.
   This Absolon, that jolif was and gay,
   This Absolon, who was elegant and gay,

Gooth with a sencer on the haliday,
Goes with a censer on the holiday,
Sensinge the wyves of the parish faste,
Censing the wives of the parish eagerly;
And many a lovely look on hem he caste,
And many a lovely look he cast on them,
235   And namely on this carpenteres wyf:
And especially on this carpenter's wife.
To loke on hire him thoughte a mery lyf.
To look on her he thought a merry life,
She was so propre and swete and likerous,
She was so attractive and sweet and flirtatious.
I dar wel seyn, if she had been a mous,
I dare well say, if she had been a mouse,
And he a cat, he wolde hire hente anon.
And he a cat, he would have grabbed her at once.
240   This parish clerk, this joly Absolon,
This parish clerk, this elegant Absolon,
Hath in his herte swich a love-longinge,
Has in his heart such a love-longing
That of no wyf ne took he noon offringe;
That of no wife took he any offering;
For curteisye, he seyde, he wolde noon.
For courtesy, he said, he would have none.
The mone, whan it was night, ful brighte shoon,
The moon, when it was night, very brightly shone,
245   And Absolon his giterne hath y-take;
And Absolon his guitar has taken;
For paramours he thoghte for to wake.
For the sake of love he intended to stay awake.
And forth he gooth, jolif and amorous,
And forth he goes, elegant and amorous,
Til he cam to the carpenteres hous
Until he came to the carpenter's house
A litel after cokkes hadde y-crowe,
A little after cocks had crowed,
250   And dressed him up by a shot-windowe
And took his place up by a casement window
That was upon the carpenteres wal.
That was upon the carpenter's wall.
He singeth in his vois gentil and smal,
He sings in his voice gentle and high,
"Now, dere lady, if thy wille be,
"Now, dear lady, if it be thy will,
I preye yow that ye wol rewe on me,"
I pray yow that you will have pity on me,"
255   Ful wel acordaunt to his giterninge.
Very well in harmony with his guitar-playing.
This carpenter awook and herde him singe,
This carpenter awoke, and heard him sing,
And spak unto his wyf, and seyde anon,
And spoke unto his wife, and said at once,
"What, Alison, herestow nat Absolon

"What! Alison! Hearest thou not Absolon,
That chaunteth thus under oure boures wal?"
That chants thus next to our bedroom's wall?"
260 And she answerde hir housbond therwithal,
And she answered her husband immediately,
"Yis, God wot, John, I here it every deel."
"Yes indeed, God knows, John, I hear it every bit."
This passeth forth; what wol ye bet than wel?
This goes on; what more would you have?
Fro day to day this joly Absolon
From day to day this elegant Absolon
So woweth hire, that him is wo bigon.
So woos her that he is in a sorry state.
265 He waketh al the night and al the day;
He stays awake all the night and all the day;
He kembeth hise lokkes brode, and made him gay;
He combs his flowing locks, and dressed himself elegantly;
He woweth hire by menes and brocage,
He woos her by go-betweens and agents,
And swoor he wolde been hir owene page;
And swore he would be her own servant;
He singeth, brokkinge as a nightingale;
He sings, trilling like a nightingale;
270 He sente hire piment, meeth, and spyced ale,
He sent her sweetened wine, mead, and spiced ale,
And wafres, pyping hote out of the glede;
And wafers, piping hot out of the fire;
And for she was of toune, he profred mede.
And, because she was a townie, he offered money;
For som folk wol ben wonnen for richesse,
For some folk will be won for riches,
And som for strokes, and som for gentillesse.
And some by force, and some for noble character.
275 Somtyme, to shewe his lightness and maistrye,
Sometimes, to show his agility and skill,
He pleyeth Herodes on a scaffold hye.
He plays Herod upon a high stage.
But what availleth him as in this cas?
But what good does it do him in this case?
She loveth so this hende Nicholas,
She so loves this clever Nicholas
That Absolon may blowe the bukkes horn;
That Absolon may go whistle;
280 He ne hadde for his labour but a scorn.
He had for his labor nothing but scorn.
And thus she maketh Absolon hire ape,
And thus she makes Absolon her fool,
And al his ernest turneth til a jape.
And turns all his earnestness into a joke.
Ful sooth is this proverbe, it is no lye,
Very true is this proverb, it is no lie,
Men seyn right thus, "Alwey the nye slye
Men say right thus: "Always the nearby sly one

285 Maketh the ferre leve to be looth."
Makes the distant loved one to be disliked."
For though that Absolon be wood or wrooth,
For though Absolon be crazed or angry,
By cause that he fer was from hir sighte,
Because he was far from her sight,
This nye Nicholas stood in his lighte.
This nearby Nicholas cast him in the shadow.
   Now bere thee wel, thou hende Nicholas!
   Now bear thyself well, thou clever Nicholas,
290 For Absolon may waille and singe "allas."
For Absolon may wail and sing "alas."
   And so bifel it on a Saterday,
   And so it happened on a Saturday,
This carpenter was goon til Osenay,
This carpenter was gone to Osenay;
And hende Nicholas and Alisoun
And clever Nicholas and Alisoun
Acorded been to this conclusioun,
Are agreed on this plan,
295 That Nicholas shal shapen him a wyle
That Nicholas shall devise a trick
This sely jalous housbond to bigyle;
To beguile this hapless jealous husband;
And if so be the game wente aright,
And if it so be the game went right,
She sholde slepen in his arm al night,
She should sleep in his arms all night,
For this was his desyr and hire also.
For this was his desire and hers also.
300 And right anon, withouten wordes mo,
And right away, without more words,
This Nicholas no lenger wolde tarie,
This Nicholas no longer would tarry,
But doth ful softe unto his chambre carie
But has carried very quietly unto his chamber
Bothe mete and drinke for a day or tweye,
Both food and drink for a day or two,
And to hire housbonde bad hire for to seye,
And told her to say to her husband,
305 If that he axed after Nicholas,
If he asked about Nicholas,
She sholde seye she niste where he was,
She should say she knew not where he was;
Of al that day she saugh him nat with yë;
Of all that day she saw him not with eye;
She trowed that he was in maladye,
She believed that he was ill,
For for no cry hir mayde coude him calle
Because, for no shout could her maid call him,
310 He nolde answere, for thing that mighte falle.
He would not answer for anything that might befall.
   This passeth forth al thilke Saterday,

This goes on all that same Saturday,
That Nicholas stille in his chambre lay,
That Nicholas still in his chamber lay,
And eet and sleep, or dide what him leste,
And ate and slept, or did what he pleased,
Til Sonday, that the sonne gooth to reste.
Until Sunday, when the sun goes to rest.

315 This sely carpenter hath greet merveyle
This hapless carpenter has great marvel
Of Nicholas, or what thing mighte him eyle,
About Nicholas, or what thing might ail him,
And seyde, "I am adrad, by Seint Thomas,
And said, "I am afraid, by Saint Thomas,
It stondeth nat aright with Nicholas.
Things are not right with Nicholas.
God shilde that he deyde sodeynly!
God forbid that he should suddenly die!

320 This world is now ful tikel, sikerly:
This world is now very ticklish, surely.
I saugh to-day a cors y-born to chirche
I saw today a corpse carried to church
That now, on Monday last, I saugh him wirche.
That just now, on last Monday, I saw him work.
Go up," quod he unto his knave anoon,
"Go up," he said unto his servant at once,
"Clepe at his dore, or knokke with a stoon,
"Call at his door, or knock with a stone.

325 Loke how it is, and tel me boldely."
Look how it is, and tell me quickly."
   This knave gooth him up ful sturdily,
   This servant goes up very resolutely,
And at the chambre dore, whyl that he stood,
And at the chamber door while he stood,
He cryde and knokked as that he were wood:
He cried and knocked as if he were crazy,
"What! how! what do ye, maister Nicholay?
"What, hey! What do you, master Nicholay?

330 How may ye slepen al the longe day?"
How can you sleep all the long day?"
But al for noght, he herde nat a word.
But all for naught; he heard not a word.
An hole he fond, ful lowe upon a bord,
He found a hole, very low upon a board,
Ther as the cat was wont in for to crepe;
Where the cat was accustomed to creep in,
And at that hole he looked in ful depe,
And through that hole he looked in very carefully,

335 And at the laste he hadde of him a sighte.
And at the last he had a sight of him.
   This Nicholas sat evere caping uprighte,
   This Nicholas sat ever gaping upward,
As he had kyked on the newe mone.
As if he were gazing on the new moon.

Adoun he gooth, and tolde his maister sone
Down he goes, and told his master immediately
In what array he saugh this ilke man.
In what condition he saw this same man.

340   This carpenter to blessen him bigan,
        This carpenter began to bless himself,
And seyde, "Help us, Seinte Frideswyde!
And said, "Help us, Saint Frideswide!
A man woot litel what him shal bityde.
A man knows little what shall happen to him.
This man is falle, with his astromye,
This man is fallen, because of his astronomy,
In som woodnesse or in som agonye;
In some madness or in some fit.

345   I thoghte ay wel how that it sholde be!
        I always thought well how it should be!
Men sholde nat knowe of Goddes privetee.
Men should not know of God's secrets.
Ye, blessed be alwey a lewed man
Yes, blessed be always an unlearned man
That noght but oonly his bileve can!
Who knows nothing but only his belief!
So ferde another clerk with astromye:
So fared another clerk with astronomy;

350   He walked in the feeldes for to prye
        He walked in the fields to look
Upon the sterres, what ther sholde bifalle,
Upon the stars, (to find) there what should happen,
Til he was in a marle-pit y-falle—
Until he was fallen in a fertilizer pit;
He saugh nat that. But yet, by Seint Thomas,
He did not see that. But yet, by Saint Thomas,
Me reweth sore of hende Nicholas.
I feel very sorry for clever Nicholas.

355   He shal be rated of his studying,
        He shall be scolded for his studying,
If that I may, by Jesus, hevene king!
If that I may, by Jesus, heaven's king!
Get me a staf, that I may underspore,
Get me a staff, that I may pry up from below,
Whyl that thou, Robin, hevest up the dore.
While thou, Robyn, lift up the door.
He shal out of his studying, as I gesse."
He shall (come) out of his studying, as I guess."

360   And to the chambre dore he gan him dresse.
        And to the chamber door he turned his attention.
His knave was a strong carl for the nones,
His servant was a strong fellow for this purpose,
And by the haspe he haf it up atones;
And by the hasp he heaved it off at once;
Into the floor the dore fil anon.
Onto the floor the door fell straightway.
This Nicholas sat ay as stille as stoon,

This Nicholas sat ever as still as stone,

365 And ever caped upward into the eir.
And ever gaped upward into the air.
This carpenter wende he were in despeir,
This carpenter supposed he was in despair,
And hente him by the sholdres mightily,
And seized him by the shoulders vigorously,
And shook him harde, and cryde spitously,
And shook him hard, and cried loudly,
"What, Nicholay! what, how! what, loke adoun!
"What! Nicholay! What, how! What, look down!

370 Awake, and thenk on Cristes passioun!
Awake, and think on Christ's passion!
I crouche thee from elves and fro wightes!"
I bless thee from elves and from evil creatures."
Therwith the night-spel seyde he anon-rightes
Therewith the night-charm he said straightway
On foure halves of the hous aboute,
On four corners of the house about,
And on the threshfold of the dore withoute:
And on the threshold of the door outside:

375 "Jesu Crist, and Seynte Benedight,
"Jesus Christ and Saint Benedict,
Blesse this hous from every wikked wight,
Bless this house from every wicked creature,
For nightes verye, the white *pater-noster*!
For evil spirits of the nights, the white pater-noster!
Where wentestow, seynt Petres soster?"
Where went thou, Saint Peter's sister?"
And atte laste this hende Nicholas
And at the last this clever Nicholas

380 Gan for to syke sore, and seyde, "Allas!
Began to sigh deeply, and said, "Alas!
Shal al the world be lost eftsones now?"
Shall all the world be lost right now?"
   This carpenter answerde, "What seystow?
   This carpenter answered, "What sayest thou?
What! thenk on God, as we don, men that swinke!"
What! Think on God, as we do, men who work."
   This Nicholas answerde, "Fecche me drinke;
   This Nicholas answered, "Fetch me drink,

385 And after wol I speke in privitee
And after will I speak in private
Of certeyn thing that toucheth me and thee;
About a certain matter that concerns me and thee.
I wol telle it non other man, certeyn."
I will tell it to no other man, certainly."
   This carpenter goth doun and comth ageyn,
   This carpenter goes down, and comes again,
And broghte of mighty ale a large quart;
And brought of strong ale a large quart;

390 And whan that ech of hem had dronke his part,
And when each of them had drunk his part,

This Nicholas his dore faste shette,
This Nicholas shut fast his door,
And doun the carpenter by him he sette.
And the carpenter sat down by him.
He seyde, "John, myn hoste lief and dere,
He said, "John, my host, beloved and dear,
Thou shalt upon thy trouthe swere me here,
Thou shalt upon thy pledged word swear to me here
395 That to no wight thou shalt this conseil wreye;
That to no person thou shalt this counsel reveal,
For it is Cristes conseil that I seye,
For it is Christ's secrets that I say,
And if thou telle it man, thou art forlore;
And if thou tell it to anyone, thou art completely lost;
For this vengeaunce thou shalt han therfore,
For this vengeance thou shalt have therefore,
That if thou wreye me, thou shalt be wood!"
That if thou betray me, thou shalt go mad."
400 "Nay, Crist forbede it, for his holy blood!"
"Nay, Christ forbid it, for his holy blood!"
Quod tho this sely man, "I nam no labbe,
Said then this hapless man, "I am no blabbermouth,
Ne, though I seye, I nam nat lief to gabbe.
And, though I say it, I do not like to gab.
Sey what thou wolt, I shal it nevere telle
Say what thou will, I shall never tell it
To child ne wyf, by him that harwed helle!"
To child nor wife, by Him that rescued souls from hell!"
405 "Now John," quod Nicholas, "I wol nat lye.
"Now John," said Nicholas, "I will not lie;
I have y-founde in myn astrologye,
I have found in my astrology,
As I have loked in the mone bright,
As I have looked on the bright moon,
That now, a Monday next, at quarter night,
That now on Monday next, after midnight,
Shal falle a reyn and that so wilde and wood,
Shall fall a rain, and that so wild and raging
410 That half so greet was nevere Noës flood.
That Noah's flood was never half so large.
This world," he seyde, "in lasse than in an hour
This world," he said, "in less than an hour
Shal al be dreynt, so hidous is the shour;
Shall all be drowned, so hideous is the shower.
Thus shal mankynde drenche and lese hir lyf."
Thus shall mankind drown, and lose their lives."
     This carpenter answerde, "Allas, my wyf!
     This carpenter answered, "Alas, my wife!
415 And shal she drenche? allas, myn Alisoun!
And shall she drown? Alas, my Alisoun!"
For sorwe of this he fil almost adoun,
For sorrow of this he almost fell down,
And seyde, "Is ther no remedie in this cas?"

And said, "Is there no remedy in this case?"
  "Why, yis, for Gode," quod hende Nicholas,
  "Why, yes indeed, by God," said clever Nicholas,
"If thou wolt werken after lore and reed;
"If thou will act in accordance with learning and (good) advice.
420 Thou mayst nat werken after thyn owene heed;
Thou mayst not act according to thine own ideas;
For thus seith Salomon, that was ful trewe,
For thus says Salomon, which was very true:
'Werk al by conseil, and thou shalt nat rewe.'
'Do all in accordance with good advice, and thou shalt not rue (it).
And if thou werken wolt by good conseil,
And if thou will act in accordance with good advice,
I undertake, withouten mast and seyl,
I guarantee, without mast and sail,
425 Yet shal I saven hire and thee and me.
Yet shall I save her and thee and me.
Hastow nat herd how saved was Noë,
Hast thou not heard how Noah was saved,
Whan that Oure Lord hadde warned him biforn
When our Lord had warned him before
That al the world with water sholde be lorn?"
That all the world should be destroyed by water?"
  "Yis," quod this carpenter, "ful yore ago."
  "Yes indeed," said this Carpenter, "very long ago."
430 "Hastow nat herd," quod Nicholas, "also
"Hast thou not heard," said Nicholas, "also
The sorwe of Noë with his felawshipe?
The sorrow of Noah with his fellowship,
Er that he mighte gete his wyf to shipe,
Before he could get his wife onto the ship?
Him hadde be levere, I dar wel undertake,
He would rather, I dare well guarantee,
At thilke tyme than alle hise wetheres blake
At that time, than have all his black sheep
435 That she hadde had a ship hirself allone.
That she had had a ship for herself alone.
And therfore, wostou what is best to done?
And therefore, knowest thou what is best to do?
This asketh haste, and of an hastif thing
This needs haste, and of a hasty thing
Men may nat preche or maken tarying.
Men may not preach nor make tarrying.
Anon go gete us faste into this in
"Right now go bring us quickly into this dwelling
440 A kneding trogh or elles a kymelyn
A kneading trough, or else a large vat,
For ech of us, but loke that they be large,
For each of us, but see that they be large,
In whiche we mowe swimme as in a barge,
In which we may float as in a barge,
And han therinne vitaille suffisant
And have therein sufficient victuals

But for a day; fy on the remenant!
But for a day—fie on the remnant!
445 The water shal aslake and goon away
The water shall recede and go away
Aboute pryme upon the nexte day.
About nine a.m. on the next day.
But Robin may nat wite of this, thy knave,
But Robin, thy knave, may not know of this,
Ne eek thy mayde Gille I may nat save.
And also thy maid Gille I can not save;
Axe nat why, for though thou aske me,
Ask not why, for though thou ask me,
450 I wol nat tellen Goddes privetee.
I will not tell God's secrets.
Suffiseth thee, but if thy wittes madde,
It suffices thee, unless thy wits go mad,
To han as greet a grace as Noë hadde.
To have as great a grace as Noah had.
Thy wyf shal I wel saven, out of doute.
Thy wife shall I well save, beyond doubt.
Go now thy wey, and speed thee heer-aboute.
Go now thy way, and speed thee on this business.
455 But whan thou hast, for hire and thee and me,
"But when thou hast, for her and thee and me,
Y-geten us thise kneding tubbes three,
Got us these three kneading tubs,
Than shaltow hange hem in the roof ful hye,
Then shalt thou hang them in the roof very high,
That no man of oure purveyaunce espye.
In a way that no man may espy our preparations.
And whan thou thus hast doon, as I have seyd,
And when thou thus hast done as I have said,
460 And hast oure vitaille faire in hem y-leyd,
And hast laid our victuals carefully in them,
And eek an ax, to smyte the corde atwo
And also an axe to smite the cord in two,
When that the water comth, that we may go,
When the water comes, so that we may go,
And breke an hole an heigh upon the gable
And break a hole on high upon the gable
Unto the gardin-ward, over the stable,
Toward the garden, over the stable,
465 That we may frely passen forth our way
That we may freely pass forth on our way
Whan that the grete shour is goon away—
When the great shower is gone away—
Than shaltow swimme as myrie, I undertake,
Then shalt thou float as merry, I guarantee,
As doth the whyte doke after hire drake.
As does the white duck after her drake.
Thanne wol I clepe, 'How, Alison! how, John!
Then I will call, 'How, Alison! how, John!
470 Be myrie, for the flood wol passe anon!'

Be merry, for the flood will soon pass!'
And thou wolt seyn, 'Hayl, maister Nicholay!
And thou will say, 'Hail, master Nicholay!
Good morwe, I se thee wel, for it is day.'
Good morrow, I see thee well, for it is day.'
And thanne shul we be lordes al oure lyf
And then shall we be lords all our life
Of al the world, as Noë and his wyf.
Of all the world, like Noah and his wife.

475 But of o thyng I warne thee ful right:
But of one thing I warn thee very sternly:
Be wel avysed on that ilke night
Be well advised on that same night
That we ben entred into shippes bord
On which we are entered onto shipboard
That noon of us ne speke nat a word,
That not one of us speak a word,
Ne clepe, ne crye, but been in his preyere;
Nor call, nor cry, but be in his prayer;

480 For it is Goddes owene heste dere.
For it is God's own dear command.
Thy wyf and thou mote hange fer atwinne,
Thy wife and thou must hang far apart,
For that bitwixe yow shal be no sinne
So that between you shall be no sin
No more in looking than ther shal in dede;
No more in looking than there shall be in deed;
This ordinance is seyd, go, God thee spede!
This ordinance is said, go, God give thee success!

485 Tomorwe at night, whan men ben alle aslepe,
Tomorrow at night, when people are all asleep,
Into oure kneding tubbes wol we crepe,
Into our kneading tubs will we creep,
And sitten ther, abyding Goddes grace.
And sit there, awaiting God's grace.
Go now thy wey, I have no lenger space
Go now thy way, I have no more time
To make of this no lenger sermoning.
To make of this any longer preaching.

490 Men seyn thus, 'Send the wyse, and sey no thing.'
Men say thus, 'Send the wise, and say nothing.'
Thou art so wys, it nedeth thee nat teche;
Thou are so wise, one needs not teach thee;
Go, save oure lyf, and that I thee biseche."
Go, save our life, and that I beseech thee."
   This sely carpenter goth forth his wey.
   This hapless carpenter goes forth his way.
Ful ofte he seith "allas" and "weylawey,"
Very often he said "alas" and "woe is me,"

495 And to his wyf he tolde his privetee;
And to his wife he told his secret;
And she was war, and knew it bet than he,
Ans she was aware, and knew it better than he,

What al this queynte cast was for to seye.
What all this ingenious scheme meant.
But nathelees she ferde as she wolde deye,
But nonetheless she acted as if she would die,
And seyde, "Allas! go forth thy wey anon,
And said, "Alas! go forth thy way quickly,
500   Help us to scape, or we ben dede echon.
Help us to escape, or we are dead each one of us.
I am thy trewe verray wedded wyf;
I am thy faithful truly wedded wife;
Go, dere spouse, and help to save oure lyf."
Go, dear spouse, and help to save our lives."
   Lo, which a greet thyng is affeccioun!
   Lo, what a great thing is emotion!
Men may dyen of imaginacioun,
One can die of imagination,
505   So depe may impressioun be take.
So deeply may a mental image be taken.
This sely carpenter biginneth quake;
This hapless carpenter begins to tremble;
Him thinketh verraily that he may see
He thinks truly that he can see
Noës flood come walwing as the see
Noah's flood come surging like the sea
To drenchen Alisoun, his hony dere.
To drown Alisoun, his honey dear.
510   He wepeth, weyleth, maketh sory chere,
He weeps, wails, looks wretched,
He syketh with ful many a sory swogh.
He sighs with very many a sorry groan.
He gooth and geteth him a kneding trogh,
He goes and gets him a kneading trough,
And after that a tubbe and a kymelyn,
And after that a tub and a large vat,
And prively he sente hem to his in,
And secretly he sent them to his dwelling,
515   And heng hem in the roof in privetee.
And hanged them in the roof secretly.
His owene hand he made laddres three,
With his own hand he made three ladders,
To climben by the ronges and the stalkes
To climb by the rungs and the uprights
Unto the tubbes hanginge in the balkes,
Unto the tubs hanging in the beams,
And hem vitailled, bothe trogh and tubbe,
And provisioned them, both trough and tub,
520   With breed and chese, and good ale in a jubbe,
With bread and cheese, and good ale in a jug,
Suffysinge right ynogh as for a day.
Sufficing just enough for a day.
But er that he had maad al this array,
But before he had made all this preparation,
He sente his knave and eek his wench also

He sent his servant and also his servant girl
Upon his nede to London for to go.
Upon his business to go to London.
525 And on the Monday, whan it drow to night,
And on the Monday, when it drew toward night,
He shette his dore withoute candel-light,
He shut his door without candlelight,
And dressed al thing as it sholde be.
And prepared everything as it should be.
And shortly, up they clomben alle three;
And shortly, up they climbed all three;
They sitten stille wel a furlong-way.
They sat still a good two and one-half minutes.
530 "Now, *Pater-noster*, clom!" seyde Nicholay,
"Now, Pater-noster, quiet!" said Nicholay.
And "clom," quod John, and "clom," seyde Alisoun.
And "quiet," said John, and "quiet," said Alisoun.
This carpenter seyde his devocioun,
This carpenter said his devotion,
And stille he sit, and biddeth his preyere,
And still he sits, and says his prayer,
Awaytinge on the reyn, if he it here.
Awaiting the rain, if he might hear it.
535 The dede sleep, for wery bisinesse,
The dead sleep, for weary business,
Fil on this carpenter right as I gesse
Fell on this carpenter right as I guess
Aboute corfew-tyme, or litel more;
About curfew-time, or a little more;
For travail of his goost he groneth sore,
For suffering of his spirit he groans deeply,
And eft he routeth, for his heed mislay.
And also he snores, for his head lay wrong.
540 Doun of the laddre stalketh Nicholay,
Down on the ladder stalks Nicholay,
And Alisoun, ful softe adoun she spedde;
And Alisoun, very quietly down she sped;
Withouten wordes mo, they goon to bedde
Without more words, they go to bed
Theras the carpenter is wont to lye.
Where the carpenter is accustomed to lie.
Ther was the revel and the melodye;
There was the revel and the sounds of festivity;
545 And thus lyth Alison and Nicholas
And thus lie Alison and Nicholas
In bisinesse of mirthe and of solas,
In business of mirth and of pleasure,
Til that the belle of Laudes gan to ringe,
Until the bell of the early morning service began to ring,
And freres in the chauncel gonne singe.
And friars in the chapel began to sing.
This parish clerk, this amorous Absolon,
This parish clerk, this amorous Absolon,

550   That is for love alwey so wo bigon,
That is for love always so woebegone,
Upon the Monday was at Oseneye
Upon the Monday was at Osney
With compaignye him to disporte and pleye,
With company to be merry and amuse himself,
And axed upon cas a cloisterer
And by chance asked a cloistered monk
Ful prively after John the carpenter;
Very discreetly about John the carpenter;
555   And he drough him apart out of the chirche,
And he drew him apart out of the church,
And seyde, "I noot, I saugh him here nat wirche
And said, "I know not, I have not seen him working here
Sin Saterday. I trow that he be went
Since Saturday. I suppose that he is gone
For timber, ther oure abbot hath him sent,
For timber, where our abbot has sent him,
For he is wont for timber for to go,
For he is accustomed to go for timber
560   And dwellen at the grange a day or two;
And dwell at the granary a day or two;
Or elles he is at his hous, certeyn.
Or else he is at his house, certainly.
Wher that he be, I can nat sothly seyn."
Where he may be, I can not truly say."
    This Absolon ful joly was and light,
    This Absolon very was jolly and happy,
And thoghte, "Now is tyme to wake al night;
And thought, "Now is time to stay awake all night;
565   For sikirly I saugh him nat stiringe
For surely I saw him not stirring
Aboute his dore sin day bigan to springe.
About his door since day began to spring.
So moot I thryve, I shal, at cokkes crowe,
As I may prosper, I shall at cock's crow,
Ful prively knokken at his windowe
Very quietly knock at his window
That stant ful lowe upon his boures wal.
That stands very low upon his bedroom's wall.
570   To Alison now wol I tellen al
To Alison now I will tell all
My love-longing, for yet I shal nat misse
My love-longing, for yet I shall not miss
That at the leste wey I shal hire kisse.
That at the very least I shall her kiss.
Som maner confort shal I have, parfay.
Some sort of comfort shall I have, by my faith.
My mouth hath icched al this longe day;
My mouth has itched all this long day;
575   That is a signe of kissing atte leste.
That is a sign of kissing at the least.
Al night me mette eek, I was at a feste.

All night I dreamed also, I was at a feast.
Therfore I wol gon slepe an houre or tweye,
Therefore I will go sleep an hour or two,
And al the night than wol I wake and pleye."
And all the night then will I stay awake and play."
   Whan that the firste cok hath crowe, anon
   When the first cock has crowed (about midnight), at once
580 Up rist this joly lovere Absolon,
Up rises the elegant lover Absolon,
And him arrayeth gay, at point-devys.
And dresses himself handsomely, in every detail.
But first he cheweth greyn and lycorys
But first he chews cardamom and licorice
To smellen swete, er he had kembd his heer.
To smell sweet, ere he had combed his hair.
Under his tonge a trewe-love he beer,
Under his tongue he had a true-love herb,
585 For therby wende he to ben gracious.
For thus he thought he would be gracious.
He rometh to the carpenteres hous,
He goes to the carpenter's house,
And stille he stant under the shot-windowe—
And he stands still under the casement window—
Unto his brest it raughte, it was so lowe—
Unto his breast it reached, it was so low—
And softe he cougheth with a semi-soun:
And softly he coughs with a gentle sound:
590 "What do ye, hony-comb, swete Alisoun,
"What do you, honey-comb, sweet Alisoun,
My faire brid, my swete cinamome?
My fair bird, my sweet cinnamon?
Awaketh, lemman myn, and speketh to me!
Awake, sweetheart mine, and speak to me!
Wel litel thenken ye upon my wo,
Well little you think upon my woe,
That for youre love I swete ther I go.
That for your love I sweat wherever I go.
595 No wonder is thogh that I swelte and swete;
No wonder is though that I swelter and sweat;
I moorne as doth a lamb after the tete.
I mourn as does a lamb after the tit.
Ywis, lemman, I have swich love-longinge,
Indeed, sweetheart, I have such love-longing,
That lyk a turtel trewe is my moorninge;
That like a true turtledove is my mourning;
I may nat ete na more than a mayde."
I can eat no more than a maiden."
600   "Go fro the window, Jakke fool," she sayde,
   "Go from the window, you idiot," she said,
"As help me God, it wol nat be 'com pa me.'
"So help me God, it will not be 'come kiss me.'
I love another, and elles I were to blame,
I love another, and else I were to blame,

Wel bet than thee, by Jesu, Absolon!
Well better than thee, by Jesus, Absolon!
Go forth thy wey or I wol caste a ston,
Go forth thy way or I will cast a stone,
605 And lat me slepe, a twenty devel wey!"
And let me sleep, in the name of twenty devils!"
  "Allas," quod Absolon, "and weylawey,
  "Alas," said Absolon, "and woe is me,
That trewe love was evere so yvel biset!
That true love was ever in such miserable circumstances!
Thanne kisse me, sin it may be no bet,
Then kiss me, since it can be no better,
For Jesus love and for the love of me."
For Jesus' love and for the love of me."
610 "Wiltow thanne go thy wey therwith?" quod she.
"Wilt thou then go thy way with that?" said she.
"Ye, certes, lemman," quod this Absolon.
"Yes, certainly, sweetheart," said this Absolon.
"Thanne make thee redy," quod she, "I come anon;"
"Then make thee ready," said she, "I come right now;"
And unto Nicholas she seyde stille,
And unto Nicholas she said quietly,
"Now hust, and thou shalt laughen al thy fille."
"Now hush, and thou shalt laugh all thy fill."
615 This Absolon doun sette him on his knees,
  This Absolon set himself down on his knees,
And seyde, "I am a lord at alle degrees;
And said, "I am a lord in every way;
For after this I hope ther cometh more.
For after this I hope there comes more.
Lemman, thy grace, and swete brid, thyn ore!"
Sweetheart, thy grace, and sweet bird, thy mercy!"
  The window she undoth, and that in haste,
  The window she undoes, and that in haste,
620 "Have do," quod she, "com of, and speed thee faste,
"Get done with it," said she, "come on, and hurry up,
Lest that oure neighebores thee espye."
Lest our neighbors espy thee."
  This Absolon gan wype his mouth ful drye:
  This Absolon wiped his mouth very dry:
Derk was the night as pich, or as the cole,
Dark was the night as pitch, or as the coal,
And at the window out she putte hir hole,
And at the window out she put her hole
625 And Absolon, him fil no bet ne wers,
And Absolon, to him it happened no better nor worse,
But with his mouth he kiste hir naked ers
But with his mouth he kissed her naked ass
Ful savourly, er he was war of this.
With great relish, before he was aware of this.
Abak he stirte, and thoghte it was amis,
Back he jumped, and thought it was amiss,
For wel he wiste a womman hath no berd;

For well he knew a woman has no beard;

630 He felte a thing al rough and long y-herd,
He felt a thing all rough and long haired,
And seyde, "Fy! allas, what have I do?"
And said, "Fie! alas! what have I done?"
   "Tehee!" quod she, and clapte the window to;
   "Tehee!" said she, and clapped the window to;
And Absolon goth forth a sory pas.
And Absolon goes forth walking sadly.
   "A berd, a berd!" quod hende Nicholas,
   "A beard, a beard!" said clever Nicholas,

635 "By Goddes *corpus*, this goth faire and weel!"
"By God's body, this goes fair and well!"
   This sely Absolon herde every deel,
   This hapless Absolon heard every bit,
And on his lippe he gan for anger byte;
And on his lip he began for anger to bite;
And to himself he seyde, "I shal thee quyte."
And to himself he said, "I shall pay thee back."
   Who rubbeth now, who froteth now his lippes
   Who rubs now, who now scrubs his lips

640 With dust, with sond, with straw, with clooth, with chippes,
With dust, with sand, with straw, with cloth, with chips,
But Absolon, that seith ful ofte, "Allas!
But Absolon, who says very often, "Alas!"
My soule bitake I unto Sathanas,
My soul I entrust to Satan,
But me wer levere than al this toun," quod he,
If I would not rather than (have) all this town," said he,
"Of this despyt awroken for to be.
"Be avenged for this insult.

645 Allas!" quod he, "allas, I ne hadde y-bleynt!"
Alas!" said he, "alas, I did not turn away!"
His hote love was cold and al y-queynt;
His hot love was cold and all extinguished;
For fro that tyme that he had kiste hir ers,
For from that time that he had kissed her ass,
Of paramours he sette nat a kers,
Love-making he thought not worth a watercress,
For he was heeled of his maladye.
For he was healed of his malady.

650 Ful ofte paramours he gan deffye,
Very often he did renounce love-making,
And weep as dooth a child that is y-bete.
And wept as does a child that is beaten.
A softe paas he wente over the street
At a slow pace he went down the street
Until a smith men cleped daun Gerveys,
To a smith men called dan Gerveys,
That in his forge smithed plough harneys:
Who in his forge made plowing equipment;

655 He sharpeth shaar and culter bisily.
He sharpens ploughshares and plough blades busily.

This Absolon knokketh al esily,
This Absolon knocked all gently,
And seyde, "Undo, Gerveys, and that anon."
And said, "Open up, Gerveys, and that right now."
  "What, who artow?" "It am I, Absolon."
  "What, who art thou?" "It am I, Absolon."
"What, Absolon! for Cristes swete tree,
"What, Absolon! for Christ's sweet cross,
660 Why ryse ye so rathe, ey, *benedicite!*
Why rise you so early, ay, bless me!
What eyleth yow? som gay gerl, God it woot,
What ails yow? some pretty girl, God knows it,
Hath broght yow thus upon the viritoot;
Hath brought you to be running around like this;
By Seynt Note, ye woot wel what I mene."
By Saint Note, you know well what I mean."
  This Absolon ne roghte nat a bene
  This Absolon cared not a bean
665 Of al his pley. No word agayn he yaf;
For all his joking. No word he gave in reply;
He hadde more tow on his distaf
He had more business on hand
Than Gerveys knew, and seyde, "Freend so dere,
Than Gerveys knew, and said, "Friend so dear,
That hote culter in the chimenee here,
That hot plough blade in the hearth here,
As lene it me: I have therwith to done,
Lend it to me; I have something to do with it,
670 And I wol bringe it thee agayn ful sone."
And I will bring it back to thee very soon."
  Gerveys answerde, "Certes, were it gold,
  Gerveys answered, "Certainly, were it gold,
Or in a poke nobles alle untold,
Or in a sack countless silver coins,
Thou sholdest have, as I am trewe smith.
Thou sholdest have it, as I am true smith.
Ey, Cristes foo! what wol ye do therwith?"
Ay, Christ's foe! What will you do with it?"
675 "Therof," quod Absolon, "be as be may:
  "Concerning that," said Absolon, "be as be may.
I shal wel telle it thee tomorwe day,"
I shall well tell it to thee to-morrow"—
And caughte the culter by the colde stele.
And caught the plough blade by the cold handle.
Ful softe out at the dore he gan to stele,
Very softly out at the door he began to steal,
And wente unto the carpenteres wal.
And went unto the carpenter's wall.
680 He cogheth first, and knokketh therwithal
He coughs first, and knocks then
Upon the windowe, right as he dide er.
Upon the window, just as he did before.
  This Alison answerde, "Who is ther

This Alison answered, "Who is there
That knokketh so? I warante it a theef."
That knocks so? I swear it is a thief."
"Why, nay," quod he, "God woot, my swete leef,
"Why, nay," said he, "God knows, my sweet beloved,
685 I am thyn Absolon, my dereling.
I am thy Absolon, my darling.
Of gold," quod he, "I have thee brought a ring—
Of gold," said he, "I have brought thee a ring.
My moder yaf it me, so God me save—
My mother gave it to me, as God may save me;
Ful fyn it is, and therto wel y-grave.
Very fine it is, and also nicely engraved.
This wol I yeve thee, if thou me kisse!"
This will I give thee, if thou kiss me."
690   This Nicholas was risen for to pisse,
This Nicholas was risen to piss,
And thoghte he wolde amenden al the jape,
And thought he would make the joke even better;
He sholde kisse his ers er that he scape.
He should kiss his ass before he escapes.
And up the windowe dide he hastily,
And he opened up the window hastily,
And out his ers he putteth prively
And he puts out his ass stealthily
695 Over the buttok, to the haunche-bon;
Over the buttock, to the thigh;
    And therwith spak this clerk, this Absolon,
    And then spoke this clerk, this Absolon,
"Spek, swete brid, I noot nat wher thou art."
"Speak, sweet bird, I know not where thou art."
This Nicholas anon leet fle a fart,
This Nicholas immediately let fly a fart
As greet as it had been a thonder-dent,
As great as if it had been a thunder-bolt,
700 That with the strook he was almost y-blent;
So that with the stroke he was almost blinded;
And he was redy with his iren hoot,
And he was ready with his hot iron,
And Nicholas amidde the ers he smoot.
And he smote Nicholas in the middle of the ass.
Of gooth the skin an hande-brede aboute,
Off goes the skin a hand's breadth about,
The hote culter brende so his toute,
The hot plough blade so burned his rump
705 And for the smert he wende for to dye.
And for the pain he thought he would die.
As he were wood, for wo he gan to crye—
As if he were crazy, for woe he began to cry,
"Help! water! water! help, for Goddes herte!"
"Help! Water! Water! Help, for God's heart!"
    This carpenter out of his slomber sterte,
    This carpenter woke suddenly out of his slumber,

And herde oon cryen "water" as he were wood,
And heard someone cry "water!" as if he were crazy,
710 And thoghte, "Allas! now comth Nowelis flood!"
And thought, "Alas, now comes Nowell's flood!"
He sit him up withouten wordes mo,
He sits up without more words,
And with his ax he smoot the corde atwo,
And with his ax he smote the cord in two,
And doun goth al; he fond neither to selle
And down goes all; he found nothing to sell (wasted no time),
Ne breed ne ale, til he cam to the celle
Neither bread nor ale, until he came to the pavement
715 Upon the floor; and ther aswowne he lay.
Upon the floor, and there he lay in a swoon.
   Up sterte hire Alison and Nicholay,
   Up started Alison and Nicholay,
And cryden "out" and "harrow" in the strete.
And cried "Out" and "Help" in the street.
The neighebores, bothe smale and grete,
The neighbors, both low-ranking and high,
In ronnen for to gauren on this man,
Run in to gawk at this man,
720 That yet aswowne lay, bothe pale and wan;
Who yet lay in a swoon, both pale and wan,
For with the fal he brosten hadde his arm.
For with the fall he had broken his arm.
But stonde he moste unto his owene harm.
But he had to stand up for himself, though it went badly;
For whan he spak, he was anon bore doun
For when he spoke, he was immediately put down
With hende Nicholas and Alisoun.
By clever Nicholas and Alisoun.
725 They tolden every man that he was wood,
They told every one that he was crazy;
He was agast so of "Nowelis flood"
He was so afraid of Nowell's flood
Thurgh fantasye, that of his vanitee
Because of his imagination that in his foolishness
He hadde y-boght him kneding tubbes three,
He had bought himself three kneading tubs,
And hadde hem hanged in the roof above;
And had hanged them in the roof above;
730 And that he preyed hem, for Goddes love,
And that he begged them, for God's love,
To sitten in the roof, *par compaignye.*
To sit in the roof, to keep him company.
   The folk gan laughen at his fantasye;
   The folk did laugh at his foolishness;
Into the roof they kyken and they cape,
Into the roof they stare and they gape,
And turned al his harm unto a jape.
And turned all his harm into a joke.
735 For what so that this carpenter answerde,

For whatever this carpenter answered,
It was for noght; no man his reson herde.
It was for naught; no one listened to his explanation,
With othes grete he was so sworn adoun,
With oaths great he was so sworn down
That he was holden wood in al the toun.
That he was considered crazy in all the town;
For every clerk anonright heeld with other:
For every clerk immediately agreed with the other.

740   They seyde, "The man is wood, my leve brother;"
They said, "The man is crazy, my dear brother";
And every wight gan laughen at this stryf.
And every person did laugh at this strife.
Thus swyved was this carpenteres wyf
Thus screwed was this carpenter's wife,
For al his keping and his jalousye;
In spite of all his guarding and his jealousy,
And Absolon hath kist hir nether yë;
And Absolon has kissed her lower eye,

745   And Nicholas is scalded in the toute.
And Nicholas is scalded in the rump.
This tale is doon, and God save al the route!
This tale is done, and God save all this company!

The Man of Law's Epilogue[1]

  Owre oost upon his stiropes stood anon
  Our Host upon his stirrups stood up at once,
And seyde "Goode men, herkeneth everych on!
And said, "Good men, listen every one!
This was a thrifty tale for the nones!
This was a excellent tale for this occasion!
Sire parissche prest," quod he, "for goddes boones,
Sir Parish Priest," said he, "for God's bones,

5   Telle us a tale as was thi forward yore.
Tell us a tale, as was thy previous agreement.
I se wel that ye lerned men in lore
I see well that you men learned in lore
Can moche good, by goddes dignete!"
Know much that is good, by God's dignity!"
The parson him answerde, "Benedicite!
The Parson him answered, "Bless me!
What eyleth the man, so synfully to swere?"
What ails the man, so sinfully to swear?"

10   Oure ost answerde, "O Janekyn, be ye there?
Our Host answered, "O Jankin, are you there?
I smelle a lollere in the wynd," quod he.
I smell a Lollard in the wind," said he.
"How! goode men", quod oure host, "herkeneth me;

---

1. The Middle English for this text is taken from the 1868 Chaucer Society edition, edited by F. J. Furnivall.

"Now! good men," said our Host, "listen to me;
Abydeth, for goddes digne passioun,
Wait, for God's worthy passion,
For we schal han a predicacioun;
For we shall have a sermon;
15   This lollere heer wil prechen us som what."
      This Lollard here will preach us something."
"Nay, by my fader soule, that schal he nat!"
"Nay, by my father's soul, that shall he not!"
Seyde the [Wife of Bath]; "heer schal he nat preche;
Said the Wife of Bath, "Here shall he not preach;
He schal no gospel glosen here ne teche.
He shall no gospel interpret here nor teach.
[W]e leven alle in the grete god," quod [she];
We all believe in the great God," said she;
20   "He wolde sowen som difficulte,
      "He would sow some difficulty,
Or springen cokkel in oure clene corn.
Or sprinkle weeds in our clean grain.
And therfore, oost, I warne thee biforn,
And therefore, Host, I warn thee beforehand,
My joly body schal a tale telle,
My handsome body shall tell a tale,
And I schal clynken you so mery a belle,
And I shall clink you so merry a bell,
25   That I schal waken al this compaignie.
      That I shall awaken all this company.
But it schal not ben of philosophie,
But it shall not be of philosophy,
Ne phislyas[?], ne termes queinte of lawe.
Nor legal cases, nor elaborate terms of law.
Ther is but litel Latyn in my mawe!
There is but little Latin in my stomach!"]

The Wife of Bath's Prologue and Tale

The Prologue

"Experience, though noon auctoritee
"Experience, though no written authority
Were in this world, is right ynough for me
Were in this world, is good enough for me
To speke of wo that is in mariage:
To speak of the woe that is in marriage;
For, lordinges, sith I twelf yeer was of age,
For, gentlemen, since I was twelve years of age,
5   Thonked be God that is eterne on lyve,
      Thanked be God who is eternally alive,
Housbondes at chirche dore I have had fyve
I have had five husbands at the church door—
(If I so ofte myghte have y-wedded be)
If I so often might have been wedded—

And alle were worthy men in hir degree.
And all were worthy men in their way.
But me was told, certeyn, nat longe agon is,
But to me it was told, certainly, it is not long ago,
10 That sith that Crist ne wente nevere but onis
That since Christ went never but once
To wedding in the Cane of Galilee,
To a wedding, in the Cana of Galilee,
That by the same ensample taughte he me
That by that same example he taught me
That I ne sholde wedded be but ones.
That I should be wedded but once.
Herkne eek, lo, which a sharp word for the nones
Listen also, lo, what a sharp word for this purpose,
15 Besyde a welle, Jesus, God and man,
Beside a well, Jesus, God and man,
Spak in repreve of the Samaritan:
Spoke in reproof of the Samaritan:
'Thou hast y-had fyve housbondes,' quod he,
'Thou hast had five husbands,' he said,
'And that ilke man that now hath thee
'And that same man that now has thee
Is noght thyn housbond—thus seyde he certeyn.
Is not thy husband,' thus he said certainly.
20 What that he mente therby, I can nat seyn,
What he meant by this, I can not say;
But that I axe, why that the fifthe man
But I ask, why the fifth man
Was noon housbond to the Samaritan?
Was no husband to the Samaritan?
How manye mighte she have in mariage?
How many might she have in marriage?
Yet herde I nevere tellen in myn age
I never yet heard tell in my lifetime
25 Upon this nombre diffinicioun.
A definition of this number.
Men may devyne and glosen up and doun,
Men may conjecture and interpret in every way,
But wel I woot expres, withoute lye,
But well I know, expressly, without lie,
God bad us for to wexe and multiplye:
God commanded us to grow fruitful and multiply;
That gentil text can I wel understonde.
That gentle text I can well understand.
30   Eek wel I woot he seyde, myn housbonde
  Also I know well, he said my husband
Sholde lete fader and moder, and take to me;
Should leave father and mother and take to me.
But of no nombre mencioun made he,
But he made no mention of number,
Of bigamye or of octogamye.
Of marrying two, or of marrying eight;
Why sholde men thanne speke of it vileinye?

Why should men then speak evil of it?

35   Lo, here the wyse king, daun Salomon;
    Lo, (consider) here the wise king, dan Salomon;
I trowe he hadde wyves mo than oon.
I believe he had wives more than one.
As wolde God it leveful were unto me
As would God it were lawful unto me
To be refresshed half so ofte as he!
To be refreshed half so often as he!
Which yifte of God hadde he for alle his wyvis!
What a gift of God he had because of all his wives!

40   No man hath swich that in this world alyve is.
No man that in this world is alive has such (a gift).
God woot this noble king, as to my wit,
God knows, this noble king, according to my judgment,
The firste night had many a mery fit
The first night had many a merry fit
With ech of hem, so wel was him on lyve!
With each of them, so well things went for him in his lifetime.
Blessed be God that I have <u>wedded fyve,</u>
Blessed be God that I have wedded five!

45   Of whiche I have pyked out the beste,
Of which I have picked out the best,
Bothe of here <u>nether purs</u> and of here cheste.
Both of their <u>lower purse (scrotum)</u> and of their strongbox.
Diverse scoles maken parfyt clerkes,
Differing schools make perfect clerks,
And diverse practyk in many sondry werkes
And differing practice in many various works
Maketh the werkman parfyt sekirly:
Makes the workman truly perfect;

50   [Of fyve husbondes scoleiyng am I.]
Of five husbands' schooling am I.
Welcome the sixte, whan that evere he shall!
Welcome the sixth, whenever he shall appear.
For sothe I wol nat kepe me chast in al.
For truly, I will not keep myself chaste in everything.
Whan myn housbond is fro the world y-gon,
When my husband is gone from the world,
Som Cristen man shal wedde me anon;
Some Christian man shall wed me straightway,

55   For thanne th'Apostle seith that I am free
For then the apostle says that I am free
To wedde, a Goddes half, <u>where it lyketh</u> me.
To wed, by God's side (I swear), wherever it pleases me.
He seith that to be wedded is no sinne:
He says that to be wedded is no sin;
Bet is to be wedded than to brinne.
It is better to be wedded than to burn.
What rekketh me thogh folk sey<u>e vileinye</u>
What do I care, though folk speak <u>evil</u>

60   Of shrewed Lameth and his bigamye?
Of cursed Lamech and his bigamy?

I woot wel Abraham was an holy man,
I know well Abraham was a holy man,
And Jacob eek, as ferforth as I can;
And Jacob also, insofar as I know;
And ech of hem hadde wyves mo than two,
And each of them had more than two wives,
And many another holy man also.
And many another holy man also.
65   Wher can ye seye, in any manere age,
       Where can you find, in any historical period,
That hye God defended mariage
That high God forbad marriage
By expres word? I pray you, telleth me.
By express word? I pray you, tell me.
Or where comanded he virginitee?
Or where commanded he virginity?
I woot as wel as ye, it is no drede,
I know as well as you, it is no doubt,
70   Th'Apostel, whan he speketh of maydenhede,
The apostle, when he speaks of maidenhood,
He seyde that precept therof hadde he noon.
He said that he had no precept concerning it.
Men may conseille a womman to been oon,
Men may advise a woman to be one,
But conseilling is no comandement:
But advice is no commandment.
He putte it in oure owene jugement. |
He left it to our own judgment;
75   For hadde God comanded maydenhede,
For had God commanded maidenhood,
Thanne hadde he dampned wedding with the dede.
Then had he damned marriage along with the act (of procreation).
And certes, if ther were no seed y-sowe,
And certainly, if there were no seed sown,
Virginitee, thanne wherof sholde it growe?
Then from what should virginity grow?
Poul dorste nat comanden, atte leste,
In any case, Paul dared not command
80   A thing of which his maister yaf noon heste.
A thing of which his master gave no command.
The dart is set up for virginitee;
The prize is set up for virginity;
Cacche who so may: who renneth best lat see.
Catch it whoever can, let's see who runs best.
But this word is nat take of every wight,
But this word does not apply to every person,
But ther as God list give it of his might.
But where God desires to give it by his power.
85   I woot wel that th'Apostel was a mayde,
I know well that the apostle was a virgin;
But natheless, thogh that he wroot and sayde
But nonetheless, though he wrote and said
He wolde that every wight were swich as he,

He would that every person were such as he,
Al nis but conseil to virginitee,
All is nothing but advice to (adopt) virginity.
And for to been a wyf, he yaf me leve
And he gave me leave to be a wife
90 Of indulgence. So nis it no repreve
By explicit permission; so it is not blameful
To wedde me, if that my make dye,
To wed me, if my mate should die,
Withoute excepcioun of bigamye,
Without objection on the grounds of bigamy.
Al were it good no womman for to touche—
Although it would be good to touch no woman—
He mente as in his bed or in his couche—
He meant in his bed or in his couch,
95 For peril is bothe fyr and tow t'assemble;
For it is perilous to assemble both fire and flax;
Ye knowe what this ensample may resemble.
You know what this example may apply to.
This al and som: he heeld virginitee
This is the sum of it: he held virginity
More parfit than wedding in freletee.
More perfect than wedding in weakness.
Freletee clepe I, but if that he and she
Weakness I call it, unless he and she
100 Wolde leden al hir lyf in chastitee.
Would lead all their life in chastity.
I graunte it wel, I have noon envye
I grant it well; I have no envy,
Thogh maydenhede preferre bigamye.
Though maidenhood may have precedence over a second marriage.
Hem lyketh to be clene, body and goost.
It pleases them to be clean, body and spirit;
Of myn estaat I nil nat make no boost:
Of my state I will make no boast,
105 For wel ye knowe, a lord in his houshold
For well you know, a lord in his household,
He hath nat every vessel al of gold;
He has not every utensil all of gold;
Somme been of tree, and doon hir lord servyse.
Some are of wood, and do their lord service.
God clepeth folk to him in sondry wyse,
God calls folk to him in various ways,
And everich hath of God a propre yifte,
And each one has of God an individual gift—
110 Som this, som that, as Him lyketh shifte.
Some this, some that, as it pleases Him to provide.
Virginitee is greet perfeccioun,
Virginity is great perfection,
And continence eek with devocioun.
And continence also with devotion,
But Crist, that of perfeccioun is welle,
But Christ, who is the source of perfection,

Bad nat every wight he sholde go selle
Did not command that every one should go sell
115 All that he hadde and give it to the pore,
All that he had, and give it to the poor,
And in swich wyse folwe him and his fore.
And in such wise follow him and his footsteps.
He spak to hem that wolde live parfitly,
He spoke to those who would live perfectly;
And lordinges, by youre leve, that am nat I.
And gentlemen, by your leave, I am not that.
I wol bistowe the flour of al myn age
I will bestow the flower of all my age
120 In the actes and in fruit of mariage.
In the acts and in fruit of marriage.
　　Telle me also, to what conclusioun
　　Tell me also, to what purpose
Were membres maad of generacioun sexual members
Were members of generation made,
And of so parfit wys a wright y-wroght?
And by so perfectly wise a Workman wrought?
　　Trusteth right wel, they were nat maad for noght.
　　Trust right well, they were not made for nothing.
125 Glose whoso wole, and seye bothe up and doun
Interpret whoever will, and say both up and down
That they were maked for purgacioun
That they were made for purgation
Of urine, and oure bothe thinges smale
Of urine, and both our small things
Were eek to knowe a femele from a male,
Were also to know a female from a male,
And for noon other cause: sey ye no?
And for no other cause—do you say no?
130 The experience woot wel it is noght so.
The experience knows well it is not so.
So that the clerkes be nat with me wrothe,
Provided that the clerks be not angry with me,
I sey this, that they maked been for bothe—
I say this: that they are made for both;
This is to seye, for office, and for ese
This is to say, for urination and for ease
Of engendrure, ther we nat God displese.
Of procreation, in which we do not displease God.
135 Why sholde men elles in hir bokes sette
Why else should men set in their books
That man shal yelde to his wyf hire dette?
That man shall pay to his wife her debt?
Now wherwith sholde he make his payement
Now with what should he make his payment,
If he ne used his sely instrument?
If he did not use his blessed instrument?
Thanne were they maad upon a creature
Then were they made upon a creature
140 To purge uryne, and eek for engendrure.

To purge urine, and also for procreation.
   But I seye noght that every wight is holde,
   But I say not that every person is required,
That hath swich harneys as I to yow tolde,
That has such equipment as I to you told,
To goon and usen hem in engendrure:
To go and use them in procreation.
Thanne sholde men take of chastitee no cure.
Then should men have no regard for chastity.

145   Crist was a mayde and shapen as a man,
Christ was a virgin and shaped like a man,
And many a seint, sith that the world bigan,
And many a saint, since the world began;
Yet lived they evere in parfit chastitee.
Yet lived they ever in perfect chastity.
I nil envye no virginitee:
I will envy no virginity.
Lat hem be breed of pured whete-seed,
Let them be bread of pure wheat-seed,

150   And lat us wyves hoten barly-breed.
And let us wives be called barley-bread;
And yet with barly-breed, Mark telle can,
And yet with barley-bread, Mark can tell it,
Oure Lord Jesu refresshed many a man.
Our Lord Jesus refreshed many a man.
In swich estaat as God hath cleped us
In such estate as God has called us
I wol persevere, I nam nat precious.
I will persevere; I am not fussy.

155   In wyfhode I wol use myn instrument
In wifehood I will use my instrument
As frely as my Makere hath it sent.
As freely as my Maker has it sent.
If I be daungerous, God yeve me sorwe!
If I be niggardly, God give me sorrow!
Myn housbond shal it have bothe eve and morwe,
My husband shall have it both evenings and mornings,
   Whan that him list com forth and paye his dette.
   When it pleases him to come forth and pay his debt.

160   An housbonde I wol have, I wol nat lette,
A husband I will have—I will not desist—
Which shal be bothe my dettour and my thral,
Who shall be both my debtor and my slave,
And have his tribulacioun withal
And have his suffering also
Upon his flessh, whyl that I am his wyf.
Upon his flesh, while I am his wife.
I have the power duringe al my lyf
I have the power during all my life

165   Upon his propre body, and noght he:
Over his own body, and not he.
Right thus th' Apostel tolde it unto me,
Right thus the Apostle told it unto me,

And bad oure housbondes for to love us weel.
And commanded our husbands to love us well.
Al this sentence me lyketh every deel."
All this sentence pleases me every bit"—

[An Interlude]

Up sterte the Pardoner, and that anon.
Up sprang the Pardoner, and that at once;
170 "Now dame," quod he, "by God and by Seint John,
"Now, madam," he said, "by God and by Saint John!
Ye been a noble prechour in this cas!
You are a noble preacher in this case.
I was aboute to wedde a wyf. Allas,
I was about to wed a wife; alas!
What sholde I bye it on my flesh so dere?
Why should I pay for it so dearly on my flesh?
Yet hadde I levere wedde no wyf to-yere!"
Yet would I rather wed no wife this year!"
175 "Abyde!" quod she, "my tale is nat bigonne.
"Wait!" she said, "my tale is not begun.
Nay, thou shalt drinken of another tonne
Nay, thou shalt drink from another barrel,
Er that I go, shal savoure wors than ale.
Before I go, which shall taste worse than ale.
And whan that I have told thee forth my tale
And when I have told thee forth my tale
Of tribulacioun in mariage,
Of suffering in marriage,
180 Of which I am expert in al myn age—
Of which I am expert in all my life—
This to seyn, myself have been the whippe—
This is to say, myself have been the whip—
Than maystow chese whether thou wolt sippe
Than may thou choose whether thou will sip
Of thilke tonne that I shal abroche.
Of that same barrel that I shall open.
Be war of it, er thou to ny approche,
Beware of it, before thou too near approach;
185 For I shall telle ensamples mo than ten.
For I shall tell examples more than ten.
'Whoso that nil be war by othere men,
'Whoever will not be warned by (the examples of) other men,
By him shul othere men corrected be.'
Shall be an example by which other men shall be corrected.'
The same wordes wryteth Ptholomee:
The same words writes Ptholomy;
Rede in his Almageste, and take it there."
Read in his Almagest, and take it there."
190 "Dame, I wolde praye yow, if youre wil it were,"
"Madam, I would pray you, if it were your will,"
Seyde this Pardoner, "as ye bigan,
Said this Pardoner, "as you began,

Telle forth youre tale, spareth for no man,
Tell forth your tale, refrain for no man,
And teche us yonge men of youre praktike."
And teach us young men of your practice."
   "Gladly," quod she, "sith it may yow lyke.
   "Gladly," she said, "since it may please you;
195 But yet I praye to al this companye,
But yet I pray to all this company,
If that I speke after my fantasye,
If I speak according to my fancy,
As taketh not agrief of that I seye;
Do not be annoyed by what I say,
For myn entente nis but for to pleye.
For my intention is only to amuse.

[The Wife Continues]

Now sires, now wol I telle forth my tale.
Now, sirs, now will I tell forth my tale.
200 As evere mote I drinken wyn or ale,
As ever may I drink wine or ale,
I shal seye sooth, tho housbondes that I hadde,
I shall speak the truth; those husbands that I had,
As three of hem were gode and two were badde.
Three of them were good, and two were bad.
The three men were gode, and riche, and olde;
The three were good men, and rich, and old;
Unnethe mighte they the statut holde
Hardly might they the statute hold (pay the debt)
205 In which that they were bounden unto me.
In which they were bound unto me.
Ye woot wel what I mene of this, pardee!
You know well what I mean of this, by God!
As help me God, I laughe whan I thinke
So help me God, I laugh when I think
How pitously a-night I made hem swinke,
How pitifully at night I made them work!
And by my fey, I tolde of it no stoor.
And, by my faith, I set no store by it.
210 They had me yeven hir lond and hir tresoor;
They had given me their land and their treasure;
Me neded nat do lenger diligence
I needed not work hard any longer
To winne hir love, or doon hem reverence.
To win their love, or do them reverence.
They loved me so wel, by God above,
They loved me so well, by God above,
That I ne tolde no deyntee of hir love!
That I reckoned little of their love!
215 A wys womman wol bisye hire evere in oon
A wise woman will be constantly busy
To gete hire love, ye, ther as she hath noon.
To get their love, yes, when she has none.

But sith I hadde hem hoolly in myn hond,
But since I had them wholly in my hand,
And sith they hadde me yeven all hir lond,
And since they had me given all their land,
What sholde I taken keep hem for to plese,
Why should I take care to please them,
220 But it were for my profit and myn ese?
Unless it were for my profit and my pleasure?
I sette hem so a-werke, by my fey,
I set them so to work, by my faith,
That many a night they songen 'weilawey!'
That many a night they sang 'Woe is me!'
The bacoun was nat fet for hem, I trowe,
The bacon was not fetched for them, I believe,
That som men han in Essex at Dunmowe.
That some men have in Essex at Dunmowe.
225 I governed hem so wel after my lawe
I governed them so well, according to my law,
That ech of hem ful blisful was and fawe
That each of them was very blissful and eager
To bringe me gaye thinges fro the fayre.
To bring me gay things from the fair.
They were ful glad whan I spak to hem fayre,
They were very glad when I spoke to them pleasantly,
For God it woot, I chidde hem spitously.
For, God knows it, I cruelly scolded them.
230 Now herkneth how I bar me proprely:
Now listen how well I conducted myself,
Ye wyse wyves, that can understonde,
You wise wives, that can understand.
Thus shul ye speke and bere hem wrong on honde,
Thus should you speak and accuse them wrongfully,
For half so boldely can ther no man
For half so boldly can there no man
Swere and lyen as a womman can.
Swear and lie, as a woman can.
235 I sey nat this by wyves that ben wyse,
I do not say this concerning wives that are wise,
But if it be whan they them misavyse.
Unless it be when they are ill advised.
A wys wyf, if that she can hir good,
A wise wife, if she knows what is good for her,
Shal beren him on hond the cow is wood,
Shall deceive him by swearing the bird is crazy,
And take witnesse of hir owene mayde
And prove it by taking witness of her own maid
240 Of hir assent. But herkneth how I sayde:
Who is in league with her. But listen how I spoke:
'Sire olde kaynard, is this thyn array?
'Sir old doddering fool, is this thy doing?
Why is my neighebores wyf so gay?
Why is my neighbor's wife so gay?
She is honoured over al ther she goth:

She is honored everywhere she goes;
I sitte at hoom, I have no thrifty cloth.
I sit at home; I have no decent clothing.
245 What dostow at my neighebores hous?
What dost thou at my neighbor's house?
Is she so fair? artow so amorous?
Is she so fair? Art thou so amorous?
What rowne ye with oure mayde? *benedicite!*
What do you whisper with our maid? Bless me!
Sire olde lechour, lat thy japes be!
Sir old lecher, let thy tricks be!
And if I have a gossib or a freend,
And if I have a close friend or an acquaintance,
250 Withouten gilt, thou chydest as a feend,
Innocently, thou scold like a fiend,
If that I walke or pleye unto his hous!
If I walk or go unto his house to amuse myself!
Thou comest hoom as dronken as a mous,
Thou comest home as drunk as a mouse,
And prechest on thy bench, with yvel preef!
And preach on thy bench, bad luck to you!
Thou seist to me, it is a greet meschief
Thou sayest to me it is a great misfortune
255 To wedde a povre womman, for costage.
To wed a poor woman, because of expense;
And if that she be riche, of heigh parage,
And if she be rich, of high birth,
Thanne seistow that it is a tormentrye
Then thou sayest that it is a torment
To suffre hire pryde and hire malencolye.
To put up with her pride and her angry moods.
And if that she be fair, thou verray knave,
And if she be fair, thou utter knave,
260 Thou seyst that every holour wol hire have:
Thou sayest that every lecher wants to have her;
She may no whyle in chastitee abyde,
She can not remain chaste for any length of time,
That is assailled upon ech a syde.
Who is assailed on every side.
    Thou seyst som folk desyren us for richesse,
    Thou sayest some folk desire us for riches,
Somme for oure shap, and somme for oure fairnesse,
Some for our shape, and some for our fairness,
265 And som for she can outher singe or daunce,
And one because she can either sing or dance,
And som for gentillesse and daliaunce,
And some because of noble descent and flirtatious talk;
Som for hir handes and hir armes smale;
Some because of their hands and their slender arms;
Thus goth al to the devel, by thy tale.
Thus goes all to the devil, according to you.
Thou seyst men may nat kepe a castel wal,
Thou sayest men may not defend a castle wall,

270 It may so longe assailled been over al.
It may so long be assailed on all sides.
And if that she be foul, thou seist that she
And if she be ugly, thou sayest that she
Coveiteth every man that she may se;
Covets every man that she may see,
For as a spaynel she wol on him lepe,
For like a spaniel she will on him leap,
Til that she finde som man hire to chepe.
Until she find some man to buy (take) her.
275 Ne noon so grey goos goth ther in the lake
Nor does any goose go there in the lake, no matter how drab,
As, seistow, that wol been withoute make.
That, thou sayest, will be without a mate.
And seyst, it is an hard thing for to welde
And thou sayest it is a hard thing to control
A thing that no man wol, his thankes, helde.
A thing that no man will, willingly, hold.
Thus seistow, lorel, whan thow goost to bedde,
Thus sayest thou, scoundrel, when thou goest to bed,
280 And that no wys man nedeth for to wedde,
And that no wise man needs to wed,
Ne no man that entendeth unto hevene.
Nor any man that hopes (to go) to heaven.
With wilde thonder-dint and firy levene
With wild thunder-bolt and fiery lightning
Mote thy welked nekke be to-broke!
May thy wrinkled neck be broken in pieces!
Thow seyst that dropping houses and eek smoke
Thou sayest that leaky houses, and also smoke,
285 And chyding wyves maken men to flee
And scolding wives make men to flee
Out of hir owene hous; a, *benedicite!*
Out of their own houses; ah, bless me!
What eyleth swich an old man for to chyde?
What ails such an old man to chide like that?
Thow seyst we wyves wol oure vyces hyde
Thou sayest we wives will hide our vices
Til we be fast, and thanne we wol hem shewe—
Until we be securely tied (in marriage), and then we will them show—
290 Wel may that be a proverbe of a shrewe!
Well may that be a proverb of a scoundrel!
Thou seist that oxen, asses, hors, and houndes,
Thou sayest that oxen, asses, horses, and hounds,
They been assayed at diverse stoundes;
They are tried out a number of times;
Bacins, lavours, er that men hem bye,
Basins, wash bowls, before men them buy,
Spones and stoles, and al swich housbondrye,
Spoons and stools, and all such household items,
295 And so been pottes, clothes, and array;
And so are pots, clothes, and adornments;
But folk of wyves maken noon assay

But folk of wives make no trial,
Til they be wedded. Olde dotard shrewe!
Until they are wedded—old doddering scoundrel!—
And thanne, seistow, we wol oure vices shewe.
And then, sayest thou, we will show our vices.
Thou seist also that it displeseth me
Thou sayest also that it displeases me
300 But if that thou wolt preyse my beautee,
Unless thou will praise my beauty,
And but thou poure alwey upon my face,
And unless thou peer always upon my face,
And clepe me "faire dame" in every place;
And call me "dear lady" in every place.
And but thou make a feste on thilke day
And unless thou make a feast on that same day
That I was born, and make me fresh and gay,
That I was born, and make me happy and gay;
305 And but thou do to my norice honour,
And unless thou do honor to my nurse,
And to my chamberere withinne my bour,
And to my chambermaid within my bedchamber,
And to my fadres folk and his allyes—
And to my father's folk and his allies—
Thus seistow, olde barel ful of lyes!
Thus sayest thou, old barrelful of lies!
And yet of oure apprentice Janekyn,
And yet of our apprentice Janekin,
310 For his crispe heer, shyninge as gold so fyn,
Because of his curly hair, shining like gold so fine,
And for he squiereth me bothe up and doun,
And because he familiarly attends me everywhere,
Yet hastow caught a fals suspecioun.
Yet hast thou caught a false suspicion.
I wol hym noght, thogh thou were deed tomorwe.
I do not want him, though thou were dead tomorrow!
  But tel me this, why hydestow, with sorwe,
  But tell me this: why hidest thou, bad luck to you,
315 The keyes of thy cheste awey fro me?
The keys of thy strongbox away from me?
It is my good as wel as thyn, pardee.
It is my property as well as thine, by God!
What, wenestow make an idiot of oure dame?
What, think thou to make a fool of the lady of the house?
Now by that lord that called is Seint Jame,
Now by that lord that is called Saint James,
Thou shalt nat bothe, thogh that thou were wood,
Thou shalt not both, though thou were crazy with anger,
320 Be maister of my body and of my good;
Be master of my body and of my property;
That oon thou shalt forgo, maugree thyne yën;
One of them thou must give up, despite anything you can do.
  What helpith thee of me to enquere or spyën?
  What helps it to inquire about me or spy?

I trowe, thou woldest loke me in thy chiste!   *metaphor*
I believe thou would lock me in thy strongbox!
325 Thou sholdest seye, "Wyf, go wher thee liste;
Thou should say, "Wife, go where you please;
Tak your disport, I wol nat leve no talis.
Enjoy yourself; I will not believe any gossip.
I knowe yow for a trewe wyf, dame Alis."
I know you for a true wife, dame Alys."
We love no man that taketh kepe or charge   *Women*
We love no man who takes notice or concern about   *freedom want*
Wher that we goon; we wol ben at oure large.
Where we go; we will be free (to do as we wish).
330 Of alle men y-blessed moot he be,
Of all men blessed may he be,
The wyse astrologien Daun Ptholome,
The wise astrologer, Dan Ptolemy,
That seith this proverbe in his Almageste:
Who says this proverb in his Almagest:
"Of alle men his wisdom is the hyeste,
"Of all men his wisdom is the highest
That rekketh nevere who hath the world in honde."   *Contrap*
Who never cares who has the world in his control."
By this proverbe thou shalt understonde,
By this proverb thou shalt understand,
335 Have thou ynogh, what thar thee recche or care
If thou have enough, why should thou take note or care
How merily that othere folkes fare?
How merrily other folks fare?
For certeyn, olde dotard, by youre leve,
For, certainly, old senile fool, by your leave,
Ye shul have queynte right ynough at eve.
You shall have pudendum right enough at eve.
He is to greet a nigard that wol werne
He is too great a miser that would refuse
340 A man to lighte a candle at his lanterne;   *metaphor*
A man to light a candle at his lantern;
He shal have never the lasse light, pardee.
He shall have never the less light, by God.
Have thou ynough, thee thar nat pleyne thee.
If thou have enough, thou need not complain.
   Thou seyst also that if we make us gay
   Thou sayest also, that if we make ourselves gay
With clothing and with precious array,
With clothing, and with precious adornments,
345 That it is peril of oure chastitee;
That it is dangerous to our chastity;
And yet, with sorwe, thou most enforce thee,
And yet—bad luck to thee!—thou must reinforce thy argument,
And seye thise wordes in th'Apostles name:
And say these words in the Apostle's name:
"In habit maad with chastitee and shame,
"In clothing made with chastity and shame
Ye wommen shul apparaille yow," quod he,

You women shall apparel yourselves," he said,
350 "And noght in tressed heer and gay perree,
"And not in carefully arranged hair and gay precious stones,
As perles, ne with gold, ne clothes riche."
Such as pearls, nor with gold, nor rich cloth."
After thy text, ne after thy rubriche
In accordance with thy text, nor in accord with thy interpretation,
I wol nat wirche as muchel as a gnat.
I will not do as much as a gnat.
Thou seydest this, that I was lyk a cat:
Thou said this, that I was like a cat;
355 For whoso wolde senge a cattes skin,
For if anyone would singe a cat's skin,
Thanne wolde the cat wel dwellen in his in;
Then would the cat well stay in his dwelling;
And if the cattes skin be slyk and gay,
And if the cat's skin be sleek and gay,
She wol nat dwelle in house half a day,
She will not stay in house half a day,
But forth she wole, er any day be dawed,
But forth she will (go), before any day be dawned,
360 To shewe hir skin and goon a-caterwawed.
To show her skin and go yowling like a cat in heat.
This is to seye, if I be gay, sire shrewe,
This is to say, if I be well dressed, sir scoundrel,
I wol renne out, my borel for to shewe.
I will run out to show my poor clothes.
Sire olde fool, what helpeth thee to spyën?
Sir old fool, what help is it for thee to spy?
Thogh thou preye Argus, with his hundred yën,
Though thou pray Argus with his hundred eyes
365 To be my warde-cors, as he can best,
To be my bodyguard, as he best knows how,
In feith, he shal nat kepe me but me lest;
In faith, he shall not keep me but as I please;
Yet coude I make his berd, so moot I thee.
Yet could I deceive him, as I may prosper!
    Thou seydest eek that ther ben thinges three,
    Thou said also that there are three things,
The whiche thinges troublen al this erthe,
The which things trouble all this earth,
370 And that no wight ne may endure the ferthe.
And that no one can endure the fourth.
O! leve sire shrewe, Jesu shorte thy lyf!
O! dear sir scoundrel, Jesus shorten thy life!
Yet prechestow and seyst an hateful wyf
Yet thou preachest and sayest a hateful wife
Y-rekened is for oon of thise meschances.
Is reckoned as one of these misfortunes.
Been ther none othere maner resemblances
Are there no other sorts of comparisons
375 That ye may lykne youre parables to,
That you can use in your sayings,

But if a sely wyf be oon of tho?
Without a poor wife's being one of them?
  Thou lykenest eek wommanes love to helle,
  Thou also compare women's love to hell,
To bareyne lond, ther water may not dwelle;
To barren land, where water may not remain.
Thou lyknest it also to wilde fyr.
Thou compare it also to Greek (inextinguishable) fire;

380 The more it brenneth, the more it hath desyr
The more it burns, the more it has desire
To consume every thing that brent wol be.
To consume every thing that will be burned.
Thou seyst that right as wormes shende a tree,
Thou sayest, just as worms destroy a tree,
Right so a wyf destroyeth hire housbonde;
Right so a wife destroys her husband;
This knowe they that been to wyves bonde.'
This know they who are bound to wives.'

385 Lordinges, right thus, as ye have understonde,
Gentlemen, right thus, as you have heard,
Bar I stifly myne olde housbondes on honde
I firmly swore to my old husbands
That thus they seyden in hir dronkenesse;
That thus they said in their drunkenness;
And al was fals, but that I took witnesse
And all was false, but I took witness
On Janekin and on my nece also.
On Janekin, and on my niece also.

390 O! Lord, the peyne I dide hem and the wo,
O! Lord! The pain I did them and the woe,
Ful giltelees, by Goddes swete pyne!
Entirely guiltless (they were), by God's sweet pain!
For as an hors I coude byte and whyne.
For like a horse I could bite and whinny.
I coude pleyne, thogh I were in the gilt,
I could complain, though I was in the wrong,
Or elles often tyme hadde I ben spilt.
Or else many times had I been ruined.

395 Whoso that first to mille comth, first grint.
Whoever first comes to the mill, first grinds;
I pleyned first: so was oure werre y-stint.
I complained first, so was our war ended.
They were ful glad to excusen hem ful blyve
They were very glad to excuse themselves quickly
Of thing of which they nevere agilte hir lyve.
Of things of which they were never guilty in their lives.
Of wenches wolde I beren hem on honde,
Of wenches would I falsely accuse them,

400 Whan that for syk unnethes mighte they stonde.
When for sickness they could hardly stand.
Yet tikled I his herte, for that he
Yet I tickled his heart, for he
Wende that I hadde of him so greet chiertee.

Believed that I had of him so great affection!
I swoor that al my walkinge out by nighte
I swore that all my walking out by night
Was for t'espye wenches that he dighte.
Was to spy out wenches with whom he had intercourse;
405 Under that colour hadde I many a mirthe,
Under that pretense I had many a mirth.
For al swich wit is yeven us in oure birthe.
For all such wit is given us in our birth;
Deceite, weping, spinning God hath yive
Deceit, weeping, spinning God has given
To wommen kindely whyl they may live.
To women naturally, while they may live.
And thus of o thing I avaunte me:
And thus of one thing I boast:
410 Atte ende I hadde the bettre in ech degree,
At the end I had the better in every way,
By sleighte, or force, or by som maner thing,
By trickery, or force, or by some such thing,
As by continuel murmur or grucching.
As by continual grumbling or grouching.
Namely abedde hadden they meschaunce:
Especially in bed they had misfortune:
Ther wolde I chyde and do hem no plesaunce;
There would I scold and do them no pleasure;
415 I wolde no lenger in the bed abyde,
I would no longer in the bed abide,
If that I felte his arm over my syde,
If I felt his arm over my side,
Til he had maad his raunson unto me;
Until he had paid his penalty to me;
Thanne wolde I suffre him do his nycetee.
Then would I allow him to do his foolishness.
And therfore every man this tale I telle,
And therefore this tale I tell to every man,
420 Winne whoso may, for al is for to selle.
Anyone can profit, for everything is for sale;
With empty hand men may none haukes lure.
One can lure no hawks with an empty hand.
For winning wolde I al his lust endure,   *sex for sale!*
For profit I would endure all his lust,
And make me a feyned appetyt—
And make me a feigned appetite;
And yet in bacon hadde I nevere delyt.
And yet in bacon (old meat) I never had delight.
425 That made me that evere I wolde hem chyde.
That made me so that I would always scold them,
For thogh the Pope had seten hem biside,
For though the pope had sat beside them,
I wolde nat spare hem at hir owene bord.
I would not spare them at their own table,
For by my trouthe, I quitte hem word for word.
For, by my troth, I paid them back word for word.

As help me verray God omnipotent,
As help me true God omnipotent,
430 Thogh I right now sholde make my testament,
Though I right now should make my will,
I ne owe hem nat a word that it nis quit.
I owe them not one word that has not been avenged.
I broghte it so aboute, by my wit,
I brought it so about by my wit
That they moste yeve it up, as for the beste,
That they had to give it up, as the best they could do,
Or elles hadde we nevere been in reste.
Or else had we never been at peace;
435 For thogh he loked as a wood leoun,
For though he looked like a furious lion,
Yet sholde he faille of his conclusioun.
Yet should he fail to attain his goal.
  Thanne wolde I seye, 'Godelief, tak keep
  Then I would say, 'Sweetheart, see
How mekely loketh Wilkin oure sheep!
How meekly looks Willy, our sheep!
Com neer, my spouse, lat me ba thy cheke!
Come near, my spouse, let me kiss thy cheek!
440 Ye sholde been al pacient and meke,
You should be all patient and meek,
And han a swete spyced conscience,
And have a sweet tender disposition,
Sith ye so preche of Jobes pacience.
Since you so preach of Job's patience.
Suffreth alwey, sin ye so wel can preche;
Suffer always, since you so well can preach;
And but ye do, certein we shal yow teche
And unless you do, certainly we shall teach
445 That it is fair to have a wyf in pees.
That it is fair to have a wife in peace.
Oon of us two moste bowen, doutelees,
One of us two must bow, doubtless,
And sith a man is more resonable
And since a man is more reasonable
Than womman is, ye moste been suffrable.
Than a woman is, you must be able to bear suffering.
What eyleth yow to grucche thus and grone?
What ails you to grouch thus and groan?
450 Is it for ye wolde have my queynte allone?
Is it because you want to have my pudendum all to yourself?
Why taak it al! lo, have it every-deel!
Why, take it all! Lo, have it every bit!
Peter! I shrewe yow but ye love it weel!
By Saint Peter! I would curse you, if you did not love it well;
For if I wolde selle my bele chose,   Sex as Commodity
For if I would sell my 'pretty thing,'
I coude walke as fresh as is a rose;
I could walk as fresh (newly clothed) as is a rose;
455 But I wol kepe it for your owene tooth.

But I will keep it for your own pleasure.
Ye be to blame. By God, I sey yow sooth.'
You are to blame, by God! I tell you the truth.'
Swiche manere wordes hadde we on honde.
Such sorts of words we had in hand.
Now wol I speken of my fourthe housbonde.
Now will I speak of my fourth husband.

My fourthe housebonde was a revelour—
My fourth husband was a reveller—
460   This is to seyn, he hadde a paramour—
This is to say, he had a mistress—
And I was yong and ful of ragerye,
And I was young and full of playfulness,
Stiborn and strong, and joly as a pye.
Stubborn and strong, and jolly as a magpie.
Wel coude I daunce to an harpe smale,
Well I could dance to a small harp,
And singe, ywis, as any nightingale,
And sing, indeed, like any nightingale,
465   Whan I had dronke a draughte of swete wyn.
When I had drunk a draft of sweet wine!
Metellius, the foule cherl, the swyn,
Metellius, the foul churl, the swine,
That with a staf birafte his wyf hir lyf
Who with a staff deprived his wife of her life,
For she drank wyn, thogh I hadde been his wyf,
Because she drank wine, if I had been his wife,
He sholde nat han daunted me fro drinke!
He should not have frightened me away from drink!
470   And after wyn on Venus moste I thinke,
And after wine on Venus must I think,
For al so siker as cold engendreth hayl,
For as surely as cold engenders hail,
A likerous mouth moste han a likerous tayl.
A gluttonous mouth must have a lecherous tail.
In wommen vinolent is no defence—
In drunken women there is no defense—
This knowen lechours by experience.
This lechers know by experience.
475   But, Lord Crist! whan that it remembreth me
But—Lord Christ!—when I remember
Upon my yowthe, and on my jolitee,
My youth, and my gaiety,
It tikleth me aboute myn herte rote.
It tickles me to the bottom of my heart.
Unto this day it dooth myn herte bote
Unto this day it does my heart good
That I have had my world as in my tyme.
That I have had my world in my time.
480   But age, allas! that al wol envenyme,
But age, alas, that all will poison,
Hath me biraft my beautee and my pith.
Has deprived me of my beauty and my vigor.

Lat go, farewel! the devel go therwith!
Let it go. Farewell! The devil go with it!
The flour is goon, ther is namore to telle:
The flour is gone; there is no more to tell;
The bren, as I best can, now moste I selle;
The bran, as I best can, now I must sell;
485 But yet to be right mery wol I fonde.
But yet I will try to be right merry.
Now wol I tellen of my fourthe housbonde. 4 *Hb*
Now will I tell of my fourth husband.
   I seye, I hadde in herte greet despyt
   I say, I had in heart great anger
That he of any other had delyt.
That he had delight in any other.
But he was quit, by God and by Seint Joce!
But he was paid back, by God and by Saint Josse
490 I made him of the same wode a croce—
I made him a cross of the same wood;
Nat of my body in no foul manere,
Not of my body, in no foul manner,
But certeinly, I made folk swich chere
But certainly, I treated folk in such a way
That in his owene grece I made him frye
That I made him fry in his own grease
For angre and for verray jalousye.
For anger, and for pure jealousy.
495 By God, in erthe I was his purgatorie,
By God, in earth I was his purgatory,
For which I hope his soule be in glorie.
For which I hope his soul may be in glory.
For God it woot, he sat ful ofte and song
For, God knows it, he sat very often and cried out in pain,
Whan that his shoo ful bitterly him wrong.
When his shoe very bitterly pinched him.
Ther was no wight, save God and he, that wiste
There was no person who knew it, save God and he,
500 In many wyse how sore I him twiste.
In many a way, how painfully I tortured him.
He deyde whan I cam fro Jerusalem,
He died when I came from Jerusalem,
And lyth y-grave under the rode-beem,
And lies buried under the rood beam,
Al is his tombe noght so curious
Although his tomb is not so elaborate
As was the sepulcre of him Darius,
As was the sepulcher of that Darius,
505 Which that Appelles wroghte subtilly;
Which Appelles wrought skillfully;
It nis but wast to burie him preciously.
It is nothing but waste to bury him expensively.
Lat him farewel, God yeve his soule reste!
Let him fare well; God give his soul rest!
He is now in the grave and in his cheste.

5th

He is now in his grave and in his casket.
   Now of my fifthe housbond wol I telle—
   Now of my fifth husband I will tell.
510 God lete his soule nevere come in helle!
God let his soul never come in hell!
And yet was he to me the moste shrewe.
And yet he was to me the greatest scoundrel;
That fele I on my ribbes al by rewe,
That feel I on my ribs one after another,
And evere shal unto myn ending day.
And ever shall unto my final day.
But in oure bed he was so fresh and gay,
But in our bed he was so lively and gay,
515 And therwithal so wel coude he me glose
And moreover he so well could deceive me,
Whan that he wolde han my *bele chose*,
When he would have my 'pretty thing';

wefe
battering?

That thogh he hadde me bet on every boon,
That though he had beat me on every bone,
He coude winne agayn my love anoon.
He could win back my love straightway
I trowe I loved him beste for that he
I believe I loved him best, because he
520 Was of his love daungerous to me.
Was of his love standoffish to me.
We wommen han, if that I shal nat lye,
We women have, if I shall not lie,
In this matere a queynte fantasye:
In this matter a curious fantasy:
Wayte what thing we may nat lightly have,
Note that whatever thing we may not easily have,
Thereafter wol we crye al day and crave.
We will cry all day and crave for it.
525 Forbede us thing, and that desyren we;
Forbid us a thing, and we desire it;
Prees on us faste, and thanne wol we flee.
Press on us fast, and then will we flee.
With daunger oute we al oure chaffare:
With niggardliness we spread out all our merchandise;
Greet prees at market maketh dere ware,
A great crowd at the market makes wares expensive,
And to greet cheep is holde at litel prys.
And too great a supply makes them of little value:
530 This knoweth every womman that is wys.
Every woman that is wise knows this.
   My fifthe housbonde, God his soule blesse!
   My fifth husband—God bless his soul!—
Which that I took for love and no richesse,
Whom I took for love, and no riches,
He som tyme was a clerk of Oxenford,
He was formerly a clerk of Oxford,
And had left scole, and wente at hoom to bord
And had left school, and came home to board

535 With my gossib, dwellinge in oure toun—
With my close friend, dwelling in our town;
God have hir soule! hir name was Alisoun.
God have her soul! Her name was Alisoun.
She knew myn herte and eek my privetee
She knew my heart, and also my secrets,
Bet than oure parisshe preest, so moot I thee!
Better than our parish priest, as I may prosper!
To hire biwreyed I my conseil al,
To her I revealed all my secrets.
540 For had myn housebonde pissed on a wal,
For had my husband pissed on a wall,
Or doon a thing that sholde han cost his lyf,
Or done a thing that should have cost his life,
To hire and to another worthy wyf,
To her, and to another worthy wife,
And to my nece, which that I loved weel,
And to my niece, whom I loved well,
I wolde han told his conseil every deel.
I would have told every one of his secrets.
545 And so I dide ful often, God it woot,
And so I did very often, God knows it,
That made his face ful often reed and hoot
That made his face very often red and hot
For verray shame, and blamed himself for he
For true shame, and blamed himself because he
Had told to me so greet a privetee.
Had told to me so great a secret.
    And so bifel that ones in a Lente—
    And so it happened that once in a Springtime—
550 So often tymes I to my gossib wente,
Since frequently I went to visit my close friend,
For evere yet I lovede to be gay,
For I always loved to be gay,
And for to walke in March, Averille, and May,
And to walk in March, April, and May,
Fro hous to hous, to here sondry talis—
From house to house, to hear various bits of gossip—
That Jankin clerk and my gossib dame Alis
That Jankin the clerk, and my close friend dame Alys,
555 And I myself into the feldes wente.
And I myself, into the fields went.
Myn housbond was at London al that Lente:
My husband was at London all that Spring;
I hadde the bettre leyser for to pleye,
I had the better opportunity to amuse myself,
And for to see, and eek for to be seye
And to see, and also to be seen
Of lusty folk. What wiste I wher my grace
By amorous folk. What did I know about where my good fortune
560 Was shapen for to be, or in what place?
Was destined to be, or in what place?
Therefore I made my visitaciouns,

Therefore I made my visitations
To vigilies and to processiouns,
To religious feasts and to processions,
To preching eek and to thise pilgrimages,
To preaching also, and to these pilgrimages,
To pleyes of miracles, and mariages,
To plays about miracles, and to marriages,
565   And wered upon my gaye scarlet gytes.
And wore my gay scarlet robes.
Thise wormes, ne thise motthes, ne thise mytes,
These worms, nor these moths, nor these mites,
Upon my peril, frete hem never a deel;
Upon my peril (I swear), chewed on them never a bit;
And wostow why? for they were used weel.
And know thou why? Because they were well used.
   Now wol I tellen forth what happed me.
   Now will I tell forth what happened to me.
570   I seye that in the feeldes walked we,
I say that in the fields we walked,
Til trewely we hadde swich daliance,
Until truly we had such flirtation,
This clerk and I, that of my purveyance
This clerk and I, that for my provision for the future
I spak to him and seyde him how that he,
I spoke to him and said to him how he,
If I were widwe, sholde wedde me.
If I were a widow, should wed me.
575   For certeinly, I sey for no bobance,
For certainly—I say this for no boast—
Yet was I nevere withouten purveyance
I was never yet without providing beforehand
Of mariage, n'of othere thinges eek.
For marriage, nor for other things also.
I holde a mouses herte nat worth a leek
I hold a mouse's heart not worth a leek
That hath but oon hole for to sterte to,
That has but one hole to flee to,
580   And if that faille, thanne is al y-do.
If that should fail, then all is lost.
I bar him on honde he hadde enchanted me—
I falsely swore that he had enchanted me—
My dame taughte me that soutiltee—
My mother taught me that trick—
And eek I seyde I mette of him al night:
And also I said I dreamed of him all night,
He wolde han slayn me as I lay upright,
He would have slain me as I lay on my back,
585   And al my bed was ful of verray blood;
And all my bed was full of real blood;
But yet I hope that he shal do me good,
But yet I hope that he shall do me good,
For blood bitokeneth gold, as me was taught.
For blood symbolizes gold, as I was taught.'

And al was fals—I dremed of it right naught,
And all was false; I dreamed of it not at all,
But as I folwed ay my dames lore
But I followed always my mother's teaching,
590 As wel of this as of othere thinges more.
As well in this as in other things more.
But now sire, lat me see, what I shal seyn?
But now, sir, let me see what I shall say.
Aha! by God, I have my tale ageyn.
A ha! By God, I have my tale again.
Whan that my fourthe housbond was on bere,
When my fourth husband was on the funeral bier,
I weep algate, and made sory chere
I wept continuously, and acted sorry,
595 As wyves moten, for it is usage,
As wives must do, for it is the custom,
And with my coverchief covered my visage;
And with my kerchief covered my face,
But for that I was purveyed of a make,
But because I was provided with a mate,
I wepte but smal, and that I undertake.
I wept but little, and that I affirm.
   To chirche was myn housbond born a-morwe
   To church was my husband carried in the morning
600 With neighebores, that for him maden sorwe;
By neighbors, who for him made sorrow;
And Jankin oure clerk was oon of tho.
And Jankin, our clerk, was one of those.
As help me God! whan that I saugh him go
As help me God, when I saw him go
After the bere, me thoughte he hadde a paire
After the bier, I thought he had a pair
Of legges and of feet so clene and faire,
Of legs and of feet so neat and fair
605 That al myn herte I yaf unto his hold.
That all my heart I gave unto his keeping.
He was, I trowe, twenty winter old,
He was, I believe, twenty years old,
And I was fourty, if I shal seye sooth;
And I was forty, if I shall tell the truth;
But yet I hadde alwey a coltes tooth.
But yet I had always a colt's tooth.
Gat-tothed I was, and that bicam me weel;
With teeth set wide apart I was, and that became me
610 I hadde the prente of Seynte Venus seel.
I had the print of Saint Venus's seal.
As help me God, I was a lusty oon,
As help me God, I was a lusty one,
And faire, and riche, and yong, and wel bigoon;
And fair, and rich, and young, and well fixed,
And trewely, as myne housbondes tolde me,
And truly, as my husbands told me,
I had the beste *quoniam* mighte be.

I had the best pudendum that might be.

615 For certes, I am al Venerien
For certainly, I am all influenced by Venus
In felinge, and myn herte is Marcien:
In feeling, and my heart is influenced by Mars.
Venus me yaf my lust, my likerousnesse,
Venus me gave my lust, my amorousness,
And Mars yaf me my sturdy hardinesse;
And Mars gave me my sturdy boldness;
Myn ascendent was Taur, and Mars therinne.
My ascendant was Taurus, and Mars was therein.
620 Allas! allas! that evere love was sinne!
Alas, alas! That ever love was sin!
I folwed ay myn inclinacioun
I followed always my inclination
By vertu of my constellacioun;
By virtue of the state of the heavens at my birth;
That made me I coude noght withdrawe
That made me that I could not withdraw
My chambre of Venus from a good felawe.
My chamber of Venus from a good fellow.
625 Yet have I Martes mark upon my face,
Yet have I Mars' mark upon my face,
And also in another privee place.
And also in another private place.
For, God so wis be my savacioun,
For as God may be my salvation,
I ne loved nevere by no discrecioun,
I never loved in moderation,
But evere folwede myn appetyt:
But always followed my appetite,
630 Al were he short or long, or blak or whyt,
Whether he were short, or tall, or black-haired, or blond;
I took no kepe, so that he lyked me,
I took no notice, provided that he pleased me,
How pore he was, ne eek of what degree.
How poor he was, nor also of what rank.
What sholde I seye but, at the monthes ende,
What should I say but, at the month's end,
This joly clerk Jankin, that was so hende,
This jolly clerk, Jankin, that was so courteous,
635 Hath wedded me with greet solempnitee,
Has wedded me with great solemnity,
And to him yaf I al the lond and fee
And to him I gave all the land and property
That evere was me yeven therbifore.
That ever was given to me before then.
But afterward repented me ful sore;
But afterward I repented very bitterly;
He nolde suffre nothing of my list.
He would not allow me anything of my desires.
640 By God, he smoot me ones on the list
By God, he hit me once on the ear,

For that I rente out of his book a leef,
Because I tore a leaf out of his book,
That of the strook myn ere wex al deef.
So that of the stroke my ear became all deaf.
Stiborn I was as is a leonesse,
I was as stubborn as is a lioness,
And of my tonge a verray jangleresse,
And of my tongue a true chatterbox,
645 And walke I wolde, as I had doon biforn,
And I would walk, as I had done before,
From hous to hous, although he had it sworn.
From house to house, although he had sworn the contrary;
For which he often tymes wolde preche,
For which he often times would preach,
And me of olde Romayn gestes teche,
And teach me of old Roman stories;
How he Simplicius Gallus lefte his wyf,
How he, Simplicius Gallus, left his wife,
650 And hire forsook for terme of al his lyf,
And forsook her for rest of all his life,
Noght but for open-heveded he hir say
Because of nothing but because he saw her bare-headed
Lokinge out at his dore upon a day.
Looking out at his door one day.
   Another Romayn tolde he me by name,
   Another Roman he told me by name,
That, for his wyf was at a someres game
Who, because his wife was at a midsummer revel
655 Withoute his witing, he forsook hire eke.
Without his knowledge, he forsook her also.
And thanne wolde he upon his Bible seke
And then he would seek in his Bible
That ilke proverbe of Ecclesiaste
That same proverb of Ecclesiasticus
Wher he comandeth and forbedeth faste
Where he commands and strictly forbids that
Man shal nat suffre his wyf go roule aboute;
Man should suffer his wife go wander about.
660 Thanne wolde he seye right thus, withouten doute:
Then would he say right thus, without doubt:
'Whoso that buildeth his hous al of salwes,
'Whoever builds his house all of willow twigs,
And priketh his blinde hors over the falwes,
And spurs his blind horse over the open fields,
And suffreth his wyf to go seken halwes,
And suffers his wife to go on pilgrimages,
Is worthy to been hanged on the galwes!'
Is worthy to be hanged on the gallows!'
665 But al for noght; I sette noght an hawe
But all for nothing, I gave not a hawthorn berry
Of his proverbes n'of his olde sawe,
For his proverbs nor for his old sayings,
Ne I wolde nat of him corrected be.

Nor would I be corrected by him.
I hate him that my vices telleth me,
I hate him who tells me my vices,
And so do mo, God woot, of us than I.
And so do more of us, God knows, than I.

670 This made him with me wood al outrely:
This made him all utterly furious with me;
I nolde noght forbere him in no cas.
I would not put up with him in any way.
    Now wol I seye yow sooth, by Seint Thomas,
    Now will I tell you the truth, by Saint Thomas,
Why that I rente out of his book a leef,
Why I tore a leaf out of his book,
For which he smoot me so that I was deef.
For which he hit me so hard that I was deaf.

675 He hadde a book that gladly, night and day,
He had a book that regularly, night and day,
For his desport he wolde rede alway.
For his amusement he would always read;
He cleped it Valerie and Theofraste,
He called it Valerie and Theofrastus,
At which book he lough alwey ful faste.
At which book he always heartily laughed.
And eek ther was somtyme a clerk at Rome,
And also there was once a clerk at Rome,

680 A cardinal, that highte Seint Jerome,
A cardinal, who is called Saint Jerome,
That made a book agayn Jovinian;
That made a book against Jovinian;
In which book eek ther was Tertulan,
In which book also there was Tertullian,
Crisippus, Trotula, and Helowys,
Crisippus, Trotula, and Heloise,
That was abbesse nat fer fro Parys;
Who was abbess not far from Paris,

685 And eek the Parables of Salomon,
And also the Parables of Salomon,
Ovydes Art, and bokes many on,
Ovid's Art, and many other books,
And alle thise were bounden in o volume.
And all these were bound in one volume.
And every night and day was his custume,
And every night and day was his custom,
Whan he hadde leyser and vacacioun
When he had leisure and spare time

690 From other worldly occupacioun,
From other worldly occupations,
To reden on this book of wikked wyves.
To read in this book of wicked wives.
He knew of hem mo legendes and lyves
He knew of them more legends and lives
Than been of gode wyves in the Bible.
Than are of good women in the Bible.

For trusteth wel, it is an impossible
For trust well, it is an impossibility
695 That any clerk wol speke good of wyves,
That any clerk will speak good of women,
But if it be of holy seintes lyves,
Unless it be of holy saints' lives,
Ne of noon other womman never the mo.
Nor of any other woman in any way.
Who peyntede the leoun, tel me, who?
Who painted the lion, tell me who?
By God, if wommen hadde writen stories,
By God, if women had written stories,
700 As clerkes han withinne hir oratories,
As clerks have within their studies,
They wolde han writen of men more wikkednesse
They would have written of men more wickedness
Than all the mark of Adam may redresse.
Than all the male sex could set right.
The children of Mercurie and of Venus
The children of Mercury (clerks) and of Venus (lovers)
Been in hir wirking ful contrarious:
Are directly contrary in their actions;
705 Mercurie loveth wisdom and science,
Mercury loves wisdom and knowledge,
And Venus loveth ryot and dispence;
And Venus loves riot and extravagant expenditures.
And, for hire diverse disposicioun,
And, because of their diverse dispositions,
Ech falleth in otheres exaltacioun,
Each falls in the other's most powerful astronomical sign.
And thus, God woot, Mercurie is desolat
And thus, God knows, Mercury is powerless
710 In Pisces wher Venus is exaltat,
In Pisces (the Fish), where Venus is exalted,
And Venus falleth ther Mercurie is reysed;
And Venus falls where Mercury is raised.
Therfore no womman of no clerk is preysed.
Therefore no woman is praised by any clerk.
The clerk, whan he is old and may noght do
The clerk, when he is old, and can not do
Of Venus werkes worth his olde sho—
Any of Venus's works worth his old shoe,
715 Thanne sit he doun and writ in his dotage
Then he sits down, and writes in his dotage
That wommen can nat kepe hir mariage!
That women can not keep their marriage!
But now to purpos why I tolde thee
But now to the point, why I told thee
That I was beten for a book, pardee.
That I was beaten for a book, by God!
Upon a night Jankin, that was our syre,
Upon a night Jankin, that was master of our house,
720 Redde on his book as he sat by the fyre

Read on his book, as he sat by the fire,
Of Eva first, that for hir wikkednesse
Of Eve first, how for her wickedness
Was al mankinde broght to wrecchednesse,
All mankind was brought to wretchedness,
For which that Jesu Crist himself was slayn,
For which Jesus Christ himself was slain,
That boghte us with his herteblood agayn.
Who bought us back with his heart's blood.

725 Lo, here expres of womman may ye finde
Lo, here clearly of woman you may find
That womman was the los of all mankinde.
That woman was the cause of the loss of all mankind.
   Tho redde he me how Sampson loste his heres:
   Then he read me how Sampson lost his hair:
Slepinge, his lemman kitte hem with hir sheres,
Sleeping, his lover cut it with her shears;
Thurgh whiche tresoun loste he bothe his yën.
Through which treason he lost both his eyes.

730   Tho redde he me, if that I shal nat lyen,
   Then he read to me, if I shall not lie,
Of Hercules and of his Dianyre,
Of Hercules and of his Dianyre,
That caused him to sette himself afyre.
Who caused him to set himself on fire.
Nothing forgat he the sorwe and the wo
He forgot not a bit of the sorrow and the woe
That Socrates had with hise wyves two—
That Socrates had with his two wives,

735 How Xantippa caste pisse upon his heed:
How Xantippa caste piss upon his head.
This sely man sat stille, as he were deed;
This poor man sat still as if he were dead;
He wyped his heed; namore dorste he seyn
He wiped his head, no more dared he say,
But 'Er that thonder stinte, comth a reyn.'
But 'Before thunder stops, there comes a rain!'
   Of Phasipha that was the quene of Crete—
   Of Phasipha, that was the queen of Crete,

740 For shrewednesse him thoughte the tale swete—
For sheer malignancy, he thought the tale sweet;
Fy! spek namore, it is a grisly thing,
Fie! Speak no more—it is a grisly thing—
   Of hire horrible lust and hir lyking.
   Of her horrible lust and her pleasure.
Of Clitermistra, for hire lecherye,
Of Clitermystra, for her lechery,
That falsly made hire housbond for to dye,
That falsely made her husband to die,

745 He redde it with ful good devocioun.
He read it with very good devotion.
   He tolde me eek for what occasioun
   He told me also for what occasion

Amphiorax at Thebes loste his lyf.
Amphiorax at Thebes lost his life.
Myn housbond hadde a legende of his wyf,
My husband had a legend of his wife,
Eriphilem, that for an ouche of gold
Eriphilem, that for a brooch of gold
750   Hath prively unto the Grekes told
Has secretly unto the Greeks told
Wher that hir housbonde hidde him in a place,
Where her husband hid him in a place,
For which he hadde at Thebes sory grace.
For which he had at Thebes a sad fate.
    Of Lyvia tolde he me, and of Lucye.
    Of Livia told he me, and of Lucie:
They bothe made hir housbondes for to dye,
They both made their husbands to die,
755   That oon for love, that other was for hate.
That one for love, that other was for hate.
Lyvia hir housbond, on an even late,
Livia her husband, on a late evening,
Empoysoned hath, for that she was his fo.
Has poisoned, because she was his foe;
Lucya, likerous, loved hire housbond so,
Lucia, lecherous, loved her husband so much
That, for he sholde alwey upon hire thinke,
That, so that he should always think upon her,
760   She yaf him swich a manere love-drinke,
She gave him such a sort of love-drink
That he was deed er it were by the morwe;
That he was dead before it was morning;
And thus algates housbondes han sorwe.
And thus always husbands have sorrow.
    Thanne tolde he me how oon Latumius
    Then he told me how one Latumius
Compleyned unto his felawe Arrius,
Complained unto his fellow Arrius,
765   That in his gardin growed swich a tree
That in his garden grew such a tree
On which he seyde how that his wyves three
On which he said how his three wives
Hanged hemself for herte despitous.
Hanged themselves for the malice of their hearts
    'O leve brother,' quod this Arrius,
    'O dear brother,' this Arrius said,
'Yif me a plante of thilke blissed tree,
'Give me a shoot of that same blessed tree,
770   And in my gardin planted shal it be!'
And in my garden shall it be planted.'
    Of latter date, of wyves hath he red
    Of latter date, of wives has he read
That somme han slayn hir housbondes in hir bed,
That some have slain their husbands in their bed,
And lete hir lechour dighte hire al the night

And let her lecher copulate with her all the night,
Whyl that the corps lay in the floor upright.
When the corpse lay in the floor flat on its back.
775 And somme han drive nayles in hir brayn
And some have driven nails in their brains,
Whyl that they slepte, and thus they han hem slayn.
While they slept, and thus they had them slain.
Somme han hem yeve poysoun in hire drinke.
Some have given them poison in their drink.
He spak more harm than herte may bithinke,
He spoke more harm than heart may imagine,
And therwithal he knew of mo proverbes
And concerning this he knew of more proverbs
780 Than in this world ther growen gras or herbes.
Than in this world there grow grass or herbs.
'Bet is,' quod he, 'thyn habitacioun
'Better is,' he said, 'thy habitation
Be with a leoun or a foul dragoun,
Be with a lion or a foul dragon,
Than with a womman usinge for to chyde.
Than with a woman accustomed to scold.
Bet is,' quod he, 'hye in the roof abyde
Better is,' he said, 'to stay high in the roof,
785 Than with an angry wyf doun in the hous;
Than with an angry wife down in the house;
They been so wikked and contrarious
They are so wicked and contrary,
They haten that hir housbondes loveth ay.'
They always hate what their husbands love.'
He seyde, 'A womman cast hir shame away
He said, 'A woman casts their shame away,
Whan she cast of hir smok;' and forthermo,
When she casts off her undergarment'; and furthermore,
790 'A fair womman, but she be chaast also,
'A fair woman, unless she is also chaste,
Is lyk a gold ring in a sowes nose.'
Is like a gold ring in a sow's nose.'
Who wolde wene, or who wolde suppose
Who would believe, or who would suppose,
The wo that in myn herte was, and pyne?
The woe that in my heart was, and pain?
    And whan I saugh he wolde nevere fyne
    And when I saw he would never cease
795 To reden on this cursed book al night,
Reading on this cursed book all night,
Al sodeynly three leves have I plight
All suddenly have I plucked three leaves
Out of his book, right as he radde, and eke
Out of his book, right as he read, and also
I with my fist so took him on the cheke
I with my fist so hit him on the cheek
That in oure fyr he fil bakward adoun.
That in our fire he fell down backwards.

800 And he upstirte as dooth a wood leoun,
And he leaped up as does a furious lion,
And with his fist he smoot me on the heed
And with his fist he hit me on the head
That in the floor I lay as I were deed.
That on the floor I lay as if I were dead.
And when he saugh how stille that I lay,
And when he saw how still I lay,
He was agast, and wolde han fled his way,
He was frightened and would have fled on his way,
805 Til atte laste out of my swogh I breyde.
Until at the last out of my swoon I awoke.
'O! hastow slayn me, false theef?' I seyde,
'O! hast thou slain me, false thief?' I said,
'And for my land thus hastow mordred me?
'And for my land thus hast thou murdered me?
Er I be deed, yet wol I kisse thee.'
Before I am dead, yet will I kiss thee.'
And neer he cam, and kneled faire adoun,
And near he came, and kneeled gently down,
810 And seyde, 'Dere suster Alisoun,
And said, 'Dear sister Alisoun,
As help me God, I shall thee nevere smyte;
So help me God, I shall never (again) smite thee!
That I have doon, it is thyself to wyte.
What I have done, it is thyself to blame (you drove me to it).
Foryeve it me, and that I thee biseke'—
Forgive it me, and that I beseech thee!'
And yet eftsones I hitte him on the cheke
And yet immediately I hit him on the cheek,
815 And seyde, 'Theef! thus muchel am I wreke.
And said, 'Thief, thus much am I avenged;
Now wol I dye: I may no lenger speke.'
Now will I die, I may no longer speak.'
    But atte laste, with muchel care and wo,
    But at the last, with much care and woe,
We fille acorded by us selven two.
We made an agreement between our two selves.
He yaf me al the brydel in myn hond,
He gave me all the control in my hand,
820 To han the governance of hous and lond,
To have the governance of house and land,
And of his tonge and of his hond also;
And of his tongue, and of his hand also;
And made him brenne his book anon right tho.
And made him burn his book immediately right then.
And whan that I hadde geten unto me,
And when I had gotten unto me,
By maistrie, al the soveraynetee,
By mastery, all the sovereignty,
825 And that he seyde, 'Myn owene trewe wyf,
And that he said, 'My own true wife,
Do as thee lust the terme of al thy lyf;

Do as you please the rest of all thy life;
Keep thyn honour, and keep eek myn estaat'—
Guard thy honor, and guard also my reputation'—
After that day we hadden never debaat.
After that day we never had an argument.
God help me so, I was to him as kinde
As God may help me, I was to him as kind

830 As any wyf from Denmark unto Inde,
As any wife from Denmark unto India,
And also trewe, and so was he to me.
And also true, and so was he to me.
I prey to God that sit in magestee,
I pray to God, who sits in majesty,
So blesse his soule for his mercy dere!
So bless his soul for his mercy dear.
Now wol I seye my tale, if ye wol here."
Now will I say my tale, if you will hear."

[Another Interruption]

[Biholde the wordes bitwene the Somonour and the Frere.]
[Behold the altercation between the Summoner and the Friar.]

835 The Frere lough whan he hadde herd al this.
The Friar laughed, when he had heard all this;
"Now, dame," quod he, "so have I joye or blis,
"Now dame," he said, "as I may have joy or bliss,
This is a long preamble of a tale!"
This is a long preamble of a tale!"
And whan the Somnour herde the Frere gale,
And when the Summoner heard the Friar cry out,
"Lo," quod the Somnour, "Goddes armes two,
"Lo," said the Summoner, "By God's two arms!

840 A frere wol entremette him everemo!
A friar will always intrude himself (in others' affairs).
Lo, gode men, a flye and eek a frere
Lo, good men, a fly and also a friar
Wol falle in every dish and eek matere.
Will fall in every dish and also every discussion.
What spekestow of preambulacioun?
What speakest thou of perambulation?
What! amble, or trotte, or [pace,] or go sit doun!
What! amble, or trot, or walk, or go sit down!

845 Thou lettest oure disport in this manere."
Thou spoil our fun in this manner."
"Ye, woltow so, sire Somnour?" quod the Frere;
"Yes, wilt thou have it thus, sir Summoner?" said the Friar;
"Now by my feith, I shal, er that I go,
"Now, by my faith I shall, before I go,
Telle of a somnour swich a tale or two
Tell of a summoner such a tale or two
That alle the folk shal laughen in this place."
That all the folk shall laugh in this place."

850 "Now elles, Frere, I wol bishrewe thy face,"

"Now otherwise, Friar, I curse thy face,"
Quod this Somnour, "and I bishrewe me
Said this Summoner, "and I curse myself,
But if I telle tales two or thre
Unless I tell tales two or three
Of freres, er I come to Sidingborne,
Of friars before I come to Siitingbourne
That I shal make thyn herte for to morne—
That I shall make thy heart to mourn,
855   For wel I woot thy pacience is goon."
For well I know thy patience is gone."
    Oure Hoste cryde "Pees! and that anoon!"
    Our Host cried "Peace! And that right now!"
And seyde, "Lat the womman telle hire tale.
And said, "Let the woman tell her tale.
Ye fare as folk that dronken been of ale.
You act like folk that are drunk on ale.
Do, dame, tel forth youre tale, and that is best."
Do, dame, tell forth your tale, and that is best."
860   "Al redy, sire," quod she, "right as yow lest,
    "All ready, sir," she said, "right as you please,
If I have licence of this worthy Frere."
If I have permission of this worthy Friar."
"Yis, dame," quod he, "tel forth, and I wol here."
"Yes, dame," he said, "tell forth, and I will hear."

The Tale

    In th'olde dayes of the King Arthour,
    In the old days of King Arthur,
Of which that Britons speken greet honour,
Of whom Britons speak great honor,
865   All was this land fulfild of fayerye.
This land was all filled full of supernatural creatures.
The elf-queen with hir joly companye
The elf-queen, with her jolly company,
Daunced ful ofte in many a grene mede.
Danced very often in many a green mead.
This was the olde opinion, as I rede—
This was the old belief, as I read;
I speke of manye hundred yeres ago—
I speak of many hundred years ago.
870   But now can no man see none elves mo.
But now no man can see any more elves,
For now the grete charitee and prayeres
For now the great charity and prayers
Of limitours and othere holy freres,
Of licensed beggars and other holy friars,
That serchen every lond and every streem,
That overrun every land and every stream,
As thikke as motes in the sonne-beem,
As thick as specks of dust in the sun-beam,
875   Blessinge halles, chambres, kichenes, boures,
Blessing halls, chambers, kitchens, bedrooms,

Citees, burghes, castels, hye toures,
Cities, towns, castles, high towers,
Thropes, bernes, shipnes, dayeryes—
Villages, barns, stables, dairies—
This maketh that ther been no fayeryes.
This makes it that there are no fairies.
For ther as wont to walken was an elf,
For where an elf was accustomed to walk
880   Ther walketh now the limitour himself
There walks now the licensed begging friar himself
In undermeles and in morweninges,
In late mornings and in early mornings,
And seyth his Matins and his holy thinges
And says his morning prayers and his holy things
As he goth in his limitacioun.
As he goes in his assigned district.
Wommen may go now saufly up and doun:
Women may go now safely up and down.
885   In every bush or under every tree
In every bush or under every tree
Ther is noon other incubus but he,
There is no other evil spirit but he,
And he ne wol doon hem but dishonour.
And he will not do them any harm except dishonor.
And so bifel that this King Arthour
And so it happened that this king Arthur
Hadde in his hous a lusty bacheler,
Had in his house a lusty bachelor,
890   That on a day cam rydinge fro river;
That on one day came riding from hawking,
And happed that, allone as he was born,
And it happened that, alone as he was born,
He saugh a mayde walkinge him biforn,
He saw a maiden walking before him,
Of whiche mayde anon, maugree hir heed,
Of which maiden straightway, despite all she could do,
By verray force he rafte hire maydenheed.
By utter force, he took away her maidenhead;
895   For which oppressioun was swich clamour
For which wrong was such clamor
And swich pursute unto the King Arthour,
And such demand for justice unto king Arthur
That dampned was this knight for to be deed
That this knight was condemned to be dead,
By cours of lawe, and sholde han lost his heed—
By course of law, and should have lost his head—
Paraventure swich was the statut tho—
Perhaps such was the statute then—
900   But that the quene and othere ladies mo
Except that the queen and other ladies as well
So longe preyeden the king of grace
So long prayed the king for grace
Til he his lyf him graunted in the place,

Until he granted him his life right there,
And yaf him to the quene al at hir wille,
And gave him to the queen, all at her will,
To chese whether she wolde him save or spille.
To choose whether she would him save or put to death.

905 The quene thanketh the king with al hir might,
The queen thanks the king with all her might,
And after this thus spak she to the knight
And after this she spoke thus to the knight,
Whan that she saugh hir tyme, upon a day:
When she saw her time, upon a day:
"Thou standest yet," quod she, "in swich array
"Thou standest yet," she said, "in such condition,
That of thy lyf yet hastow no suretee.
That of thy life yet thou hast no assurance

910 I grante thee lyf, if thou canst tellen me
I grant thee life, if thou canst tell me
What thing is it that wommen most desyren.
What thing it is that women most desire.
Be war, and keep thy nekke-boon from yren.
Beware, and keep thy neck-bone from iron (axe)!
And if thou canst nat tellen it anon,
And if thou canst not tell it right now,
Yet wol I yeve thee leve for to gon
Yet I will give thee leave to go

915 A twelf-month and a day, to seche and lere
A twelvemonth and a day, to seek to learn
An answere suffisant in this matere.
A satisfactory answer in this matter;
And suretee wol I han, er that thou pace,
And I will have, before thou go, a pledge
Thy body for to yelden in this place."
To surrender thy body in this place."

Wo was this knight and sorwefully he syketh.
Woe was this knight, and sorrowfully he sighs;

920 But what! he may nat do al as him lyketh,
But what! He can not do all as he pleases.
And at the laste he chees him for to wende,
And at the last he chose to leave
And come agayn, right at the yeres ende,
And come again, exactly at the year's end,
With swich answere as God wolde him purveye;
With such answer as God would provide him;
And taketh his leve and wendeth forth his weye.
And takes his leave, and goes forth on his way.

925 He seketh every hous and every place
He seeks every house and every place
Wheras he hopeth for to finde grace,
Where he hopes to have the luck
To lerne what thing wommen loven most;
To learn what thing women love most,
But he ne coude arryven in no cost
But he could not arrive in any region

Wheras he mighte finde in this matere
Where he might find in this matter
930   Two creatures accordinge in-fere.
Two creatures agreeing together.
   Somme seyde wommen loven best richesse,
   Some said women love riches best,
Somme seyde honour, somme seyde jolynesse;
Some said honor, some said gaiety,
Somme riche array, somme seyden lust abedde,
Some rich clothing, some said lust in bed,
And ofte tyme to be widwe and wedde.
And frequently to be widow and wedded.
935   Somme seyde that oure hertes been most esed
Some said that our hearts are most eased
Whan that we been y-flatered and y-plesed.
When we are flattered and pleased.
He gooth ful ny the sothe, I wol nat lye:
He goes very near the truth, I will not lie.
A man shal winne us best with flaterye;
A man shall win us best with flattery,
And with attendance and with bisinesse
And with attentions and with solicitude
940   Been we y-lymed, bothe more and lesse.
We are caught, every one of us.
   And somme seyn how that we loven best
   And some say that we love best
For to be free and do right as us lest,
To be free and do just as we please,
And that no man repreve us of oure vyce,
And that no man reprove us for our vices,
But seye that we be wyse, and no thing nyce.
But say that we are wise and not at all silly.
945   For trewely, ther is noon of us alle,
For truly there is not one of us all,
If any wight wol clawe us on the galle,
If any one will scratch us on the sore spot,
That we nil kike for he seith us sooth:
That we will not kick back, because he tells us the truth.
Assay, and he shal finde it that so dooth.
Try it, and whoever so does shall find it true;
For be we never so vicious withinne,
For, be we never so vicious within,
950   We wol been holden wyse, and clene of sinne.
We want to be considered wise and clean of sin.
   And somme seyn that greet delyt han we
   And some say that we have great delight
For to ben holden stable and eek secree,
To be considered steadfast, and also (able to keep a) secret,
And in o purpos stedefastly to dwelle,
And in one purpose steadfastly to remain,
And nat biwreye thing that men us telle—
And not reveal things that men tell us.
955   But that tale is nat worth a rake-stele.

But that tale is not worth a rake handle.
Pardee, we wommen conne nothing hele:
By God, we women can hide nothing;
Witnesse on Myda—wol ye here the tale?
Witness on Midas—will you hear the tale?
    Ovyde, amonges othere thinges smale,
    Ovid, among other small matters,
Seyde Myda hadde under his longe heres,
Said Midas had, under his long hair,
960 Growinge upon his heed two asses eres,
Two ass's ears, growing upon his head,
The whiche vyce he hidde as he best mighte
The which vice he hid as he best could
Ful subtilly from every mannes sighte,
Very skillfully from every man's sight,
That, save his wyf, ther wiste of it namo.
That, except for his wife, there knew of it no others.
He loved hire most, and trusted hire also;
He loved her most, and trusted her also;
965 He preyede hire that to no creature
He prayed her that to no creature
She sholde tellen of his disfigure.
She should tell of his disfigurement.
She swoor him nay, for al this world to winne,
She swore him, "Nay"; for all this world to win,
She nolde do that vileinye or sinne,
She would not do that dishonor or sin,
To make hir housbond han so foul a name.
To make her husband have so foul a reputation.
970 She nolde nat telle it for hir owene shame.
She would not tell it for her own shame.
But nathelees, hir thoughte that she dyde
But nonetheless, she thought that she would die
That she so longe sholde a conseil hyde.
If she should hide a secret so long;
Hir thoughte it swal so sore aboute hir herte
She thought it swelled so sore about her heart
That nedely som word hire moste asterte,
That necessarily some word must escape her;
975 And sith she dorste telle it to no man,
And since she dared tell it to no man,
Doun to a mareys faste by she ran.
She ran down to a marsh close by—
Til she came there hir herte was afyre,
Until she came there her heart was afire—
And as a bitore bombleth in the myre,
And as a bittern bumbles in the mire,
She leyde hir mouth unto the water doun:
She laid her mouth down unto the water:
980 "Biwreye me nat, thou water, with thy soun,"
"Betray me not, thou water, with thy sound,"
Quod she, "to thee I telle it, and namo;
She said; "to thee I tell it and no others;

Myn housbond hath longe asses eres two!
My husband has two long asses ears!
Now is myn herte all hool, now is it oute.
Now is my heart all whole; now is it out.
I mighte no lenger kepe it, out of doute."
I could no longer keep it, without doubt."

985 Heer may ye se, thogh we a tyme abyde,
Here you may see, though we a time abide,
Yet out it moot, we can no conseil hyde.
Yet out it must come; we can hide no secret.
The remenant of the tale if ye wol here,
The remnant of the tale if you will hear,
Redeth Ovyde, and ther ye may it lere.
Read Ovid, and there you may learn it.
    This knight of which my tale is specially,
    This knight, of whom my tale is in particular,

990 Whan that he saugh he mighte nat come therby,
When he saw he might not come to that—
This is to seye, what wommen loven moost,
This is to say, what women love most—
Withinne his brest ful sorweful was the goost,
Within his breast very sorrowful was the spirit.
But hoom he gooth, he mighte nat sojourne.
But home he goes; he could not linger;
The day was come that hoomward moste he tourne,
The day was come that homeward he must turn.

995 And in his wey it happed him to ryde
And in his way he happened to ride,
In al this care under a forest-syde,
In all this care, near a forest side,
Wheras he saugh upon a daunce go
Where he saw upon a dance go
Of ladies foure and twenty and yet mo;
Ladies four and twenty, and yet more;
Toward the whiche daunce he drow ful yerne,
Toward the which dance he drew very eagerly,

1000 In hope that som wisdom sholde he lerne.
In hope that he should learn some wisdom.
But certeinly, er he came fully there,
But certainly, before he came fully there,
Vanisshed was this daunce, he niste where.
Vanished was this dance, he knew not where.
No creature saugh he that bar lyf,
He saw no creature that bore life,
Save on the grene he saugh sitting a wyf—
Save on the green he saw sitting a woman—

1005 A fouler wight ther may no man devyse.
There can no man imagine an uglier creature.
Agayn the knight this olde wyf gan ryse,
At the knight's coming this old wife did rise,
And seyde, "Sire knight, heerforth ne lyth no wey.
And said, "Sir knight, there lies no road out of here.
Tel me what that ye seken, by youre fey!

Tell me what you seek, by your faith!
Paraventure it may the bettre be:
Perhaps it may be the better;
1010 Thise olde folk can muchel thing," quod she.
These old folk know many things," she said.
   "My leve mooder," quod this knight, "certeyn
   "My dear mother," said this knight, "certainly
I nam but deed, but if that I can seyn
I am as good as dead unless I can say
What thing it is that wommen most desyre.
What thing it is that women most desire.
Coude ye me wisse, I wolde wel quyte your hyre."
If you could teach me, I would well repay you."
1015   "Plighte me thy trouthe, heer in myn hand," quod she,
   "Pledge me thy word here in my hand," she said,
"The nexte thing that I require thee,
"The next thing that I require of thee,
Thou shalt it do, if it lye in thy might,
Thou shalt do it, if it lies in thy power,
And I wol telle it yow er it be night."
And I will tell it to you before it is night."
   "Have heer my trouthe," quod the knight, "I grante."
   "Have here my pledged word," said the knight, "I agree."
1020   "Thanne," quod she, "I dar me wel avante
   "Then," she said, "I dare me well boast
Thy lyf is sauf, for I wol stonde therby.
Thy life is safe, for I will stand thereby;
Upon my lyf, the queen wol seye as I.
Upon my life, the queen will say as I.
Lat see which is the proudeste of hem alle,
Let's see which is the proudest of them all
That wereth on a coverchief or a calle,
That wears a kerchief or a hairnet
1025 That dar seye nay of that I shal thee teche.
That dares say 'nay' of what I shall teach thee.
Lat us go forth withouten lenger speche."
Let us go forth without longer speech."
Tho rouned she a pistel in his ere,
Then she whispered a message in his ear,
And bad him to be glad and have no fere.
And commanded him to be glad and have no fear.
   Whan they be comen to the court, this knight
   When they are come to the court, this knight
1030 Seyde he had holde his day, as he hadde hight,
Said he had held his day, as he had promised,
And redy was his answere, as he sayde.
And his answer was ready, as he said.
Ful many a noble wyf, and many a mayde,
Very many a noble wife, and many a maid,
And many a widwe—for that they ben wyse—
And many a widow, because they are wise,
The quene hirself sittinge as a justyse,
The queen herself sitting as a justice,

1035 Assembled been, his answere for to here;
Are assembled, to hear his answer;
And afterward this knight was bode appere.
And afterward this knight was commanded to appear.
To every wight comanded was silence,
Silence was commanded to every person,
And that the knight sholde telle in audience
And that the knight should tell in open court
What thing that worldly wommen loven best.
What thing (it is) that worldly women love best.
1040 This knight ne stood nat stille as doth a best,
This knight stood not silent as does a beast,
But to his questioun anon answerde
But to his question straightway answered
With manly voys, that al the court it herde:
With manly voice, so that all the court heard it:
  "My lige lady, generally," quod he,
  "My liege lady, without exception," he said,
"Wommen desyren to have sovereyntee
"Women desire to have sovereignty
1045 As wel over hir housbond as hir love,
As well over her husband as her love,
And for to been in maistrie him above.
And to be in mastery above him.
This is youre moste desyr, thogh ye me kille.
This is your greatest desire, though you kill me.
Doth as yow list—I am heer at your wille."
Do as you please; I am here subject to your will."
  In al the court ne was ther wyf, ne mayde,
  In all the court there was not wife, nor maid,
1050 Ne widwe that contraried that he sayde,
Nor widow that denied what he said,
But seyden he was worthy han his lyf.
But said that he was worthy to have his life.
  And with that word up stirte the olde wyf,
  And with that word up sprang the old woman,
Which that the knight saugh sittinge in the grene:
Whom the knight saw sitting on the green:
"Mercy," quod she, "my sovereyn lady quene!
"Mercy," she said, "my sovereign lady queen!
1055 Er that youre court departe, do me right.
Before your court departs, do me justice.
I taughte this answere unto the knight;
I taught this answer to the knight;
For which he plighte me his trouthe there,
For which he pledged me his word there,
The firste thing I wolde of him requere
The first thing that I would ask of him
He wolde it do, if it lay in his might.
He would do, if it lay in his power.
1060 Bifore the court thanne preye I thee, sir knight,"
Before the court then I pray thee, sir knight,"
Quod she, "that thou me take unto thy wyf,

Said she, "that thou take me as thy wife,
For wel thou wost that I have kept thy lyf.
For well thou know that I have saved thy life.
If I sey fals, sey nay, upon thy fey!"
If I say false, say 'nay,' upon thy faith!"
   This knight answerde, "Allas and weylawey!
   This knight answered, "Alas and woe is me!
1065   I woot right wel that swich was my biheste.
I know right well that such was my promise.
For Goddes love, as chees a newe requeste:
For God's love, choose a new request!
Tak al my good, and lat my body go."
Take all my goods and let my body go."
   "Nay thanne," quod she, ' "I shrewe us bothe two!
   "Nay, then," she said, "I curse both of us two!
For thogh that I be foul and old and pore,
For though I am ugly, and old, and poor
1070   I nolde for al the metal ne for ore
I would not for all the metal, nor for ore
That under erthe is grave or lyth above
That under earth is buried or lies above,
But if thy wyf I were, and eek thy love."
Have anything except that I were thy wife, and also thy love."
   "My love?" quod he, "Nay, my dampnacioun!
   "My love?" he said, "nay, my damnation!
Allas! that any of my nacioun
Alas, that any of my family
1075   Sholde evere so foule disparaged be!"
Should ever be so foully degraded!"
But al for noght, the ende is this, that he
But all for naught; the end is this, that he
Constreyned was: he nedes moste hire wedde,
Constrained was; he must by necessity wed her,
And taketh his olde wyf and gooth to bedde.
And takes his old wife, and goes to bed.
   Now wolden som men seye, paraventure,
   Now would some men say, perhaps,
1080   That for my necligence I do no cure
That because of my negligence I make no effort
To tellen yow the joye and al th'array
To tell you the joy and all the rich display
That at the feste was that ilke day.
That was at the (wedding) feast that same day.
To whiche thing shortly answere I shal:
To which thing shortly I shall answer:
I seye ther nas no joye ne feste at al;
I say there was no joy nor feast at all;
1085   Ther nas but hevinesse and muche sorwe,
There was nothing but heaviness and much sorrow.
For prively he wedded hire on morwe,
For he wedded her in private in the morning,
And al day after hidde him as an oule,
And all day after hid himself like an owl,

So wo was him, his wyf looked so foule.
So woeful was he, his wife looked so ugly.
   Greet was the wo the knight hadde in his thoght,
   Great was the woe the knight had in his thought,

1090 Whan he was with his wyf abedde y-broght;
When he was brought to bed with his wife;
He walweth, and he turneth to and fro.
He wallows and he turns to and fro.
His olde wyf lay smylinge everemo,
His old wife lay smiling evermore,
And seyde, "O dere housbond, *benedicite!*
And said, "O dear husband, bless me!
Fareth every knight thus with his wyf as ye?
Does every knight behave thus with his wife as you do?

1095 Is this the lawe of King Arthures hous?
Is this the law of king Arthur's house?
Is every knight of his so dangerous?
Is every knight of his so aloof?
I am youre owene love and eek youre wyf;
I am your own love and also your wife;
I am she which that saved hath youre lyf;
I am she who has saved your life,
And certes yet dide I yow nevere unright.
And, certainly, I did you never wrong yet;

1100 Why fare ye thus with me this firste night?
Why behave you thus with me this first night?
Ye faren lyk a man had lost his wit!
You act like a man who had lost his wit.
What is my gilt? for Goddes love, tel me it,
What is my offense? For God's love, tell it,
And it shal been amended, if I may."
And it shall be amended, if I can."
   "Amended?" quod this knight, "allas! nay, nay!
   "Amended?" said this knight, "Alas, nay, nay!

1105 It wol nat been amended nevere mo!
It will not be amended ever more.
Thou art so loothly, and so old also,
Thou art so loathsome, and so old also,
And therto comen of so lowe a kinde,
And moreover descended from such low born lineage,
That litel wonder is thogh I walwe and winde.
That little wonder is though I toss and twist about.
So wolde God myn herte wolde breste!"
So would God my heart would burst!"

1110   "Is this," quod she, "the cause of youre unreste?"
   "Is this," she said, "the cause of your distress?"
   "Ye, certainly," quod he, "no wonder is."
   "Yes, certainly," he said, "it is no wonder."
   "Now, sire," quod she, "I coude amende al this,
   "Now, sir," she said, "I could amend all this,
If that me liste, er it were dayes three,
If I pleased, before three days were past,
So wel ye mighte bere yow unto me.

Providing that you might behave well towards me.

1115   But for ye speken of swich gentillesse
    "But, since you speak of such nobility
As is descended out of old richesse—
As is descended out of old riches,
That therfore sholden ye be gentil men—
That therefore you should be noble men,
Swich arrogance is nat worth an hen.
Such arrogance is not worth a hen.
Loke who that is most vertuous alway,
Look who is most virtuous always,

1120 Privee and apert, and most entendeth ay
In private and public, and most intends ever
To do the gentil dedes that he can,
To do the noble deeds that he can;
And tak him for the grettest gentil man.
Take him for the greatest noble man.
Crist wol we clayme of him oure gentillesse,
Christ wants us to claim our nobility from him,
Nat of oure eldres for hire old richesse.
Not from our ancestors for their old riches.

1125 For thogh they yeve us al hir heritage—
For though they give us all their heritage,
For which we clayme to been of heigh parage—
For which we claim to be of noble lineage,
Yet may they nat biquethe, for no thing,
Yet they can not bequeath by any means
To noon of us hir vertuous living
To any of us their virtuous living,
That made hem gentil men y-called be,
That made them be called noble men,

1130 And bad us folwen hem in swich degree.
And commanded us to follow them in such matters.
    Wel can the wyse poete of Florence,
    "Well can the wise poet of Florence,
That highte Dant, speken in this sentence;
Who is called Dante, speak on this matter.
Lo, in swich maner rym is Dantes tale:
Lo, in such sort of rime is Dante's speech:
'Ful selde up ryseth by his branches smale
'Very seldom grows up from its small branches

1135 Prowesse of man, for God of his goodnesse
Nobility of man, for God, of his goodness,
Wol that of him we clayme oure gentillesse;'
Wants us to claim our nobility from him';
For of oure eldres may we no thing clayme
For from our ancestors we can claim no thing
But temporel thing, that man may hurte and mayme.
Except temporal things, that may hurt and injure a man.
Eek every wight wot this as wel as I,
"Also every person knows this as well as I,

1140 If gentillesse were planted naturelly
If nobility were planted naturally

Unto a certeyn linage doun the lyne,
Unto a certain lineage down the line,
Privee and apert, than wolde they nevere fyne
Then in private and in public they would never cease
To doon of gentillesse the faire offyce—
To do the just duties of nobility;
They mighte do no vileinye or vyce.
They could do no dishonor or vice.

1145   Tak fyr, and ber it in the derkeste hous
        "Take fire and bear it in the darkest house
Bitwix this and the Mount of Caucasus,
Between this and the mount of Caucasus,
And lat men shette the dores and go thenne,
And let men shut the doors and go away;
Yet wol the fyr as faire lye and brenne,
Yet will the fire as brightly blaze and burn
As twenty thousand men mighte it biholde:
As if twenty thousand men might it behold;

1150   His office naturel ay wol it holde,
        Its natural function it will always hold,
Up peril of my lyf, til that it dye.
On peril of my life (I say), until it dies.
Heer may ye see wel how that genterye
"Here may you see well that nobility
Is nat annexed to possessioun,
Is not joined with possession,
Sith folk ne doon hir operacioun
Since folk not do behave as they should

1155   Alwey, as dooth the fyr, lo, in his kinde.
        Always, as does the fire, lo, in its nature.
For, God it woot, men may wel often finde
For, God knows it, men may well often find
A lordes sone do shame and vileinye;
A lord's son doing shame and dishonor;
And he that wol han prys of his gentrye
And he who will have praise for his noble birth,
For he was boren of a gentil hous,
Because he was born of a noble house

1160   And hadde his eldres noble and vertuous,
        And had his noble and virtuous ancestors,
And nil himselven do no gentil dedis,
And will not himself do any noble deeds
Ne folwe his gentil auncestre that deed is,
Nor follow his noble ancestry that is dead,
He nis nat gentil, be he duk or erl;
He is not noble, be he duke or earl,
For vileyns sinful dedes make a cherl.
For churlish sinful deeds make a churl.

1165   For gentillesse nis but renomee
        For nobility is nothing but renown
Of thyne auncestres, for hire heigh bountee,
Of thy ancestors, for their great goodness,

Which is a straunge thing to thy persone.
Which is a thing not naturally part of thy person.
Thy gentillesse cometh fro God allone.
Thy nobility comes from God alone.
Thanne comth oure verray gentillesse of grace:
Then our true nobility comes from grace ;
1170   It was nothing biquethe us with oure place.
It was not at all bequeathed to us with our social rank.
Thenketh how noble, as seith Valerius,
"Think how noble, as says Valerius,
Was thilke Tullius Hostilius,
Was that same Tullius Hostillius,
That out of povert roos to heigh noblesse.
That out of poverty rose to high nobility.
Redeth Senek, and redeth eek Boëce:
Read Seneca, and read also Boethius;
1175   Ther shul ye seen expres that it no drede is
There shall you see clearly that it is no doubt
That he is gentil that doth gentil dedis.
That he is noble who does noble deeds.
And therfore, leve housbond, I thus conclude:
And therefore, dear husband, I thus conclude:
Al were it that myne auncestres were rude,
Although it is so that my ancestors were rude,
Yet may the hye God, and so·hope I,
Yet may the high God, and so hope I,
1180   Grante me grace to liven vertuously.
Grant me grace to live virtuously.
Thanne am I gentil, whan that I biginne
Then am I noble, when I begin
To liven vertuously and weyve sinne.
To live virtuously and abandon sin.
    And ther as ye of povert me repreve,
    "And whereas you reprove me for poverty,
The hye God, on whom that we bileve,
The high God, on whom we believe,
1185   In wilful povert chees to live his lyf.
In voluntary poverty chose to live his life.
And certes every man, mayden, or wyf,
And certainly every man, maiden, or woman
May understonde that Jesus, hevene king,
Can understand that Jesus, heaven's king,
Ne wolde nat chese a vicious living.
Would not choose a vicious form of living.
Glad povert is an honest thing, certeyn;
Glad poverty is an honest thing, certain;
1190   This wol Senek and othere clerkes seyn.
This will Seneca and other clerks say.
Whoso that halt him payd of his poverte,
Whoever considers himself satisfied with his poverty,
I holde him riche, al hadde he nat a sherte.
I consider him rich, although he had not a shirt.

He that coveyteth is a povre wight,
He who covets is a poor person,
For he wolde han that is nat in his might.
For he would have that which is not in his power;
1195 But he that noght hath, ne coveyteth have,
But he who has nothing, nor covets to have anything,
Is riche, although ye holde him but a knave.
Is rich, although you consider him but a knave.
Verray povert, it singeth proprely.
True poverty, it rightly sings;
Juvenal seith of povert merily:
Juvenal says of poverty merrily:
'The povre man, whan he goth by the weye,
The poor man, when he goes along the roadway,
1200 Bifore the theves he may singe and pleye.'
Before the thieves he may sing and play.'
Poverte is hateful good, and as I gesse,
Poverty is a hateful good and, as I guess,
A ful greet bringere out of bisinesse;
A very great remover of cares;
A greet amendere eek of sapience
A great amender also of wisdom
To him that taketh it in pacience.
To him that takes it in patience.
1205 Poverte is this, although it seme elenge,
Poverty is this, although it may seem miserable:
Possessioun that no wight wol chalenge;
A possession that no one will challenge.
Poverte ful ofte, whan a man is lowe,
Poverty very often, when a man is low,
Maketh his God and eek himself to knowe;
Makes him know his God and also himself.
Poverte a spectacle is, as thinketh me,
Poverty is an eye glass, as it seems to me,
1210 Thurgh which he may his verray frendes see.
Through which one may see his true friends.
And therfore, sire, sin that I noght yow greve,
And therefore, sir, since I do not injure you,
Of my povert namore ye me repreve.
You (should) no longer reprove me for my poverty.
   Now, sire, of elde ye repreve me:
   "Now, sir, of old age you reprove me;
And certes, sire, thogh noon auctoritee
And certainly, sir, though no authority
1215 Were in no book, ye gentils of honour
Were in any book, you gentlefolk of honor
Seyn that men sholde an old wight doon favour
Say that men should be courteous to an old person
And clepe him fader, for youre gentillesse;
And call him father, because of your nobility;
And auctours shal I finden, as I gesse.
And authors shall I find, as I guess.

Now ther ye seye that I am foul and old,
"Now where you say that I am ugly and old,
1220 Than drede you noght to been a cokewold,
Than do not fear to be a cuckold;
For filthe and elde, also moot I thee,
For filth and old age, as I may prosper,
Been grete wardeyns upon chastitee.
Are great guardians of chastity.
But nathelees, sin I knowe youre delyt,
But nonetheless, since I know your delight,
I shal fulfille youre worldly appetyt.
I shall fulfill your worldly appetite.
1225 Chese now," quod she, "oon of thise thinges tweye:
"Choose now," she said, "one of these two things:
To han me foul and old til that I deye
To have me ugly and old until I die,
And be to yow a trewe humble wyf,
And be to you a true, humble wife,
And nevere yow displese in al my lyf,
And never displease you in all my life,
Or elles ye wol han me yong and fair,
Or else you will have me young and fair,
1230 And take youre aventure of the repair
And take your chances of the crowd
That shal be to youre hous, by cause of me,
That shall be at your house because of me,
Or in som other place, may wel be.
Or in some other place, as it may well be.
Now chese yourselven whether that yow lyketh."
Now choose yourself, whichever you please."
This knight avyseth him and sore syketh,
This knight deliberates and painfully sighs,
1235 But atte laste he seyde in this manere:
But at the last he said in this manner:
"My lady and my love, and wyf so dere,
"My lady and my love, and wife so dear,
I put me in youre wyse governance:
I put me in your wise governance;
Cheseth youreself which may be most plesance
Choose yourself which may be most pleasure
And most honour to yow and me also.
And most honor to you and me also.
1240 I do no fors the whether of the two,
I do not care which of the two,
For as yow lyketh, it suffiseth me."
For as it pleases you, is enough for me."
"Thanne have I gete of yow maistrye," quod she,
"Then have I gotten mastery of you," she said,
"Sin I may chese and governe as me lest?"
"Since I may choose and govern as I please?"
"Ye, certes, wyf," quod he, "I holde it best."
"Yes, certainly, wife," he said, "I consider it best."

1245 "Kis me," quod she. "We be no lenger wrothe,
"Kiss me," she said, "we are no longer angry,
For by my trouthe, I wol be to yow bothe,
For, by my troth, I will be to you both—
This is to seyn, ye, bothe fair and good.
This is to say, yes, both fair and good.
I prey to God that I mot sterven wood,
I pray to God that I may die insane
But I to yow be also good and trewe
Unless I to you be as good and true
1250 As evere was wyf, sin that the world was newe.
As ever was wife, since the world was new.
And but I be to-morn as fair to sene
And unless I am tomorrow morning as fair to be seen
As any lady, emperyce, or quene,
As any lady, empress, or queen,
That is bitwixe the est and eke the west,
That is between the east and also the west,
Doth with my lyf and deeth right as yow lest.
Do with my life and death right as you please.
1255 Cast up the curtin: loke how that it is."
Cast up the curtain, look how it is."
  And whan the knight saugh verraily al this,
  And when the knight saw truly all this,
That she so fair was and so yong therto,
That she so was beautiful, and so young moreover,
For joye he hente hire in his armes two;
For joy he clasped her in his two arms.
His herte bathed in a bath of blisse.
His heart bathed in a bath of bliss.
1260 A thousand tyme a-rewe he gan hire kisse,
A thousand time in a row he did her kiss,
And she obeyed him in every thing
And she obeyed him in every thing
That mighte doon him plesance or lyking.
That might do him pleasure or enjoyment.
And thus they live unto hir lyves ende
And thus they live unto their lives' end
In parfit joye. And Jesu Crist us sende
In perfect joy; and Jesus Christ us send
1265 Housbondes meke, yonge, and fresshe abedde,
Husbands meek, young, and vigorous in bed,
And grace t'overbyde hem that we wedde.
And grace to outlive them whom we wed;
And eek I preye Jesu shorte hir lyves
And also I pray Jesus shorten their lives
That noght wol be governed by hir wyves;
That will not be governed by their wives;
And olde and angry nigardes of dispence,
And old and angry misers in spending,
1270 God sende hem sone verray pestilence.
God send them soon the very pestilence!

The Pardoner's Prologue and Tale

The Introduction

* * *

"By corpus bones! but I have triacle,
By corpus' bones! unless I have medicine,
Or elles a draught of moyste and corny ale,
Or else a draught of fresh and strong ale,
Or but I here anon a mery tale,
Or unless I hear right now a merry tale,
Myn herte is lost for pitee of this mayde.
My heart is lost for pity of this maid.
30   Thou bel amy, thou Pardoner," he seyde,
    Thou fair friend (rascal), thou Pardoner," he said,
"Tel us som mirthe or japes right anon."
"Tell us some mirth or comic tales right away."
    "It shall be doon," quod he, "by Seint Ronyon!
    "It shall be done," said he, "by Saint Ronyon!
But first," quod he, "heer at this ale-stake
But first," said he, "here at this ale stake (tavern sign)
I wol both drinke and eten of a cake."
I will both drink and eat of a cake."
35   But right anon thise gentils gonne to crye,
    But right away these gentlefolk began to cry,
"Nay! lat him telle us of no ribaudye;
"Nay, let him tell us of no ribaldry!
Tel us som moral thing, that we may lere
Tell us some moral thing, that we may learn
Som wit, and thanne wol we gladly here."
Some useful knowledge, and then will we gladly hear."
    "I graunte, ywis," quod he, "but I mot thinke
    "I agree, indeed," said he, "but I must think
40 Upon som honest thing whyl that I drinke."
About some respectable thing while I drink."

The Prologue

"Lordinges," quod he, "in chirches whan I preche,
"Gentlemen," he said, "in churches when I preach,
I peyne me to han an hauteyn speche,
I take pains to have a loud voice,
And ringe it out as round as gooth a belle,
And ring it out as round as goes a belle,
For I can al by rote that I telle.
For I know all by rote that I tell.
45 My theme is alwey oon, and evere was—
My theme is always the same, and ever was—
Radix malorum est Cupiditas.
'Greed is the root of all evil.'
First I pronounce whennes that I come,
"First I pronounce from whence I come,

And thanne my bulles shewe I, alle and somme.
And then my papal bulls I show, each and every one.
Oure lige lordes seel on my patente,
Our liege lord's seal on my letter of authorization,
50 That shewe I first, my body to warente,
I show that first, to protect my body,
That no man be so bold, ne preest ne clerk,
So that no man be so bold, neither priest nor clerk,
Me to destourbe of Cristes holy werk;
To hinder me from (doing) Christ's holy work.
And after that thanne telle I forth my tales.
And after that then I tell forth my tales;
Bulles of popes and of cardinales,
Indulgences of popes and of cardinals,
55 Of patriarkes, and bishoppes I shewe,
Of patriarchs and bishops I show,
And in Latyn I speke a wordes fewe,
And in Latin I speak a few words,
To saffron with my predicacioun,
With which to add spice to my preaching,
And for to stire hem to devocioun.
And to stir them to devotion.
   Thanne shewe I forth my longe cristal stones,
   Then I show forth my long crystal stones,
60 Y-crammed ful of cloutes and of bones—
Crammed full of rags and of bones—
Reliks been they, as wenen they echoon.
Relics they are, as suppose they each one.
Thanne have I in latoun a sholder-boon
Then I have mounted in latten (brass-like alloy) a shoulder-bone
Which that was of an holy Jewes shepe.
Which was of a holy Jew's sheep.
'Goode men,' seye I, 'tak of my wordes kepe:
'Good men,' I say, 'take heed of my words;
65 If that this boon be wasshe in any welle,
If this bone be washed in any well,
If cow, or calf, or sheep, or oxe swelle,
If cow, or calf, or sheep, or ox swell
That any worm hath ete, or worm y-stonge,
That any worm has eaten, or worm stung,
Tak water of that welle, and wash his tonge,
Take water of that well and wash its tongue,
And it is hool anon; and forthermore,
And it is whole right away; and furthermore,
70 Of pokkes and of scabbe and every sore
Of pocks and of scab, and every sore
Shal every sheep be hool, that of this welle
Every sheep shall be whole that of this well
Drinketh a draughte. Tak kepe eek what I telle:
Drinks a draft. Take heed also what I say:
If that the good man that the bestes oweth
If the householder who owns the beasts
Wol every wike, er that the cok him croweth,

Will every week, before the cock crows,
75 Fastinge, drinken of this welle a draughte—
Fasting, drink of this well a draft,
As thilke holy Jewe oure eldres taughte—
As that same holy Jew taught our elders,
His bestes and his stoor shal multiplye.
His beasts and his possessions shall multiply.
  And, sires, also it heleth jalousye:
  'And, sirs, it also heals jealousy;
For though a man be falle in jalous rage,
For though a man be fallen in jealous rage,
80 Let maken with this water his potage,
Have his potage made with this water,
And nevere shal he more his wyf mistriste,
And he shall never more mistrust his wife,
Though he the sooth of hir defaute wiste—
Though he knew the truth of her misdeed,
Al had she taken preestes two or three.
Although she had taken two or three priests.
  Heer is a miteyn eek, that ye may see:
  'Here is a mitten also, that you may see.
85 He that his hond wol putte in this miteyn,
He that will put his hand in this mitten,
He shal have multiplying of his greyn
He shall have multiplying of his grain,
Whan he hath sowen, be it whete or otes,
When he has sown, be it wheat or oats,
So that he offre pens, or elles grotes.
Providing that he offer pennies, or else fourpences.
Goode men and wommen, o thing warne I yow:
'Good men and women, one thing I warn you:
90 If any wight be in this chirche now,
If any person be in this church now
That hath doon sinne horrible, that he
Who has done such horrible sin, that he
Dar nat for shame of it y-shriven be,
Dare not, for shame, be confessed of it,
Or any womman, be she yong or old,
Or any woman, be she young or old,
That hath y-maked hir housbonde cokewold,
Who has made her husband cuckold,
95 Swich folk shul have no power ne no grace
Such folk shall have no power nor no grace
To offren to my reliks in this place.
To offer to my relics in this place.
And whoso findeth him out of swich blame,
And whoever finds himself out of such blame,
He wol com up and offre a Goddes name,
He will come up and offer in God's name,
And I assoille him by the auctoritee
And I will absolve him by the authority
100 Which that by bulle y-graunted was to me.'
Which by papal bull was granted to me.'

By this gaude have I wonne, yeer by yeer,
"By this trick have I won, year after year,
An hundred mark sith I was pardoner.
An hundred marks since I was pardoner.
I stonde lyk a clerk in my pulpet,
I stand like a clerk in my pulpit,
And whan the lewed peple is doun y-set,
And when the ignorant people are set down,
105 I preche, so as ye han herd bifore,
I preach as you have heard before
And telle an hundred false japes more.
And tell a hundred more false tales.
Thanne peyne I me to strecche forth the nekke,
Then I take pains to stretch forth the neck,
And est and west upon the peple I bekke
And east and west upon the people I nod,
As doth a dowve, sittinge on a berne.
As does a dove sitting on a barn.
110 Myn hondes and my tonge goon so yerne
My hands and my tongue go so quickly
That it is joye to see my bisinesse.
That it is joy to see my business.
Of avaryce and of swich cursednesse
Of avarice and of such cursedness
Is al my preching, for to make hem free
Is all my preaching, to make them generous
To yeven hir pens, and namely unto me.
To give their pennies, and namely unto me.
115 For myn entente is nat but for to winne,
For my intention is only to make a profit,
And nothing for correccioun of sinne:
And not at all for correction of sin.
I rekke nevere, whan that they ben beried,
I care not a bit, when they are buried,
Though that hir soules goon a-blakeberied!
Though their souls go picking blackberries!
For certes, many a predicacioun
For certainly, many a sermon
120 Comth ofte tyme of yvel entencioun:
For certainly, many a sermon
Som for plesaunce of folk and flaterye,
Some for pleasure of folk and flattery,
To been avaunced by ypocrisye,
To be advanced by hypocrisy,
And som for veyne glorie, and som for hate.
And some for vain glory, and some for hate.
For whan I dar non other weyes debate,
For when I dare debate no other ways,
125 Than wol I stinge him with my tonge smerte
Then I will sting him with my sharp tongue
In preching, so that he shal nat asterte
In preaching, so that he shall not escape
To been defamed falsly, if that he

To be defamed falsely, if he
Hath trespased to my brethren or to me.
Has trespassed to my brethren or to me.
For, though I telle noght his propre name,
For though I tell not his proper name,
130 Men shal wel knowe that it is the same
Men shall well know that it is the same,
By signes and by othere circumstances.
By signs, and by other details.
Thus quyte I folk that doon us displesances;
Thus I repay folk who make trouble for us pardoners;
Thus spitte I out my venim under hewe
Thus I spit out my venom under hue
Of holynesse, to semen holy and trewe.
Of holinesses, to seem holy and true.
135 But shortly myn entente I wol devyse:
"But shortly my intention I will tell:
I preche of no thing but for coveityse.
I preach of nothing but for greed.
Therfore my theme is yet, and evere was,
Therefore my theme is yet, and ever was,
Radix malorum est cupiditas.
'Greed is the root of all evil.'
　　Thus can I preche agayn that same vyce
　　Thus I can preach against that same vice
140 Which that I use, and that is avaryce.
Which I use, and that is avarice.
But though myself be gilty in that sinne,
But though myself be guilty of that sin,
Yet can I maken other folk to twinne
Yet I can make other folk to turn away
From avaryce, and sore to repente.
From avarice and bitterly to repent.
But that is nat my principal entente:
But that is not my principal intention;
145 I preche nothing but for coveityse.
I preach nothing but for greed.
Of this matere it oughte ynogh suffyse.
Concerning this matter this ought to be enough.
Than telle I hem ensamples many oon
"Then I tell them illustrative tales many a one
Of olde stories longe tyme agoon,
Of old stories from long time ago.
For lewed peple loven tales olde;
For ignorant people love old tales;
150 Swich thinges can they wel reporte and holde.
Such things they can well repeat and hold in memory.
What, trowe ye, the whyles I may preche
What, do you suppose, that while I can preach,
And winne gold and silver for I teche,
And win gold and silver because I teach,
That I wol live in povert wilfully?
That I will live in poverty voluntarily?

Nay, nay, I thoghte it nevere, trewely!
Nay, nay, I never thought it, truly!
155 For I wol preche and begge in sondry londes;
For I will preach and beg in various lands;
I wol nat do no labour with myn hondes,
I will not do any labor with my hands,
Ne make baskettes, and live therby,
Nor make baskets and live thereby,
By cause I wol nat beggen ydelly.
Because I will not beg idly.
I wol non of the Apostles counterfete:
I will imitate none of the apostles;
160 I wol have money, wolle, chese, and whete,
I will have money, wool, cheese, and wheat,
Al were it yeven of the povereste page,
Although it were given by the poorest servant boy,
Or of the povereste widwe in a village,
Or by the poorest widow in a village,
Al sholde hir children sterve for famyne.
Even though her children should die of hunger.
Nay! I wol drinke licour of the vyne,
Nay, I will drink liquor of the vine,
165 And have a joly wenche in every toun.
And have a pretty wench in every town.
But herkneth, lordinges, in conclusioun:
But listen, gentlemen, in conclusion:
Youre lyking is that I shall telle a tale.
Your desire is that I shall tell a tale.
Now have I dronke a draughte of corny ale,
Now I have drunk a draft of strong ale,
By God, I hope I shal yow telle a thing
By God, I hope I shall tell you a thing
170 That shal by resoun been at youre lyking.
That shall, for good reason, be to your liking.
For though myself be a ful vicious man,
For though myself be a very vicious man,
A moral tale yet I yow telle can,
Yet I can tell you a moral tale,
Which I am wont to preche for to winne.
Which I am accustomed to preach in order to profit.
Now holde youre pees, my tale I wol beginne."
Now hold your peace! My tale I will begin."

The Tale

175 In Flaundres whylom was a compaignye
In Flanders once was a company
Of yonge folk, that haunteden folye—
Of young folk who practiced folly,
As ryot, hasard, stewes, and tavernes,
Such as debauchery, gambling, brothels, and taverns,
Where as with harpes, lutes, and giternes,

Where with harps, lutes, and guitars,
They daunce and pleyen at dees bothe day and night,
They dance and play at dice both day and night,
180   And eten also and drinken over hir might,
And also eat and drink beyond their capacity,
Thurgh which they doon the devel sacrifyse
Through which they do the devil sacrifice
Withinne that develes temple, in cursed wyse,
Within that devil's temple in cursed manner
By superfluitee abhominable.
By abominable excess.
Hir othes been so grete and so dampnable,
Their oaths are so great and so damnable
185   That it is grisly for to here hem swere.
That it is grisly to hear them swear.
Our blissed Lordes body they totere—
Our blessed Lord's body they tore in pieces—
Hem thoughte Jewes rente him noght ynough—
They thought that the Jews did not tear him enough—
And ech of hem at otheres sinne lough.
And each of them laughed at the other's sin.
And right anon thanne comen tombesteres
And right away then come dancing girls
190   Fetys and smale, and yonge fruytesteres,
Elegantly shaped and slim, and girls selling fruits,
Singeres with harpes, baudes, wafereres,
Singers with harps, bawds, girls selling wafers,
Whiche been the verray develes officeres
Which are the very devil's officers
To kindle and blowe the fyr of lecherye
To kindle and blow the fire of lechery,
That is annexed unto glotonye:
That is joined unto gluttony.
195   The Holy Writ take I to my witnesse
The Bible I take as my witness
That luxurie is in wyn and dronkenesse.
That lechery is in wine and drunkenness.
Lo, how that dronken Loth unkindely
Lo, how that drunken Lot, unnaturally,
Lay by his doghtres two, unwitingly;
Lay by his two daughters, unwittingly;
So dronke he was, he niste what he wroghte.
So drunk he was, he knew not what he did.
200   Herodes, whoso wel the stories soghte,
Herod, whoever should seek well the histories (would learn),
Whan he of wyn was repleet at his feste,
When he was filled with wine at his feast,
Right at his owene table he yaf his heste
Right at his own table he gave his command
To sleen the Baptist John ful giltelees.
To slay John the Baptist, full guiltless.
   Senek seith a good word doutelees:

Seneca says a good word, doubtless;
205 He seith, he can no difference finde
He says he can find no difference
Bitwix a man that is out of his minde
Between a man that is out of his mind
And a man which that is dronkelewe,
And a man that is drunk,
But that woodnesse, y-fallen in a shrewe,
Except that madness, fallen in an evil person,
Persevereth lenger than doth dronkenesse.
Lasts longer than does drunkenness.
210 O glotonye, ful of cursednesse!
O gluttony, full of cursedness!
O cause first of oure confusioun!
O first cause of our ruin!
O original of oure dampnacioun,
O origin of our damnation,
Til Crist had boght us with his blood agayn!
Until Christ had bought us with his blood again!
Lo, how dere, shortly for to sayn,
Lo, how dearly, shortly to say,
215 Aboght was thilke cursed vileinye;
Was bought that same cursed villainy!
Corrupt was al this world for glotonye!
Corrupt was all this world for gluttony.
Adam oure fader and his wyf also
Adam our fader, and his wife also,
Fro Paradys to labour and to wo
From Paradise to labor and to woe
Were driven for that vyce, it is no drede.
Were driven for that vice, there is no doubt.
220 For whyl that Adam fasted, as I rede,
For while Adam fasted, as I read,
He was in Paradys; and whan that he
He was in Paradise; and when he
Eet of the fruyt defended on the tree,
Ate of the forbidden fruit on the tree,
Anon he was outcast to wo and peyne.
Immediately he was cast out to woe and pain.
O glotonye, on thee wel oghte us pleyne!
O gluttony, on thee well we ought to complain!
225 O, wiste a man how manye maladyes
O, if a man knew how many evils
Folwen of excesse and of glotonyes,
Follow of excess and of gluttony,
He wolde been the more mesurable
He would be the more moderate
Of his diete, sittinge at his table.
Of his diet, sitting at his table.
Allas! the shorte throte, the tendre mouth,
Alas, the short throat, the tender mouth,
230 Maketh that, est and west, and north and south,
Makes that east and west and north and south,

In erthe, in eir, in water, men to swinke
In earth, in air, in water, men work
To gete a glotoun deyntee mete and drinke!
To get a glutton dainty food and drink!
Of this matere, O Paul, wel canstow trete:
Of this matter, O Paul, well can thou treat
"Mete unto wombe, and wombe eek unto mete,
"Food unto belly, and belly also unto food,
235   Shal God destroyen bothe," as Paulus seith.
God shall destroy both," as Paul says.
Allas! a foul thing is it, by my feith,
Alas, a foul thing it is, by my faith,
To seye this word, and fouler is the dede,
To say this word, and fouler is the deed,
Whan man so drinketh of the whyte and rede
When man so drinks of the white and red
That of his throte he maketh his privee,
That he makes his privy of his throat
240   Thurgh thilke cursed superfluitee.
Through that same cursed excess.
    The apostel, weping, seith ful pitously,
    The apostle weeping says full piteously,
"Ther walken manye of whiche yow told have I"—
"There walk many of whom I have told you—
I seye it now weping with pitous voys—
I say it now weeping, with piteous voice—
"They been enemys of Cristes croys,
They are enemies of Christ's cross,
245   Of which the ende is deeth: wombe is her god!"
Of which the end is death; belly is their god!"
O wombe! O bely! O stinking cod,
O gut! O belly! O stinking bag,
Fulfild of donge and of corrupcioun!
Filled with dung and with corruption!
At either ende of thee foul is the soun.
At either end of thee the sound is foul.
How greet labour and cost is thee to finde!
How great labor and cost it is to feed thee!
250   Thise cookes, how they stampe, and streyne, and grinde,
These cooks, how they pound, and strain, and grind,
And turnen substance into accident,
And turn substance into outward appearance
To fulfille al thy likerous talent!
To fulfill all thy gluttonous desire!
Out of the harde bones knokke they
Out of the hard bones they knock
The mary, for they caste noght awey
The marrow, for they throw nothing away
255   That may go thurgh the golet softe and swote;
That may go through the gullet softly and sweetly.
Of spicerye of leef, and bark, and rote
Of seasonings of leaf, and bark, and root
Shal been his sauce y-maked by delyt,

Shall his sauce be made for delight,
To make him yet a newer appetyt.
To make him yet a newer appetite.
But certes, he that haunteth swich delyces
But, certainly, he who habitually seeks such delicacies
260 Is deed, whyl that he liveth in tho vyces.
Is dead, while he lives in those vices.
   A lecherous thing is wyn, and dronkenesse
   A lecherous thing is wine, and drunkenness
Is ful of stryving and of wrecchednesse.
Is full of striving and of wretchedness.
O dronke man, disfigured is thy face,
O drunken man, disfigured is thy face,
Sour is thy breeth, foul artow to embrace,
Sour is thy breath, foul art thou to embrace,
265 And thurgh thy dronke nose semeth the soun
And through thy drunken nose the sound seems
As though thou seydest ay "Sampsoun, Sampsoun";
As though thou said always "Sampson, Sampson!"
And yet, God wot, Sampsoun drank nevere no wyn.
And yet, God knows, Sampson never drank any wine.
Thou fallest, as it were a stiked swyn;
Thou fallest like a stuck pig;
Thy tonge is lost, and al thyn honest cure,
Thy tongue is lost, and all thy care for decency,
270 For dronkenesse is verray sepulture
For drunkenness is truly the sepulcher
Of mannes wit and his discrecioun.
Of man's wit and his discretion.
In whom that drinke hath dominacioun,
In whom drink has domination
He can no conseil kepe, it is no drede.
He can keep no secrets; there is no doubt.
Now kepe yow fro the whyte and fro the rede—
Now guard yourself from the white and from the red,
275 And namely fro the whyte wyn of Lepe
And namely from the white wine of Lepe
That is to selle in Fishstrete or in Chepe.
That is for sale in Fishstreet or in Cheapside.
This wyn of Spaigne crepeth subtilly
This wine of Spain creeps subtly
In othere wynes growinge faste by,
Into other wines, growing near by,
Of which ther ryseth swich fumositee,
Of which there rise such bodily vapors
280 That whan a man hath dronken draughtes three
That when a man has drunk three drafts,
And weneth that he be at hoom in Chepe,
And supposes that he is at home in Cheapside,
He is in Spaigne, right at the toune of Lepe,
He is in Spain, right at the town of Lepe—
Nat at The Rochel, ne at Burdeux toun;
Not at La Rochelle, nor at Bordeaux town—

And thanne wol he seye, "Sampsoun, Sampsoun."
And then will he say "Sampson, Sampson!"

285   But herkneth, lordinges, o word I yow preye,
     But listen, gentlemen, one word, I pray you,
That alle the sovereyn actes, dar I seye,
That all the great deeds, I dare say,
Of victories in the Olde Testament,
Of victories in the Old Testament,
Thurgh verray God, that is omnipotent,
Through true God, who is omnipotent,
Were doon in abstinence and in preyere:
Were done in abstinence and in prayer.

290   Loketh the Bible, and ther ye may it lere.
Look in the Bible, and there you can learn it.
     Loke Attila, the grete conquerour,
     Consider how Attila, the great conqueror,
Deyde in his sleep, with shame and dishonour,
Died in his sleep, with shame and dishonor,
Bledinge ay at his nose in dronkenesse:
Bleeding ever at his nose in drunkenness.
A capitayn shoulde live in sobrenesse.
A captain should live in sobriety.

295   And over al this, avyseth yow right wel
     And beyond all this, consider right well
What was comaunded unto Lamuel—
What was commanded unto Lamuel—
Nat Samuel, but Lamuel, seye I—
Not Samuel, but Lamuel, I say;
Redeth the Bible, and finde it expressly
Read the Bible, and find it explicitly
Of wyn-yeving to hem that han justyse.
About giving wine to those that have the duty of doing justice.

300   Namore of this, for it may wel suffyse.
No more of this, for it may well suffice.
     And now that I have spoke of glotonye,
     And now that I have spoken of gluttony,
Now wol I yow defenden hasardrye.
Now I will forbid you gambling.
Hasard is verray moder of lesinges,
Dicing is the true mother of lies,
And of deceite and cursed forsweringes,
And of deceit, and cursed perjuries,

305   Blaspheme of Crist, manslaughtre, and wast also
Blasphemy of Christ, manslaughter, and waste also
Of catel and of tyme; and forthermo,
Of possessions and of time; and furthermore,
It is repreve and contrarie of honour
It is a disgrace and contrary to honor
For to ben holde a commune hasardour.
To be considered a common dice player.
And ever the hyer he is of estaat
And ever the higher he is of estate,

310   The more is he y-holden desolaat:

The more is he considered abandoned (to shame).
If that a prince useth hasardrye,
If a prince plays at dicing,
In alle governaunce and policye
In all governance and policy
He is, as by commune opinioun,
He is, by common opinion,
Y-holde the lasse in reputacioun.
Held the less in reputation.

315   Stilbon, that was a wys embassadour,
       Stilboun, who was a wise ambassador,
Was sent to Corinthe in ful greet honour,
Was sent to Corinth in very great honor
Fro Lacidomie to make hire alliaunce.
From Sparta to make their alliance.
And whan he cam, him happede par chaunce
And when he came, it happened, by chance,
That alle the grettest that were of that lond,
That all the greatest men that were of that land,
320   Pleyinge atte hasard he hem fond.
       Playing at dice he found them.
For which, as sone as it mighte be,
For which, as soon as it could be,
He stal him hoom agayn to his contree,
He stole home again to his country,
And seyde, "Ther wol I nat lese my name,
And said, "There I will not lose my reputation,
Ne I wol nat take on me so greet defame,
Nor will I take on me so great infamy,
325   Yow for to allye unto none hasardours.
       To ally you unto any dice-players.
Sendeth othere wyse embassadours—
Send other wise ambassadors;
For by my trouthe, me were levere dye
For, by my troth, I would rather die
Than I yow sholde to hasardours allye.
Than I should ally you to dice-players.
For ye that been so glorious in honours
For you, that are so glorious in honors,
330   Shul nat allyen yow with hasardours
       Shall not ally yourselves with dice-players
As by my wil, ne as by my tretee."
By my will, nor by my negotiation."
This wyse philosophre, thus seyde he.
This wise philosopher, thus said he.
    Loke eek that to the king Demetrius
    Consider also that to the king Demetrius
The king of Parthes, as the book seith us,
The king of Parthia, as the book tells us,
335   Sente him a paire of dees of gold in scorn,
       Sent him a pair of dice of gold in scorn,
For he hadde used hasard ther-biforn;
Because he had played at dicing before that;

For which he heeld his glorie or his renoun
For which he held his glory or his renown
At no value or reputacioun.
At no value or esteem.
Lordes may finden other maner pley
Lords may find other sorts of play
340 Honeste ynough to dryve the day awey.
Respectable enough to pass the time.
　　Now wol I speke of othes false and grete
　　Now will I speak of oaths false and great
A word or two, as olde bokes trete.
A word or two, as old books treat them.
　　Gret swering is a thing abhominable,
　　Great swearing is an abominable thing,
And false swering is yet more reprevable.
And false swearing is yet more worthy of reproof.
345 The heighe God forbad swering at al—
The high God forbad swearing at al,
Witnesse on Mathew—but in special
Witness on Matthew; but in special
Of swering seith the holy Jeremye,
Of swearing says the holy Jeremiah,
"Thou shalt swere sooth thyn othes and nat lye,
"Thou shall swear truly thine oaths, and not lie,
And swere in dome, and eek in rightwisnesse;"
And in judgement and also in righteousness";
350 But ydel swering is a cursednesse.
But idle swearing is a cursed thing.
　　Bihold and see, that in the first table
　　Behold and see that in the first three
Of heighe Goddes hestes honurable,
Of high God's honorable commandments,
How that the seconde heste of him is this:
How the second of his commands is this:
"Tak nat my name in ydel or amis."
"Take not my name in vain nor amiss."
355 Lo, rather he forbedeth swich swering
Lo, he forbids such swearing rather
Than homicyde or many a cursed thing—
Than homicide or many a cursed thing;
I seye that, as by ordre, thus it stondeth—
I say that, so far as order is concerned, thus it stands;
This knoweth, that his hestes understondeth,
He who understands his commandments knows this,
How that the second heste of God is that.
How that is the second command of God.
360 And forther over, I wol thee telle al plat
And furthermore, I will tell thee flatly
That vengeance shal nat parten from his hous
That vengeance shall not part from his house
That of his othes is to outrageous.
Who of his oaths is too excessive.
"By Goddes precious herte," and "By his nayles,"

"By God's precious heart," and "By his nails,"
And "By the blode of Crist that is in Hayles,
And "By the blood of Christ that is in Hales Abbey,
365 Seven is my chaunce, and thyn is cink and treye;"
Seven is my number, and thine is five and three!"
"By Goddes armes, if thou falsly pleye,
"By God's arms, if thou falsely play,
This dagger shal thurghout thyn herte go!"
This dagger shall go throughout thy heart!"—
This fruyt cometh of the bicched bones two—
This fruit comes of the two cursed dice,
Forswering, ire, falsnesse, homicyde.
Perjury, anger, falseness, homicide.
370 Now for the love of Crist that for us dyde,
Now, for the love of Christ, who for us died,
Lete youre othes, bothe grete and smale.
Leave aside your oaths, both great and small.
But, sires, now wol I telle forth my tale.
But, sirs, now will I tell forth my tale.
 Thise ryotoures three of which I telle,
 These three rioters of whom I tell,
Longe erst er pryme rong of any belle,
Long before prime rang of any bell,
375 Were set hem in a taverne for to drinke;
Had set themselves in a tavern to drink,
And as they sat, they herde a belle clinke
And as they sat, they heard a bell clink
Biforn a cors was caried to his grave.
Before a corpse, which was carried to its grave.
That oon of hem gan callen to his knave,
The one of them did call to his servant:
"Go bet," quod he, "and axe redily,
"Go quickly," he said, "and ask at once
380 What cors is this that passeth heer forby;
What corpse is this that passes by here;
And looke that thou reporte his name wel."
And see that thou report his name correctly."
 "Sire," quod this boy, "it nedeth never-a-del.
 "Sir," said this boy, "that is not at all necessary;
It was me told, er ye cam heer two houres.
It was told me two hours before you came here.
He was, pardee, an old felawe of youres;
He was, indeed, an old fellow of yours,
385 And sodeynly he was y-slayn tonight,
And suddenly he was slain last night,
Fordronke, as he sat on his bench upright.
Completely drunk, as he sat on his bench upright.
Ther cam a privee theef men clepeth Deeth,
There came a stealthy thief men call Death,
That in this contree al the peple sleeth,
Who slays all the people in this country,
And with his spere he smoot his herte atwo,
And with his spear he struck his heart in two,

390 And wente his wey withouten wordes mo.
And went his way without more words.
He hath a thousand slayn this pestilence.
He has slain a thousand (during) this pestilence.
And maister, er ye come in his presence,
And, master, before you come in his presence,
Me thinketh that it were necessarie
It seems to me that it would be necessary
For to be war of swich an adversarie:
To beware of such an adversary.
395 Beth redy for to mete him everemore.
Always be ready to meet him;
Thus taughte me my dame, I sey namore."
Thus taught me my mother; I say no more."
   "By Seinte Marie," seyde this taverner,
   "By Saint Mary!" said this tavern-keeper,
"The child seith sooth, for he hath slayn this yeer,
"The child says truth, for he has slain this year,
Henne over a myle, withinne a greet village,
Over a mile from here, within a great village,
400 Bothe man and womman, child, and hyne, and page;
Both man and woman, child, and laborer, and servant boy;
I trowe his habitacioun be there.
I suppose his habitation is there.
To been avysed greet wisdom it were,
It would be great wisdom to be forewarned,
Er that he dide a man a dishonour."
Before he did a man any harm."
   "Ye, Goddes armes," quod this ryotour,
   "Yea, God's arms!" said this rioter,
405 "Is it swich peril with him for to mete?
"Is it such peril to meet with him?
I shal him seke by wey and eek by strete,
I shall seek him by path-way and also by street (everywhere),
I make avow to Goddes digne bones!
I make a vow to God's honorable bones!
Herkneth felawes, we three been al ones:
Listen, fellows, we three are all agreed;
Lat ech of us holde up his hond til other,
Let each of us hold up his hand to other,
410 And ech of us bicomen otheres brother,
And each of us become the others' brother,
And we wol sleen this false traytour Deeth.
And we will slay this false traitor Death.
He shal be slayn, he that so manye sleeth,
He shall be slain, he who slays so many,
By Goddes dignitee, er it be night."
By God's dignity, before it be night!"
   Togidres han thise three hir trouthes plight
   Together have these three pledged their troths
415 To live and dyen ech of hem for other,
To live and die each of them for other,
As though he were his owene y-boren brother.

As though he were his own born brother.
And up they sterte, al dronken in this rage,
And up they leaped, all drunken in this rage,
And forth they goon towardes that village
And forth they go towards that village
Of which the taverner hadde spoke biforn,
Of which the tavern-keeper had spoken before.

420 And many a grisly ooth thanne han they sworn,
And many a grisly oath then have they sworn,
And Cristes blessed body they to-rente—
And Christ's blessed body they tore to pieces—
Deeth shal be deed, if that they may him hente.
Death shall be dead, if they can catch him!
    Whan they han goon nat fully half a myle,
    When they have gone not fully half a mile,
Right as they wolde han troden over a style,
Right as they would have stepped over a fence,

425 An old man and a povre with hem mette.
An old and poor man met with them.
This olde man ful mekely hem grette,
This old man full meekly greeted them,
And seyde thus, "Now, lordes, God yow see!"
And said thus, "Now, lords, may God look after you!"
    The proudest of thise ryotoures three
    The proudest of these three rioters
Answerde agayn, "What, carl, with sory grace!
Answered in reply, "What, churl, bad luck to you!

430 Why artow al forwrapped save thy face?
Why art thou all wrapped up except for thy face?
Why livestow so longe in so greet age?"
Why live thou so long in such old age?"
    This olde man gan loke in his visage,
    This old man did look in his face,
And seyde thus, "For I ne can nat finde
And said thus: "Because I can not find
A man, though that I walked into Inde,
A man, though I walked to India,

435 Neither in citee nor in no village,
Neither in city nor in any village,
That wolde chaunge his youthe for myn age;
That would change his youth for my age;
And therfore moot I han myn age stille,
And therefore I must have my age still,
As longe time as it is Goddes wille.
As long a time as it is God's will.
    Ne Deeth, allas! ne wol nat han my lyf.
    Nor Death, alas, will not have my life.

440 Thus walke I, lyk a restelees caityf,
Thus I walk, like a restless wretch,
And on the ground, which is my modres gate,
And on the ground, which is my mother's gate,
I knokke with my staf bothe erly and late,
I knock with my staff, both early and late,

And seye, 'Leve moder, leet me in!
And say 'Dear mother, let me in!
Lo, how I vanish, flesh, and blood, and skin!
Lo how I waste away, flesh, and blood, and skin!
445   Allas! whan shul my bones been at reste?
Alas, when shall my bones be at rest?
Moder, with yow wolde I chaunge my cheste
Mother, with you would I exchange my strongbox
That in my chambre longe tyme hath be,
That in my chamber long time has been,
Ye, for an heyre clout to wrappe me!'
Yea, for an hair shirt to wrap me!'
But yet to me she wol nat do that grace,
But yet to me she will not do that favor,
450   For which ful pale and welked is my face.
For which full pale and withered is my face.
But sires, to yow it is no curteisye
"But, sirs, to you it is no courtesy
To speken to an old man vileinye,
To speak rudeness to an old man,
But he trespasse in worde or elles in dede.
Unless he trespass in word or else in deed.
In Holy Writ ye may yourself wel rede,
In Holy Writ you may yourself well read:
455   'Agayns an old man, hoor upon his heed,
'In the presence of an old man, gray upon his head,
Ye sholde aryse.' Wherfor I yeve yow reed:
You should rise;' therefore I give you advice,
Ne dooth unto an old man noon harm now,
Do no harm now unto an old man,
Namore than that ye wolde men did to yow
No more than you would want men to do to you
In age, if that ye so longe abyde.
In old age, if you live so long.
460   And God be with yow, wher ye go or ryde;
And God be with you, wherever you walk or ride!
I moot go thider as I have to go."
I must go thither where I have to go."
    "Nay, olde cherl, by God, thou shalt nat so,"
    "Nay, old churl, by God, thou shall not so,"
Seyde this other hasardour anon;
Said this other dice-player quickly;
"Thou partest nat so lightly, by Seint John!
"Thou depart not so quickly, by Saint John!
465   Thou spak right now of thilke traitour Deeth
Thou spoke right now of that same traitor Death.
That in this contree alle oure frendes sleeth.
That slays all our friends in this country.
Have heer my trouthe, as thou art his espye,
Have here my pledge, as thou art his spy,
Telle wher he is, or thou shalt it abye,
Tell where he is or thou shall pay for it,
By God, and by the holy sacrament!

By God and by the holy sacrament!

470 For soothly thou art oon of his assent
For truly thou art in league with him
To sleen us yonge folk, thou false theef!"
To slay us young folk, thou false thief!"
   "Now, sires," quod he, "if that yow be so leef
   "Now, sirs," said he, "if you are so eager
To finde Deeth, turne up this croked wey,
To find Death, turn up this crooked way,
For in that grove I lafte him, by my fey,
For in that grove I left him, by my faith,

475 Under a tree, and there he wol abyde:
Under a tree, and there he will wait;
Nat for youre boost he wole him nothing hyde.
He will not in any way hide himself because of your boast.
See ye that ook? right ther ye shul him finde.
Do you see that oak? Right there you shall find him.
God save yow, that boghte agayn mankinde,
God save you, He who redeemed mankind,
And yow amende!" Thus seyde this olde man.
And amend you!" Thus said this old man;

480   And everich of thise ryotoures ran,
   And every one of these rioters ran
Til he cam to that tree, and ther they founde
Until he came to that tree, and there they found
Of florins fyne of golde y-coyned rounde
Of fine round florins of coined gold
Wel ny an eighte busshels, as hem thoughte.
Well nigh eight bushels, as they thought.
No lenger thanne after Deeth they soughte,
No longer then after Death they sought,

485 But ech of hem so glad was of that sighte—
But each of them was so glad of that sight,
For that the florins been so faire and brighte—
Because the florins are so faire and bright,
That doun they sette hem by this precious hord.
That they set themselves down by this precious hoard.
The worste of hem he spake the firste word.
The worst of them, he spoke the first word.
   "Brethren," quod he, "take kepe what that I seye:
   "Brethren," he said, "take heed of what I say;

490 My wit is greet, though that I bourde and pleye.
My wit is great, though I jest and play.
This tresor hath Fortune unto us yiven
Fortune has given this treasure unto us
In mirthe and jolitee our lyf to liven,
In mirth and jollity to live our life,
And lightly as it comth, so wol we spende.
And as easily as it comes, so will we spend it.
Ey! Goddes precious dignitee! who wende
Ah, God's precious dignity! Who would have supposed

495 Today that we sholde han so fair a grace?

To-day that we should have such good fortune?
But mighte this gold be caried fro this place
But if this gold could be carried from this place
Hoom to myn hous—or elles unto youres—
Home to my house, or else unto yours—
For wel ye woot that al this gold is oures—
For well you know that all this gold is ours—
Thanne were we in heigh felicitee.
Then we would be in great happiness.

500   But trewely, by daye it may nat be:
But truly, it may not be (done) by day.
Men wolde seyn that we were theves stronge,
Men would say that we were arrant thieves,
And for oure owene tresor doon us honge.
And for our own treasure have us hanged.
This tresor moste y-caried be by nighte,
This treasure must be carried by night
As wysly and as slyly as it mighte.
As wisely and as slyly as it can be.

505   Wherfore I rede that cut among us alle
Wherefore I advise that among us all straws
Be drawe, and lat se wher the cut wol falle;
Be drawn, and let's see where the lot will fall;
And he that hath the cut with herte blithe
And he who has the shortest straw with happy heart
Shal renne to the toune, and that ful swythe,
Shall run to the town, and that very quickly,
And bringe us breed and wyn ful prively.
And very secretly bring us bread and wine.

510   And two of us shul kepen subtilly
And two of us shall carefully guard
This tresor wel; and if he wol nat tarie,
This treasure well; and if he will not tarry,
Whan it is night we wol this tresor carie,
When it is night, we will carry this treasure,
By oon assent, where as us thinketh best."
By mutual agreement, where we think best."
That oon of hem the cut broughte in his fest,
That one of them brought the straws in his fist,

515   And bad hem drawe, and loke wher it wol falle;
And commanded them to draw and see where it will fall;
And it fil on the yongeste of hem alle,
And it fell on the youngest of them all,
And forth toward the toun he wente anon.
And forth toward the town he went right away.
And also sone as that he was agon,
And as soon as he was gone,
That oon of hem spak thus unto that other:
The one of them spoke thus unto that other:

520   "Thou knowest wel thou art my sworne brother;
"Thou knowest well thou art my sworn brother;
Thy profit wol I telle thee anon.

Thy profit will I tell thee straightway.
Thou woost wel that oure felawe is agon,
Thou knowest well that our fellow is gone.
And heer is gold, and that ful greet plentee,
And here is gold, and that a full great quantity,
That shal departed been among us three.
That shall be divided among us three.
525 But natheles, if I can shape it so
But nevertheless, if I can arrange things so
That it departed were among us two,
That it were divided among us two,
Hadde I nat doon a freendes torn to thee?"
Had I not done a good turn to thee?"
    That other answerde, "I noot how that may be:
    That other answered, "I know not how that can be.
He woot how that the gold is with us tweye.
He knows that the gold is with us two;
530 What shal we doon? what shal we to him seye?"
What shall we do? What shall we say to him?"
    "Shal it be conseil?" seyde the firste shrewe;
    "Shall it be (our) secret plan?" said the first scoundrel,
"And I shal tellen in a wordes fewe
"And I shall tell in a few words
What we shal doon, and bringe it wel aboute."
What we shall do, and bring it well about."
    "I graunte," quod that other, "out of doute,
    "I agree," said that other, "without doubt,
535 That, by my trouthe, I wol thee nat biwreye."
That, by my troth, I will not betray thee."
"Now," quod the firste, "thou woost wel we be tweye,
"Now," said the first, "thou knowest well we are two,
And two of us shul strenger be than oon.
And two of us shall be stronger than one.
Looke whan that he is set, that right anoon
Look, when he has set down, right away
Arys as though thou woldest with him pleye;
Arise as though thou would with him play,
540 And I shal ryve him thurgh the sydes tweye
And I shall stab him through the two sides
Whyl that thou strogelest with him as in game,
While thou struggle with him as in game,
And with thy dagger looke thou do the same;
And with thy dagger see that thou do the same;
And thanne shall al this gold departed be,
And then shall all this gold be divided,
My dere freend, bitwixen me and thee.
My dear friend, between me and thee.
545 Thanne may we bothe oure lustes al fulfille,
Then we both can fulfill all our desires,
And pleye at dees right at oure owene wille."
And play at dice just as we wish,"
And thus acorded been thise shrewes tweye
And thus these two scoundrels are agreed

To sleen the thridde, as ye han herd me seye.
To slay the third, as you have heard me say.
  This yongest, which that wente unto the toun,
  This youngest, who went to the town,
550 Ful ofte in herte he rolleth up and doun
Very often in heart he rolls up and down
The beautee of thise florins newe and brighte.
The beauty of these florins new and bright.
"O Lord!" quod he, "if so were that I mighte
"O Lord!" he said, "if it would be that I might
Have al this tresor to myself allone,
Have all this treasure to myself alone,
Ther is no man that liveth under the trone
There is no man that lives under the throne
555 Of God that sholde live so mery as I!"
Of God that should live so merrily as I!"
And atte laste the feend, our enemy,
And at the last the fiend, our enemy,
Putte in his thought that he shold poyson beye,
Put in his thought that he should buy poison,
With which he mighte sleen his felawes tweye—
With which he might slay his two fellows;
For-why the feend fond him in swich lyvinge
Because the fiend found him in such a manner of living
560 That he had leve him to sorwe bringe:
That he had leave bring him to sorrow.
For this was outrely his fulle entente,
For this was utterly his full intention,
To sleen hem bothe, and nevere to repente.
To slay them both and never to repent.
  And forth he gooth—no lenger wolde he tarie—
  And forth he goes, no longer would he tarry,
Into the toun, unto a pothecarie,
Into the town, unto an apothecary,
465 And preyed him that he him wolde selle
And prayed him that he would sell him
Som poyson, that he mighte his rattes quelle,
Some poison, that he might kill his rats;
And eek ther was a polcat in his hawe,
And also there was a polecat in his yard,
That, as he seyde, his capouns hadde y-slawe,
That, as he said, had slain his capons,
And fayn he wolde wreke him, if he mighte,
And he would gladly revenge himself, if he could,
470 On vermin, that destroyed him by nighte.
On vermin that ruined him by night.
  The pothecarie answerde, "And thou shalt have
  The apothecary answered, "And thou shall have
A thing that, also God my soule save,
A thing that, as God may save my soul,
In al this world ther nis no creature,
In all this world there is no creature
That ete or dronke hath of this confiture

That has eaten or drunk of this concoction
575 Noght but the mountance of a corn of whete,
Only so much as the amount of a seed of wheat,
That he ne shal his lyf anon forlete.
That he shall not immediately lose his life;
Ye, sterve he shal, and that in lasse whyle
Yea, he shall die, and that in less time
Than thou wolt goon a paas nat but a myle,
Than thou will go at a walk but only a mile,
This poyson is so strong and violent."
This poison is so strong and violent."
580 This cursed man hath in his hond y-hent
This cursed man has in his hand taken
This poyson in a box, and sith he ran
This poison in a box, and then he ran
Into the nexte strete unto a man,
Into the next street unto a man,
And borwed [of] him large botels three,
And borrowed [of] him three large bottles,
And in the two his poyson poured he—
And in the two he poured his poison;
585 The thridde he kepte clene for his drinke—
The third he kept clean for his drink.
For al the night he shoop him for to swinke
For all the night he intended to work
In caryinge of the gold out of that place.
In carrying of the gold out of that place.
And whan this ryotour, with sory grace,
And when this rioter, bad luck to him,
Hadde filled with wyn his grete botels three,
Had filled his three big bottles with wine,
590 To his felawes agayn repaireth he.
He goes back again to his fellows.
   What nedeth it to sermone of it more?
   What needs it to preach of it more?
For right as they hadde cast his deeth bifore,
For right as they had planned his death before,
Right so they han him slayn, and that anon.
Right so they have him slain, and that immediately.
And whan that this was doon, thus spak that oon:
And when this was done, thus spoke that one:
595 "Now lat us sitte and drinke, and make us merie,
"Now let us sit and drink, and make us merry,
And afterward we wol his body berie."
And afterward we will bury his body."
And with that word it happed him, par cas,
And with that word it happened to him, by chance,
To take the botel ther the poyson was,
To take the bottle where the poison was,
And drank, and yaf his felawe drink also,
And drank, and gave his fellow drink also,
600 For which anon they storven bothe two.
For which straightway they died, both of the two.
   But certes, I suppose that Avicen

But certainly, I suppose that Avicenna
Wroot nevere in no canon, ne in no fen,
Wrote never in any authoritative book, nor in any chapter,
Mo wonder signes of empoisoning
More wondrous symptoms of poisoning
Than hadde thise wrecches two, er hir ending.
Than had these two wretches, before their ending.

605 Thus ended been thise homicydes two,
Thus ended are these two homicides,
And eek the false empoysoner also.
And also the false poisoner as well.
   O cursed sinne of alle cursednesse!
   O cursed sin of all cursedness!
O traytours homicyde, O wikkednesse!
O treacherous homicide, O wickedness!
O glotonye, luxurie, and hasardrye!
O gluttony, lechery, and dicing!

610 Thou blasphemour of Crist with vileinye
Thou blasphemer of Christ with churlish speech
And othes grete, of usage and of pryde!
And great oaths, out of habit and out of pride!
Allas! mankinde, how may it bityde
Alas, mankind, how may it happen
That to thy Creatour which that thee wroghte,
That to thy creator, who made thee
And with his precious herte-blood thee boghte,
And with his precious heart's blood redeemed thee,

615 Thou art so fals and so unkinde, allas!
Thou art so false and so unnatural, alas?
   Now, goode men, God forgeve yow youre trespas,
   Now, good men, God forgive you your trespass,
And ware yow fro the sinne of avaryce.
And guard yourselves from the sin of avarice!
Myn holy pardoun may yow alle waryce—
My holy pardon can cure you all,
So that ye offre nobles or sterlinges,
Providing that you offer gold coins or silver pennies,

620 Or elles silver broches, spones, ringes.
Or else silver brooches, spoons, rings.
Boweth youre heed under this holy bulle!
Bow your head under this holy papal bull!
Cometh up, ye wyves, offreth of youre wolle!
Come up, you wives, offer some of your wool!
Youre names I entre heer in my rolle anon:
Your names I enter here in my roll immediately;
Into the blisse of hevene shul ye gon.
Into the bliss of heaven you shall go.

625 I yow assoile, by myn heigh power—
I absolve you, by my high power,
Yow that wol offre—as clene and eek as cleer
You who will offer, as clean and also as clear (of sin)
As ye were born.—And, lo, sires, thus I preche.
As you were born.—And lo, sirs, thus I preach.
And Jesu Crist, that is our soules leche,

And Jesus Christ, that is our souls' physician,
So graunte yow his pardon to receyve,
So grant you to receive his pardon,
630   For that is best; I wol yow nat deceyve.
For that is best; I will not deceive you.

[The Epilogue]

"But sires, o word forgat I in my tale:
   But, sirs, one word I forgot in my tale:
I have relikes and pardon in my male
I have relics and pardons in my bag,
As faire as any man in Engelond,
As fine as any man in England,
Whiche were me yeven by the Popes hond.
Which were given to me by the pope's hand.
635   If any of yow wol of devocioun
If any of you will, of devotion,
Offren and han myn absolucioun,
Offer and have my absolution,
Cometh forth anon, and kneleth heer adoun,
Come forth straightway, and kneel down here,
And mekely receyveth my pardoun;
And meekly receive my pardon;
Or elles, taketh pardon as ye wende,
Or else take pardon as you travel,
640   Al newe and fresh, at every myles ende—
All new and fresh at every mile's end,
So that ye offren alwey newe and newe
Providing that you offer, again and again,
Nobles or pens, which that be gode and trewe.
Gold coins or silver pennies, which are good and true.
It is an honour to everich that is heer
It is an honor to every one that is here
That ye mowe have a suffisant pardoner
That you may have a pardoner with sufficient power
645   T'assoille yow, in contree as ye ryde,
To absolve you in the countryside as you ride,
For aventures whiche that may bityde.
For accidents that may happen.
Peraventure ther may falle oon or two
Perhaps there may fall one or two
Doun of his hors, and breke his nekke atwo.
Down off his horse and break his neck in two.
Look which a seuretee is it to you alle
Look what a safeguard is it to you all
650   That I am in youre felaweship y-falle,
That I happen to be in your fellowship,
That may assoille yow, bothe more and lasse,
Who can absolve you, both more and less (every one),
Whan that the soule shal fro the body passe.
When the soul shall from the body pass.
I rede that oure Host heer shal biginne,
I advise that our Host here shall begin,

For he is most envoluped in sinne.
For he is most enveloped in sin.
655 Com forth, sire Hoste, and offre first anon,
Come forth, sir Host, and offer first right now,
And thou shalt kisse the reliks everichon,
And thou shall kiss the relics every one,
Ye, for a grote: unbokel anon thy purs."
Yea, for a fourpence coin! Unbuckle thy purse right now."
   "Nay, nay," quod he, "thanne have I Cristes curs!
   "Nay, nay!" he said, "then I will have Christ's curse!
Lat be," quod he, "it shal nat be, so theech!
Let it be," he said, "it shall not be, as I may prosper!
660 Thou woldest make me kisse thyn olde breech
   Thou would make me kiss thine old underpants,
And swere it were a relik of a seint,
And swear it was a relic of a saint,
Thogh it were with thy fundement depeint!
Though it were stained by thy fundament!
But by the croys which that Seint Eleyne fond,
But, by the cross that Saint Helen found,
I wolde I hadde thy coillons in myn hond
I would I had thy testicles in my hand
665 In stede of relikes or of seintuarie.
Instead of relics or a container for relics.
Lat cutte hem of! I wol thee helpe hem carie.
Have them cut off, I will help thee carry them;
Thay shul be shryned in an hogges tord!"
They shall be enshrined in a hog's turd!"
This Pardoner answerde nat a word;
This Pardoner answered not a word;
So wrooth he was, no word ne wolde he seye.
So angry he was, no word would he say.
670   "Now," quod our Host, "I wol no lenger pleye
   "Now," said our Host, "I will no longer joke
With thee, ne with noon other angry man."
With thee, nor with any other angry man."
   But right anon the worthy Knight bigan,
   But immediately the worthy Knight began,
Whan that he saugh that al the peple lough,
When he saw that all the people laughed,
"Namore of this, for it is right ynough!
"No more of this, for it is right enough!
675 Sire Pardoner, be glad and mery of chere;
Sir Pardoner, be glad and merry of cheer;
And ye, sire Host, that been to me so dere,
And you, sir Host, who are so dear to me,
I prey yow that ye kisse the Pardoner.
I pray you that you kiss the Pardoner.
And Pardoner, I prey thee, drawe thee neer,
And Pardoner, I pray thee, draw thyself nearer,
And, as we diden, lat us laughe and pleye."
And, as we did, let us laugh and play."
680 Anon they kiste, and riden forth hir weye.
At once they kissed, and rode forth their way.

The Nun's Priest's Tale

A povre widwe, somdel stape in age,
A poor widow, somewhat advanced in age,
Was whylom dwelling in a narwe cotage,
Was once dwelling in a small cottage,
Bisyde a grove, stondinge in a dale.
Beside a grove, standing in a dale.
This widwe of which I telle yow my tale,
This widow, of whom I tell you my tale,
5 Sin thilke day that she was last a wyf,
Since that same day that she was last a wife
In pacience ladde a ful simple lyf,
In patience led a very simple life,
For litel was hir catel and hir rente.
For little was her possessions and her income.
By housbondrye of such as God hire sente
By husbandry of such as God sent her
She fond hirself and eek hir doghtren two.
She provided for herself and also her two daughters.
10 Three large sowes hadde she and namo,
She had three large sows, and no more,
Three kyn, and eek a sheep that highte Malle.
Three cows, and also a sheep that is called Malle.
Ful sooty was hire bour, and eek hir halle,
Full sooty was her bedchamber and also her hall,
In which she eet ful many a sclendre meel.
In which she ate very many a scanty meal.
Of poynaunt sauce hir neded never a deel:
She needed not a bit of spicy sauce.
15 No deyntee morsel passed thurgh hir throte.
No dainty morsel passed through her throat;
Hir diete was accordant to hir cote—
Her diet was such as her farm produced.
Repleccioun ne made hir never syk.
Overeating never made her sick;
Attempree diete was al hir phisyk,
Moderate diet was all her medical treatment,
And exercyse, and hertes suffisaunce.
And exercise, and a contented heart.
20 The goute lette hire nothing for to daunce,
The gout not at all prevented her from dancing,
N'apoplexye shente nat hir heed.
And apoplexy harmed not her head.
No wyn ne drank she, neither whyt ne reed;
No wine she drank, neither white nor red;
Hir bord was served most with whyt and blak—
Her board was provided mostly with white and black—
Milk and broun breed—in which she fond no lak,
Milk and dark bread, in which she found no lack,
25 Seynd bacoun, and somtyme an ey or tweye,
Broiled bacon, and sometimes an egg or two,

For she was as it were a maner deye.
For she was, as it were, a sort of dairywoman.
A yerd she hadde, enclosed al aboute
She had a yard, enclosed all around
With stikkes, and a drye dich withoute,
With sticks, and a dry ditch outside it,
In which she hadde a cok hight Chauntecleer:
In which she had a cock, called Chauntecleer.
30 In al the land of crowing nas his peer.
In all the land, there was not his peer in crowing.
His voys was merier than the mery orgon
His voice was merrier than the merry organ
On messe-dayes that in the chirche gon;
That goes in the church on mass-days.
Wel sikerer was his crowing in his logge
Well more accurate was his crowing in his lodge
Than is a clokke or an abbey orlogge.
Than is a clock or an abbey timepiece.
35 By nature knew he ech ascencioun
By nature he knew (the hour of) each ascension
Of the equinoxial in thilke toun:
Of the celestial equator in that same town;
For whan degrees fiftene were ascended,
For when degrees fifteen were ascended,
Thanne crew he, that it mighte nat ben amended.
Then he crowed so that it could not be improved.
His comb was redder than the fyn coral,
His comb was redder than the fine coral,
40 And batailed as it were a castel wal.
And notched with battlements as if it were a castle wall;
His bile was blak, and as the jeet it shoon;
His bill was black, and it shone like the jet stone;
Lyk asur were his legges and his toon;
Like azure were his legs and his toes;
His nayles whytter than the lilie flour,
His nails whiter than the lily flour,
And lyk the burned gold was his colour.
And like the burnished gold was his color.
45 This gentil cok hadde in his governaunce
This gentle cock had in his governance
Sevene hennes, for to doon al his plesaunce,
Seven hens to do all his pleasure,
Whiche were his sustres and his paramours,
Which were his sisters and his concubines,
And wonder lyk to him, as of colours;
And wonderfully like him, in their colors;
Of whiche the faireste hewed on hir throte
Of which the fairest colored on her throat
50 Was cleped faire damoysele Pertelote.
Was called fair demoiselle Pertelote.
Curteys she was, discreet, and debonaire,
Courteous she was, discreet, and gracious,
And compaignable, and bar hirself so faire,

And companionable, and bore herself so fair
Sin thilke day that she was seven night old,
Since that same day that she was seven nights old
That trewely she hath the herte in hold
That truly she has in possession the heart
55 Of Chauntecleer, loken in every lith;
Of Chauntecleer, locked in every limb (completely);
He loved hire so, that wel was him therwith.
He loved her so that well was him because of that.
But such a joye was it to here hem singe,
But such a joy it was to hear them sing,
Whan that the brighte sonne gan to springe,
When the bright sun began to spring,
In swete acord, "my lief is faren in londe."
In sweet accord, "My love has gone to the country!"—
60 For thilke tyme, as I have understonde,
For in that same time, as I have understood,
Bestes and briddes coude speke and singe.
Beasts and birds could speak and sing.
    And so bifel that in a daweninge,
    And so befell that in a dawning,
As Chauntecleer among his wyves alle
As Chauntecleer among all his wives
Sat on his perche that was in the halle,
Sat on his perch, that was in the hall,
65 And next him sat this faire Pertelote,
And next to him sat this faire Pertelote,
This Chauntecleer gan gronen in his throte
This Chauntecleer began to groan in his throat,
As man that in his dreem is drecched sore.
As one that in his dream is deeply troubled.
    And whan that Pertelote thus herde him rore,
    And when Pertelote thus heard him roar,
She was agast, and seyde, "Herte dere,
She was aghast and said, "Dear heart,
70 What eyleth yow to grone in this manere?
What ails you, to groan in this manner?
Ye been a verray sleper, fy for shame!"
You are a true (sound) sleeper; fie, for shame!"
    And he answerde and seyde thus, "Madame,
    And he answered, and said thus: "Madame,
I pray yow, that ye take it nat agrief:
I pray you that you take it not amiss.
By God, me mette I was in swich meschief
By God, I dreamed I was in such mischief
75 Right now, that yet myn herte is sore afright.
Right now that yet my heart is grievously frightened.
Now God," quod he, "my swevene recche aright,
Now God," said he, "interpret my dream correctly,
And keep my body out of foul prisoun!
And keep my body out of foul prison!
Me mette how that I romed up and doun
I dreamed how I roamed up and down

Withinne our yerde, wher as I saugh a beste,
Within our yard, where I saw a beast
80 Was lyk an hound and wolde han maad areste
Was like a hound, and would have seized
Upon my body, and wolde han had me deed.
Upon my body, and would have had me dead.
His colour was bitwixe yelow and reed,
His color was between yellow and red,
And tipped was his tail and bothe his eres
And tipped was his tail and both his ears
With blak, unlyk the remenant of his heres;
With black, unlike the rest of his hair;
85 His snowte smal, with glowinge eyen tweye.
His snout small, with two glowing eyes.
Yet of his look for fere almost I deye:
Yet for fear of his look I almost die;
This caused me my groning, doutelees."
This caused my groaning, doubtless."
    "Avoy!" quod she, "fy on yow, hertelees!
    "Shame!" said she, "fie on you, coward!
Allas!" quod she, "for, by that God above,
Alas," said she, "for, by that God above,
90 Now han ye lost myn herte and al my love.
Now have you lost my heart and all my love!
I can nat love a coward, by my feith!
I can not love a coward, by my faith!
For certes, what so any womman seith,
For certainly, whatever any woman says,
We alle desiren, if it mighte be,
We all desire, if it might be,
To han housbondes hardy, wyse, and free,
To have husbands hardy, wise, and generous,
95 And secree, and no nigard, ne no fool,
And secret—and no miser, nor no fool,
Ne him that is agast of every tool,
Nor him who is afraid of every weapon,
Ne noon avauntour. By that God above,
Nor any boaster, by that God above!
How dorste ye seyn for shame unto your love
How dare you say, for shame, unto your love
That any thing mighte make yow aferd?
That any thing might make you afraid?
100 Have ye no mannes herte, and han a berd?
Have you no man's heart, and have a beard?
Allas! and conne ye been agast of swevenis?
Alas! And can you be frightened of dreams?
Nothing, God wot, but vanitee in sweven is.
Nothing, God knows, but foolishness is in dreams.
Swevenes engendren of replecciouns,
Dreams are produced by overeating,
And ofte of fume, and of complecciouns,
And often by stomach vapors and by the mixture of bodily humors,
105 Whan humours been to habundant in a wight.

When humors are too abundant in a person.
Certes this dreem, which ye han met tonight,
Certainly this dream, which you have dreamed to-night,
Cometh of the grete superfluitee
Comes of the great superfluity
Of youre rede *colera*, pardee,
Of your red choleric humor, indeed,
Which causeth folk to dreden in hir dremes
Which causes folk in their dreams to be afraid
110 Of arwes, and of fyr with rede lemes,
Of arrows, and of fire with red flames,
Of rede bestes, that they wol hem byte,
Of red beasts, (fearing) that they will bite them,
Of contek, and of whelpes grete and lyte;
Of strife, and of dogs, big and little;
Right as the humour of malencolye
Right as the humor of melancholy
Causeth ful many a man in sleep to crye
Causes very many a man in sleep to cry
115 For fere of blake beres, or boles blake,
For fear of black bears, or black bulls,
Or elles, blake develes wole hem take.
Or else black devils will take them.
Of othere humours coude I telle also
Of other humors could I tell also
That werken many a man in sleep ful wo;
That cause many a man much woe (in) sleep;
But I wol passe as lightly as I can.
But I will pass over as lightly as I can.
120 Lo Catoun, which that was so wys a man,
"Lo Cato, who was so wise a man,
Seyde he nat thus, 'Ne do no fors of dremes'?
Said he not thus, 'Attach no importance to dreams'?
Now, sire," quod she, "whan we flee fro the bemes,
"Now sir," said she, "when we fly from the beams,
For Goddes love, as tak some laxatyf.
For God's love, take some laxative.
Up peril of my soule and of my lyf
Upon peril of my soul and of my life,
125 I counseille yow the beste, I wol nat lye,
I counsel you the best—I will not lie—
That bothe of colere and of malencolye
That both of choler and of melancholy
Ye purge yow; and for ye shul nat tarie,
You purge yourself; and so that you shall not delay,
Though in this toun is noon apothecarie,
Though in this town is no apothecary,
I shal myself to herbes techen yow,
I shall myself guide you to herbs
130 That shul ben for youre hele and for youre prow;
That shall be for your health and for your benefit;
And in oure yerd tho herbes shal I finde
And in our yard I shall find those herbs

The whiche han of hire propretee by kinde
The which by nature have the power
To purgen yow binethe and eek above.
To purge you beneath and also above.
Forget not this, for Goddes owene love!
Forget not this, for God's own love!
135 Ye been ful colerik of compleccioun.
You are dominated by the choleric humor;
Ware the sonne in his ascencioun
Beware the sun when it is high in the sky
Ne fynde yow nat repleet of humours hote;
And do not find yourself with an excess of hot humors.
And if it do, I dar wel leye a grote,
And if there be an excess, I dare well bet four pence,
That ye shul have a fevere terciane,
That you shall have a fever recurring every three days,
140 Or an agu, that may be youre bane.
Or an ague that may be your death.
A day or two ye shul have digestyves
A day or two you shall have digestives
Of wormes, er ye take your laxatyves,
Of worms, before you take your laxatives
Of lauriol, centaure, and fumetere,
Of spurge laurel, centaury, and fumitory,
Or elles of ellebor that groweth there,
Or else of hellebore, that grows there,
145 Of catapuce, or of gaytres beryis,
Of caper-spurge, or of rhamus,
Of erbe yve, growing in oure yerd, ther mery is.
Of ground ivy, growing in our yard, where it is pleasant;
Pekke hem up right as they growe, and ete hem in.
Peck them up right as they grow and eat them in.
Be mery, housbond, for youre fader kin!
Be merry, husband, for your father's kin!
Dredeth no dreem: I can say yow namore."
Dread no dream; I can say you no more."
150   "Madame," quod he, "graunt mercy of youre lore.
"Madame," said he, "great thanks for your learning.
But nathelees, as touching daun Catoun,
But nonetheless, as touching dan Cato,
That hath of wisdom swich a greet renoun,
That has of wisdom such a great renoun,
Though that he bad no dremes for to drede,
Though he commanded (us) to dread no dreams,
By God, men may in olde bokes rede
By God, men may in old books read
155 Of many a man, more of auctoritee
Of many a man of more authority
Than ever Catoun was, so mote I thee,
Than Cato ever was, as I may prosper,
That al the revers seyn of his sentence,
Who say all the reverse of this sentence,
And han wel founden by experience,

And have well found by experience
That dremes ben significaciouns
That dreams are significations
160 As wel of joye as tribulaciouns
As well of joy as of tribulations
That folk enduren in this lyf present.
That folk endure in this present life.
Ther nedeth make of this noon argument:
There need be no argument about this;
The verray preve sheweth it in dede.
The proof itself shows it in the deed.
   Oon of the gretteste auctours that men rede
   "One of the greatest author that men read
165 Seith thus, that whylom two felawes wente
Says thus: that once two fellows went
On pilgrimage, in a ful good entente;
On pilgrimage, with a very good intention,
And happed so thay come into a toun,
And it so happened, they came in a town
Wher as ther was swich congregacioun
Where there was such a gathering
Of peple, and eek so streit of herbergage,
Of people, and also such a scantiness of lodging,
170 That they ne founde as muche as o cotage
That they found not so much as one cottage
In which they bothe mighte y-logged be.
In which they both might be lodged.
Wherfor thay mosten of necessitee,
Therefore they must of necessity,
As for that night, departen compaignye;
For that night, part company;
And ech of hem goth to his hostelrye,
And each of them goes to his hostelry,
175 And took his logging as it wolde falle.
And took his lodging as it would befall.
That oon of hem was logged in a stalle,
The one of them was lodged in a stall,
Fer in a yerd, with oxen of the plough;
Far in a yard, with oxen of the plough;
That other man was logged wel ynough,
That other man was lodged well enough,
As was his aventure or his fortune,
As was his adventure or his fortune,
180 That us governeth alle as in commune.
Which us governs all in common.
And so bifel that, longe er it were day,
"And it so befell that, long before it was day,
This man mette in his bed, ther as he lay,
This man dreamed in his bed, where he lay,
How that his felawe gan upon him calle,
How his fellow began to call upon him,
And seyde, 'Allas! for in an oxes stalle
And said, 'Alas, for in an oxen's stall

185   This night I shal be mordred ther I lye.
This night I shall be murdered where I lie!
Now help me, dere brother, or I dye;
Now help me, dear brother, or I die.
In alle haste com to me,' he sayde.
In all haste come to me!' he said.
    This man out of his sleep for fere abrayde,
    This man out of his sleep for fear awakened suddenly;
But whan that he was wakened of his sleep,
But when he was wakened of his sleep,
190   He turned him, and took of this no keep:
He turned himself and took no heed of this.
Him thoughte his dreem nas but a vanitee.
He thought his dream was nothing but a fantasy.
Thus twyes in his sleping dremed he;
Thus twice in his sleeping he dreamed;
And atte thridde tyme yet his felawe
And at third time yet his fellow
Cam, as him thoughte, and seide, 'I am now slawe.
Came, as it seemed to him, and said, 'I am now slain.
195   Bihold my blody woundes, depe and wyde!
Behold my bloody wounds deep and wide!
Arys up erly in the morwe tyde,
Arise up early in the morning time,
And at the west gate of the toun,' quod he,
And at the west gate of the town,' he said,
'A carte ful of donge ther shaltow see,
'A cart full of dung there shalt thou see,
In which my body is hid ful prively:
In which my body is hid very secretly;
200   Do thilke carte aresten boldely.
Have that same cart immediately seized.
My gold caused my mordre, sooth to sayn;'
My gold caused my murder, to say the truth,'
And tolde him every poynt how he was slayn,
And told him in full detail how he was slain,
With a ful pitous face, pale of hewe.
With a very piteous face, pale of hue.
And truste wel, his dreem he fond ful trewe,
And trust well, his dream he found very true,
205   For on the morwe, as sone as it was day,
For on the morrow, as soon as it was day,
To his felawes in he took the way;
To his fellow's inn he took the way;
And whan that he cam to this oxes stalle,
And when he came to this oxen's stall,
After his felawe he bigan to calle.
After his fellow he began to call.
    The hostiler answered him anon,
    "The innkeeper answered him straightway,
210   And seyde, 'Sire, your felawe is agon:
And said, 'Sir, your fellow is gone.
As sone as day he wente out of the toun.'

As soon as it was day he went out of the town.'
This man gan fallen in suspecioun,
"This man began to fall in suspicion,
Remembringe on his dremes that he mette,
Remembering his dreams that he dreamed,
And forth he goth, no lenger wolde he lette,
And forth he goes—no longer would he delay—
215 Unto the west gate of the toun, and fond
Unto the west gate of the town, and found
A dong-carte, wente as it were to donge lond,
A dung-cart, which went as if it were to dung land,
That was arrayed in the same wyse
That was drawn up in that same manner
As ye han herd the dede man devyse.
As you have heard the dead man tell.
And with an hardy herte he gan to crye,
And with a hardy heart he began to cry for
220 'Vengeaunce and justice of this felonye!
Vengeance and justice of this felony:
My felawe mordred is this same night,
'My fellow is murdered this same night,
And in this carte he lyth gapinge upright.
And in this cart he lies gaping upright.
I crye out on the ministres,' quod he,
I cry out on the officials,' said he,
'That sholden kepe and reulen this citee,
'Who should guard and rule this city.
225 Harrow! allas! heer lyth my felawe slayn!'
Help! Alas! Here lies my fellow slain!'
What sholde I more unto this tale sayn?
What should I more unto this tale say?
The peple out sterte, and caste the cart to grounde,
The people rushed out and cast the cart to ground,
And in the middel of the dong they founde
And in the middle of the dung they found
The dede man, that mordred was al newe.
The dead man, who was just recently murdered.
230 O blisful God, that art so just and trewe!
"O blissful God, that art so just and true,
Lo, how that thou biwreyest mordre alway!
Lo, how thou always reveal murder!
Mordre wol out, that see we day by day.
Murder will out; we see that day by day.
Mordre is so wlatsom and abhominable
Murder is so disgusting and abominable
To God, that is so just and resonable,
To God, who is so just and reasonable,
235 That he ne wol nat suffre it heled be.
That He will not suffer it to be hidden,
Though it abyde a yeer, or two, or three,
Though it may wait a year, or two, or three.
Mordre wol out, this my conclusioun.
Murder will out, this is my conclusion.

And right anoon, ministres of that toun
And immediately, officials of that town
Han hent the carter and so sore him pyned,
Have seized the carter and so painfully tortured him,
240 And eek the hostiler so sore engyned,
And also the hosteller so grievously tortured,
That thay biknewe hir wikkednesse anoon,
That they straightway acknowledged their wickedness,
And were anhanged by the nekke-boon.
And were hanged by the neck-bone.
Here may men seen that dremes been to drede.
"Here men may seen that dreams are to be feared.
    And certes, in the same book I rede,
    And certainly in the same book I read,
245 Right in the nexte chapitre after this—
Right in the next chapter after this—
I gabbe nat, so have I joye or blis—
I do not lie, as I may have joy or bliss—
Two men that wolde han passed over see,
Two men that would have passed over see,
For certeyn cause, into a fer contree,
For a certain reason, into a far country,
If that the wind ne hadde been contrarie:
If that the wind had not been contrary,
250 That made hem in a citee for to tarie
That made them to tarry in a city
That stood ful mery upon an haven syde.
That stood very merrily upon an haven-side;
But on a day, agayn the even-tyde,
But on a day, toward the evening time,
The wind gan chaunge, and blew right as hem leste.
The wind began to change, and blew exactly as they desired.
Jolif and glad they wente unto hir reste,
Jolly and glad they went unto their rest,
255 And casten hem ful erly for to saille;
And they planned to sail very early.
    But herkneth! To that oo man fil a greet mervaille.
    But listen! To that one man befell a great marvel:
That oon of hem, in sleping as he lay,
The one of them, in sleeping as he lay,
Him mette a wonder dreem, agayn the day:
He dreamed a wondrous dream before the day.
Him thoughte a man stood by his beddes syde,
He thought a man stood by his bed's side,
260 And him comaunded that he sholde abyde,
And commanded him that he should stay,
And seyde him thus, 'If thou tomorwe wende,
And said to him thus: 'If thou travel tomorrow,
Thou shalt be dreynt: my tale is at an ende.'
Thou shalt be drowned; my tale is at an end.'
    He wook, and tolde his felawe what he mette,
    He woke, and told his fellow what he dreamed,
And preyde him his viage for to lette;

And prayed him to delay his voyage;
265 As for that day, he preyde him to byde.
For that day, he prayed him to wait.
   His felawe, that lay by his beddes syde,
   His fellow, that lay by his bed's side,
Gan for to laughe, and scorned him ful faste.
Began to laugh, and vigorously scorned him.
'No dreem' quod he, 'may so myn herte agaste
'No dream,' said he, 'may so frighten my heart
That I wol lette for to do my thinges.
That I will desist from doing my tasks.
270 I sette not a straw by thy dreminges,
I set not a straw by (put no value on) thy dreams,
For swevenes been but vanitees and japes.
For dreams are but fantasies and foolishness.
Men dreme alday of owles or of apes,
Men dream all the time of owls and of apes,
And eke of many a mase therwithal;
And also of many a source of amazement indeed;
Men dreme of thing that nevere was ne shal.
Men dream of a thing that never was nor shall be.
275 But sith I see that thou wolt heer abyde,
But since I see that thou will remain here,
And thus forsleuthen wilfully thy tyde,
And thus willfully waste thy tide,
God woot it reweth me; and have good day.'
God knows, it makes me sorry; and have good day!'
And thus he took his leve, and wente his way.
And thus he took his leave, and went his way.
But er that he hadde halfe his cours y-seyled,
But before he had sailed half his course,
280 Noot I nat why, ne what mischaunce it eyled,
I know not why, nor what mischance harmed it,
But casuelly the shippes botme rente,
But by chance the ship's bottom broke open,
And ship and man under the water wente
And ship and man went under the water
In sighte of othere shippes it byside,
In sight of other ships beside it,
That with hem seyled at the same tyde.
That with them sailed on the same tide.
285 And therfore faire Pertelote so dere,
And therefore, faire Pertelote so dear,
By swiche ensamples olde maistow lere
By such old examples thou may learn
That no man sholde been to recchelees
That no man should be too heedless
Of dremes, for I sey thee, doutelees,
Of dreams; for I say to thee, doubtless,
That many a dreem ful sore is for to drede.
That many a dream is very greatly to be feared.
290   Lo, in the lyf of Seint Kenelm I rede,
   "Lo, I read in the life of Saint Kenelm,

That was Kenulphus sone, the noble king
That was son of Kenulphus, the noble king
Of Mercenrike, how Kenelm mette a thing
Of Mercia, how Kenelm dreamed a thing.
A lyte er he was mordred on a day.
A little before he was murdered, on a day,
His mordre in his avisioun he say.
He saw his murder in his vision.

295   His norice him expouned every del
His nurse completely explained to him
His sweven, and bad him for to kepe him wel
His dream, and ordered him to guard himself well
For traisoun; but he nas but seven yeer old,
From treason; but he was only seven years old,
And therfore litel tale hath he told
And therefore he put little store
Of any dreem, so holy was his herte.
In any dream, so holy was his heart.

300   By God, I hadde lever than my sherte
By God! I had rather than my shirt (give my shirt)
That ye had rad his legende as have I.
That you had read his legend, as have I.
   Dame Pertelote, I sey yow trewely,
   "Dame Pertelote, I say you truly,
Macrobeus, that writ the avisioun
Macrobius, that wrote the vision
In Affrike of the worthy Cipioun,
In Africa of the worthy Scipio,

305   Affermeth dremes, and seith that they been
Affirms (the value of) dreams, and says that they are
Warninge of thinges that men after seen.
Warnings of things that men later see (come to pass)
   And forthermore, I pray yow loketh wel
   And furthermore, I pray you, look well
In the Olde Testament, of Daniel,
In the Old Testament, concerning Daniel,
If he held dremes any vanitee.
If he held dreams (to be) any foolishness.

310   Reed eek of Ioseph, and ther shul ye see
   Read also of Joseph, and there shall you see
Wher dremes ben somtyme (I sey nat alle)
Whether dreams are sometimes—I say not all—
Warninge of thinges that shul after falle.
Warnings of things that shall afterward befall.
   Loke of Egipte the king, daun Pharao,
   Consider the king of Egypt, dan Pharaoh,
His bakere and his boteler also,
His baker and his butler also,

315   Wher they ne felte noon effect in dremes.
Whether or not they felt any effect in dreams.
Whoso wol seken actes of sondry remes
Whoever will seek out the histories of various nations
May rede of dremes many a wonder thing.

May read many a wonderful thing about dreams.
   Lo Cresus, which that was of Lyde king,
   Lo Croesus, who was king of Lydia,
Mette he nat that he sat upon a tree,
Dreamed he not that he sat upon a tree,
320   Which signified he sholde anhanged be?
   Which signified he should be hanged?
   Lo heer Andromacha, Ectores wyf,
   Lo here Andromacha, Hector's wife,
That day that Ector sholde lese his lyf,
That day that Hector should lose his life,
She dremed on the same night biforn,
She dreamed on the same night before
How that the lyf of Ector sholde be lorn
How the life of Hector should be lost,
325   If thilke day he wente into bataille;
   If that same day he went into battle.
She warned him, but it mighte nat availle;
She warned him, but it might not avail;
He wente for to fighte nathelees,
He went to fight nonetheless,
But he was slayn anoon of Achilles.
But he was slain straightway by Achilles.
But thilke tale is al to long to telle,
But that same tale is all too long to tell,
330   And eek it is ny day, I may nat dwelle.
   And also it is nigh day; I may not delay.
Shortly I seye, as for conclusioun,
Shortly I say, as for conclusion,
That I shal han of this avisioun
That I shall have of this vision
Adversitee; and I seye forthermore,
Adversity; and I say furthermore,
That I ne telle of laxatyves no store,
That I put no store in laxatives,
335   For they ben venimous, I woot it wel;
   For they are poisonous, I know it well;
I hem defye, I love hem never a del.
I renounce them, I love them not at all!
   Now let us speke of mirthe and stinte al this;
   "Now let us speak of mirth, and stop all this.
Madame Pertelote, so have I blis,
Madame Pertelote, as I may have bliss,
Of o thing God hath sent me large grace:
Of one thing God has sent me a great favor;
340   For whan I see the beautee of your face—
   For when I see the beauty of your face,
Ye ben so scarlet reed about your yën—
You are so scarlet red about your eyes,
It maketh al my drede for to dyen.
It makes all my dread die;
For, also siker as *In principio,*
For as surely as 'In the beginning,

Mulier est hominis confusio.
'Woman is the ruin of man—'
345   Madame, the sentence of this Latin is
'Woman is the ruin of man—'
'Womman is mannes joye and al his blis.'
'Woman is man's joy and all his bliss.'
For whan I fele a-night your softe syde,
For when I feel at night your soft side—
Al be it that I may nat on you ryde,
Although I can not on you ride,
For that our perche is maad so narwe, alas!
Because our perch is made so narrow, alas—
350   I am so ful of joye and of solas
I am so full of joy and of pleasure,
That I defye bothe sweven and dreem."
That I renounce both vision and dream."
And with that word he fley doun fro the beem,
And with that word he flew down from the beam,
For it was day, and eek his hennes alle,
For it was day, and also all his hens,
And with a chuk he gan hem for to calle,
And with a cluck he began to call them,
355   For he had founde a corn lay in the yerd.
Because he had found a seed, which lay in the yard.
Real he was, he was namore aferd;
Royal he was, he was no longer afraid.
He fethered Pertelote twenty tyme,
He embraced Pertelote twenty times,
And trad hir eke as ofte, er it was pryme.
And copulated with her also as often, before it was 6 a.m.
He loketh as it were a grim leoun,
He looks as if he were a grim lion,
360   And on his toos he rometh up and doun—
And on his toes he roams up and down;
Him deyned not to sette his foot to grounde.
He deigned not to set his foot to ground.
He chukketh whan he hath a corn y-founde,
He clucks when he has found a seed,
And to him rennen thanne his wyves alle.
And then his wives all run to him.
Thus royal, as a prince is in his halle,
Thus royal, as a prince is in his hall,
365   Leve I this Chauntecleer in his pasture;
Leave I this Chauntecleer in his feeding place,
And after wol I telle his aventure.
And after I will tell his adventure.
    Whan that the month in which the world bigan,
    When the month in which the world began,
That highte March, whan God first maked man,
Which is called March, when God first made man,
Was complet, and passed were also,
Was complete, and passed were also,
370   Sin March bigan, thritty dayes and two,

Since March had begun, thirty days and two,
Bifel that Chauntecleer, in al his pryde,
Befell that Chauntecleer in all his pride,
His seven wyves walkinge by his syde,
His seven wives walking by his side,
Caste up his eyen to the brighte sonne,
Cast up his eyes to the bright sun,
That in the signe of Taurus hadde y-ronne
That in the sign of Taurus had run
375 Twenty degrees and oon, and somwhat more;
Twenty degrees and one, and somewhat more,
And knew by kynde, and by noon other lore,
And knew by nature, and by none other knowledge,
That it was pryme, and crew with blisful stevene.
That it was prime, and crowed with blissful voice.
"The sonne," he sayde, "is clomben up on hevene
"The sun," he said, "has climbed up on heaven
Fourty degrees and oon, and more, ywis.
Forty degrees and one, and more indeed.
380 Madame Pertelote, my worldes blis,
Madame Pertelote, my world's bliss,
Herkneth thise blisful briddes how they singe,
Listen to these blissful birds, how they sing,
And see the fresshe floures how they springe;
And see the fresh flowers, how they spring;
Ful is myn herte of revel and solas."
My heart is full of revel and pleasure!"
But sodeinly him fil a sorweful cas,
But suddenly to him befell a sorrowful situation,
385 For ever the latter ende of joye is wo.
For ever the latter end of joy is woe.
God woot that worldly joye is sone ago;
God knows that worldly joy is soon gone;
And if a rethor coude faire endyte,
And if a rhetorician could fairly compose,
He in a cronique saufly mighte it wryte
He in a chronicle confidently could write it
As for a sovereyn notabilitee.
As a supremely important fact.
390 Now every wys man, lat him herkne me:
Now every wise man, let him listen to me;
This storie is also trewe, I undertake,
This story is as true, I declare,
As is the book of Launcelot de Lake,
As is the Book of Lancelot of the Lake,
That wommen holde in ful gret reverence.
Which women hold in very great reverence.
Now wol I torne agayn to my sentence.
Now will I turn again to my subject matter.
395   A col-fox, ful of sly iniquitee,
   A fox, full of sly iniquity,
That in the grove hadde woned yeres three,
That in the grove had dwelled three years,

By heigh imaginacioun forncast,
By exalted imagination predestined,
The same night thurghout the hegges brast
The same night through the hedges broke
Into the yerd, ther Chauntecleer the faire
Into the yard where the handsome Chauntecleer
400   Was wont, and eek his wyves, to repaire;
Was accustomed, and also his wives, to repair;
And in a bed of wortes stille he lay,
And in a bed of cabbages he lay quietly
Til it was passed undren of the day,
Until it had passed 9 a.m. of the day,
Waytinge his tyme on Chauntecleer to falle,
Waiting his time on Chauntecleer to fall,
As gladly doon thise homicydes alle,
As habitually do all these homicides
405   That in awayt liggen to mordre men.
That in ambush lie to murder men.
O false mordrour, lurkinge in thy den!
O false murderer, lurking in thy den!
O newe Scariot, newe Genilon!
O new Judas Iscariot, new Genylon,
False dissimilour, O Greek Sinon,
False deceiver, O Greek Synon,
That broghtest Troye al outrely to sorwe!
That brought all Troy completely to sorrow!
410   Chauntecleer, acursed be that morwe,
Chauntecleer, cursed be that morning
That thou into that yerd flough fro the bemes!
That thou flew from the beams into that yard!
Thou were ful wel y-warned by thy dremes
Thou were very well warned by thy dreams
That thilke day was perilous to thee.
That that same day was perilous to thee;
But what that God forwoot mot nedes be,
But what God knows beforehand must by necessity be,
415   After the opinioun of certeyn clerkis.
According to the opinion of certain scholars.
Witnesse on him that any perfit clerk is
Take witness of him that is a thoroughly competent scholar,
That in scole is gret altercacioun
That in the university is great disagreement
In this matere, and greet disputisoun,
In this matter, and great disputation,
And hath ben of an hundred thousand men.
And has been (disputed) by a hundred thousand men.
420   But I ne can not bulte it to the bren,
But I can not separate the valid and invalid arguments
As can the holy doctour Augustyn,
As can the holy doctor Augustine,
Or Boece, or the bishop Bradwardyn,
Or Boethius, or the Bishop Bradwardyn,
Whether that Goddes worthy forwiting

Whether God's worthy foreknowledge
Streyneth me nedely for to doon a thing
Constrains me by need to do a thing—
425 ("Nedely" clepe I simple necessitee);
"Need" I call simple necessity—
Or elles, if free choys be graunted me
Or else, if free choice be granted to me
To do that same thing or do it noght,
To do that same thing, or do it not,
Though God forwoot it er that I was wroght;
Though God knew it before I was born;
Or if his witing streyneth never a del
Or if his knowledge constrains not at all
430 But by necessitee condicionel.
But by conditional necessity.
I wol not han to do of swich matere;
I will not have to do with such matter;
My tale is of a cok, as ye may here,
My tale is of a cock, as you may hear,
That took his counseil of his wyf, with sorwe,
Who took his counsel from his wife, with sorrow,
To walken in the yerd upon that morwe
To walk in the yard upon that morning
435 That he had met the dreem that I yow tolde.
That he had dreamed that dream of which I told you.
Wommennes counseils been ful ofte colde;
Women's counsels are very often fatal;
Wommannes counseil broghte us first to wo,
Woman's counsel brought us first to woe
And made Adam fro Paradys to go,
And made Adam to go from Paradise,
Ther as he was ful mery and wel at ese.
Where he was very merry and well at ease.
440 But for I noot to whom it mighte displese,
But because I know not to whom it might displease,
If I counseil of wommen wolde blame,
If I would blame counsel of women,
Passe over, for I seyde it in my game.
Pass over, for I said it as a joke.
Rede auctours, wher they trete of swich matere,
Read authors, where they treat of such matter,
And what thay seyn of wommen ye may here.
And what they say of women you may hear.
445 Thise been the cokkes wordes, and nat myne;
These are the cock's words, and not mine;
I can noon harm of no womman divyne.
I know no harm of any woman divine.
    Faire in the sond, to bathe hire merily,
    Fair in the sand, to bathe her merrily,
Lyth Pertelote, and alle hire sustres by,
Lies Pertelote, and all her sisters by her,
Agayn the sonne; and Chauntecleer so free
In the sunshine, and Chauntecleer so noble

450   Song merier than the mermayde in the see—
      Sang more merrily than the mermaid in the sea
      For Phisiologus seith sikerly
      (For Phisiologus says surely
      How that they singen wel and merily—
      How they sing well and merrily).
          And so bifel that, as he caste his yë
          And so befell that, as he cast his eye
      Among the wortes, on a boterflye,
      On a butterfly among the cabbages,
455   He was war of this fox that lay ful lowe.
      He was aware of this fox, that lay very low.
      Nothing ne liste him thanne for to crowe,
      Not at all then did he want to crow,
      But cryde anon, "Cok cok!" and up he sterte,
      But cried straightway, "Cock! cock!" and up he leaped
      As man that was affrayed in his herte.
      As one that was frightened in his heart.
      For naturelly a beest desyreth flee
      For naturally a beast desires to flee
460   Fro his contrarie, if he may it see,
      From his natural opponent, if he may see it,
      Though he never erst had seyn it with his yë.
      Though he never before had seen it with his eye.
      This Chauntecleer, whan he gan him espye,
      This Chauntecleer, when he did espy him,
      He wolde han fled, but that the fox anon
      He would have fled, but that the fox straightway
      Seyde, "Gentil sire, allas! wher wol ye gon?
      Said, "Gentle sir, alas, where will you go?
465   Be ye affrayed of me that am your freend?
      Are you afraid of me who is your friend?
      Now certes, I were worse than a feend,
      Now, certainly, I would be worse than a fiend,
      If I to yow wolde harm or vileinye.
      If I to you would do harm or villainy!
      I am nat come your counseil for t'espye,
      I am not come to spy on your secrets,
      But trewely, the cause of my cominge
      But truly, the cause of my coming
470   Was only for to herkne how that ye singe.
      Was only to hear how you sing.
      For trewely ye have as mery a stevene
      For truly, you have as merry a voice
      As eny aungel hath that is in hevene;
      As has any angel that is in heaven.
      Therwith ye han in musik more feelinge
      Therewith you have in music more feeling
      Than hadde Boece, or any that can singe.
      Than had Boethius, or any that knows how to sing.
475   My lord your fader (God his soule blesse!)
      My lord your father—God bless his soul!—
      And eek your moder, of hire gentilesse,

And also your mother, of her graciousness,
Han in myn hous y-been, to my gret ese;
Have been in my house to my great pleasure;
And certes, sire, ful fayn wolde I yow plese.
And certainly, sir, I would very eagerly please you.
   But for men speke of singing, I wol saye,
   But, insofar as men speak of singing, I will say—
480 So mote I brouke wel myn eyen tweye,
As I may well have use of my two eyes—
Save yow, I herde never man so singe
Except for you, I heard never man so sing
As dide your fader in the morweninge.
As did your father in the morning.
Certes, it was of herte, al that he song.
Certainly, it came from the heart, all that he sang.
And for to make his voys the more strong,
And to make his voice the more strong,
485 He wolde so peyne him that with bothe his yën
He would so exert himself that with both his eyes
He moste winke, so loude he wolde cryen,
He had to wink, so loud he would cry,
And stonden on his tiptoon therwithal,
And stand on his tiptoes simultaneously,
And strecche forth his nekke long and smal.
And stretch forth his neck long and small.
And eek he was of swich discrecioun
And also he was of such sound judgment
490 That ther nas no man in no regioun
That there was no man in any region
That him in song or wisdom mighte passe.
That might pass him in song or wisdom.
I have wel rad in 'Daun Burnel the Asse,'
I have well read in 'Dan Burnel the Ass,'
Among his vers, how that ther was a cok,
Among his verses, how there was a cock,
For that a preestes sone yaf him a knok
Because a priest's son gave him a knock
495 Upon his leg, whyl he was yong and nyce,
Upon his leg while he was young and foolish,
He made him for to lese his benefyce.
He made him lose his benefice.
But certeyn, ther nis no comparisoun
But certainly, there is no comparison
Bitwix the wisdom and discrecioun
Between the wisdom and discretion
Of youre fader, and of his subtiltee.
Of your father and of his subtlety.
500 Now singeth, sire, for seinte charitee!
Now sing, sir, for Saint Charity;
Let see, conne ye your fader countrefete?"
Let's see; can you imitate your father?"
   This Chauntecleer his winges gan to bete,
   This Chauntecleer began to beat his wings,

As man that coude his tresoun nat espye,
As one that could not espy his treason,
So was he ravisshed with his flaterye.
He was so ravished with his flattery.
505   Allas! ye lordes, many a fals flatour
    Alas, you lords, many a false flatterer
Is in your courtes, and many a losengeour,
Is in your courts, and many a sycophant,
That plesen yow wel more, by my feith,
Who please you well more, by my faith,
Than he that soothfastnesse unto yow seith.
Than he who says the truth unto you.
Redeth Ecclesiaste of flaterye;
Read Ecclesiastes about flattery;
510   Beth war, ye lordes, of hir trecherye.
    Beware, you lords, of their treachery.
      This Chauntecleer stood hye upon his toos,
        This Chauntecleer stood high upon his toes,
Strecching his nekke, and heeld his eyen cloos,
Stretching his neck, and held his eyes closed,
And gan to crowe loude for the nones;
And began to crow loud for the occasion.
And daun Russel the fox sterte up at ones
And dan Russell the fox leaped up at once,
515   And by the gargat hente Chauntecleer,
    And grabbed Chauntecleer by the throat,
And on his bak toward the wode him beer,
And carried him on his back toward the woods,
For yet ne was ther no man that him sewed.
For yet there was no one that pursued him.
      O destinee, that mayst nat been eschewed!
        O destiny, that may not be escaped!
Allas, that Chauntecleer fleigh fro the bemes!
Alas, that Chauntecleer flew from the beams!
520   Allas, his wyf ne roghte nat of dremes!
    Alas, his wife took no heed of dreams!
And on a Friday fil al this meschaunce.
And on a Friday befell all this misfortune.
      O Venus, that art goddesse of plesaunce,
        O Venus, who art goddess of pleasure,
Sin that thy servant was this Chauntecleer,
Since this Chauntecleer was thy servant,
And in thy service dide al his poweer,
And in thy service did all his power,
525   More for delyt than world to multiplye,
    More for delight than to people the world,
Why woldestow suffre him on thy day to dye?
Why wouldest thou allow him to die on thy day?
      O Gaufred, dere mayster soverayn,
        O Gaufred, dear supreme master,
That whan thy worthy king Richard was slayn
Who when thy worthy king Richard was slain
With shot, compleynedest his deth so sore,

By shot of an arrow, complained his death so grievously,

530 Why ne hadde I now thy sentence and thy lore,
Why had I not now thy wisdom and thy learning,
The Friday for to chide, as diden ye?
To chide the Friday, as you did?
(For on a Friday soothly slayn was he.)
For on a Friday, truly, he was slain.
Than wolde I shewe yow how that I coude pleyne
Then would I show you how that I could complain
For Chauntecleres drede, and for his peyne.
For Chanticleer's dread and for his pain.

535   Certes, swich cry ne lamentacioun
Certainly, such cry nor lamentation
Was never of ladies maad when Ilioun
Was never made by ladies when Ilion (Troy)
Was wonne, and Pirrus with his streite swerd,
Was won, and Pirrus with his drawn sword,
Whan he hadde hent king Priam by the berd,
When he had seized king Priam by the beard,
And slayn him (as saith us *Eneydos*),
And slain him, as the Aeneid tells us,

540 As maden alle the hennes in the clos,
As all the hens made in the yard,
Whan they had seyn of Chauntecleer the sighte.
When they had seen the sight of Chauntecleer.
But sovereynly dame Pertelote shrighte
But supremely dame Pertelote shrieked
Ful louder than dide Hasdrubales wyf,
Much louder than did Hasdrubales' wife,
Whan that hir housbond hadde lost his lyf,
When her husband had lost his life

545 And that the Romayns hadde brend Cartage:
And the Romans had burned Carthage.
She was so ful of torment and of rage
She was so full of torment and of rage
That wilfully into the fyr she sterte,
That willfully into the fire she leaped
And brende hirselven with a stedfast herte.
And burned herself with a steadfast heart.
     O woful hennes, right so cryden ye
O woeful hens, exactly so you cried

550 As, whan that Nero brende the citee
As when Nero burned the city
Of Rome, cryden senatoures wyves,
Of Rome senators' wives cried
For that hir housbondes losten alle hir lyves;
Because their husbands lost all their lives—
Withouten gilt this Nero hath hem slayn.
Without guilt this Nero has them slain.
Now wol I torne to my tale agayn.
Now will I turn to my tale again.

555   This sely widwe and eek hir doghtres two
This poor widow and also her two daughters

Herden thise hennes crye and maken wo,
Heard these hens cry and make woe,
And out at dores sterten they anoon,
And out at doors they rush anon,
And syen the fox toward the grove goon,
And see the fox go toward the grove,
And bar upon his bak the cok away;
And carried the cock away upon his back,
560 And cryden, "Out! harrow! and weylaway!
And cried, "Help! Help and alas!
Ha, ha, the fox!" and after him they ran,
Ha, ha! The fox!" and after him they ran,
And eek with staves many another man;
And also with staves many another man.
Ran Colle our dogge, and Talbot, and Gerland,
Ran Colle our dog, and Talbot and Gerland,
And Malkin, with a distaf in hir hand;
And Malkyn, with a distaff in her hand;
565 Ran cow and calf, and eek the verray hogges,
Ran cow and calf, and also the very hogs,
So fered for the berking of the dogges
So frightened for the barking of the dogs
And shouting of the men and wimmen eke,
And shouting of the men and women also
They ronne so hem thoughte hir herte breke.
They ran so hard that they thought their hearts would break.
They yelleden as feendes doon in helle;
They yelled as fiends do in hell;
570 The dokes cryden as men wolde hem quelle;
The ducks cried as if men would them kill;
The gees for fere flowen over the trees;
The geese for fear flew over the trees;
Out of the hyve cam the swarm of bees;
Out of the hive came the swarm of bees.
So hidous was the noyse, a! benedicite!
So hideous was the noise—a, bless me!—
Certes, he Jakke Straw and his meynee
Certainly, he Jack Straw and his company
575 Ne made nevere shoutes half so shrille
Never made shouts half so shrill
Whan that they wolden any Fleming kille,
When they would any Fleming kill,
As thilke day was maad upon the fox.
As that same day was made upon the fox.
Of bras thay broghten bemes, and of box,
They brought trumpets of brass, and of box-wood,
Of horn, of boon, in whiche they blewe and pouped,
Of horn, of bone, in which they blew and puffed,
580 And therwithal thay shryked and they houped:
And with that they shrieked and they whooped.
It seemed as that heven sholde falle.
It seemed as if heaven should fall.
    Now, gode men, I pray yow herkneth alle!

Now, good men, I pray you all to listen:
Lo, how Fortune turneth sodeinly
Lo, how Fortune turns suddenly
The hope and pryde eek of hir enemy!
The hope and pride also of her enemy!

585   This cok, that lay upon the foxes bak,
This cock, that lay upon the fox's back,
In al his drede unto the fox he spak,
In all his dread unto the fox he spoke,
And seyde, "Sire, if that I were as ye,
And said, "Sir, if I were you,
Yet sholde I seyn, as wis God helpe me,
Yet should I say, as God may help me,
'Turneth agayn, ye proude cherles alle!
'Turn again, all you proud churls!

590   A verray pestilence upon yow falle!
May a true pestilence fall upon you!
Now I am come unto this wodes syde,
Now I am come unto the wood's side;
Maugree your heed, the cok shal heer abyde;
Despite all you could do, the cock shall here remain.
I wol him ete in feith, and that anon.'"
I will eat him, in faith, and that right away!'"

    The fox answerde, "In feith, it shal be don,"
*   The fox answered, "In faith, it shall be done."*

595   And as he spak that word, al sodeinly
And as he spoke that word, all suddenly
This cok brak from his mouth deliverly,
This cock nimbly broke from his mouth,
And heighe upon a tree he fleigh anon.
And high upon a tree he quickly flew.

    And whan the fox saugh that the cok was gon,
*   And when the fox saw that the cock was gone,*
"Allas!" quod he, "O Chauntecleer, allas!
"Alas!" said he, "O Chauntecleer, alas!

600   I have to yow," quod he, "y-doon trespas,
I have to you," said he, "done offense,
In as muche as I maked yow aferd
In as much as I made you afraid
When I yow hente and broghte out of the yerd.
When I seized you and brought you out of the yard.
But, sire, I dide it in no wikke entente;
But, sir, I did it with no wicked intention.
Com doun, and I shal telle yow what I mente.
Come down, and I shall tell you what I meant;

605   I shal seye sooth to yow, God help me so."
I shall say the truth to you, as God may help me!"

    "Nay, than," quod he, "I shrewe us bothe two,
*   "Nay then," said he, "I curse both of us two.*
And first I shrewe myself, bothe blood and bones,
And first I curse myself, both blood and bones,
If thou bigyle me ofter than ones.
If thou trick me more often than once.

Thou shalt namore, thurgh thy flaterye,
Thou shalt no more through thy flattery
610 Do me to singe and winke with myn yë.
Make me sing and close my eyes;
For he that winketh whan he sholde see,
For he that closes his eyes, when he should see,
Al wilfully, God lat him never thee!"
All willfully, God let him never prosper!"
  "Nay," quod the fox, "but God yeve him meschaunce,
  "Nay," said the fox, "but God give him misfortune,
That is so undiscreet of governaunce
Who is so indiscreet of governance
615 That jangleth whan he sholde holde his pees."
That he chatters when he should hold his peace."
    Lo, swich it is for to be recchelees
    Lo, such it is to be careless
And necligent, and truste on flaterye.
And negligent, and trust on flattery.
But ye that holden this tale a folye,
But you who hold this tale a folly,
As of a fox, or of a cok and hen,
As of a fox, or of a cock and hen,
620 Taketh the moralitee, goode men.
Take the morality, good men.
For Seint Paul seith that al that writen is,
For Saint Paul says that all that is written,
To our doctryne it is y-write, ywis.
Is written for our instruction, indeed;
Taketh the fruyt, and lat the chaf be stille.
Take the fruit, and let the chaff be still.
Now, gode God, if that it be thy wille,
Now, good God, if it be thy will,
625 As seith my lord, so make us alle good men,
As says my lord, make us all good men,
And bringe us to his heighe bliss. Amen.
And bring us to his high bliss! Amen.

From The Parson's Tale

The Introduction

By that the Maunciple hadde his tale al ended,
By the time that the Manciple had his tale all ended,
The sonne fro the south lyne was descended
The sun from the meridian was descended
So lowe, that he nas nat, to my sighte,
So low that it was not, to my sight,
Degrees nyne and twenty as in highte.
More than nine and twenty degrees in altitude.
5 Foure of the clokke it was tho, as I gesse,
Four of the clock it was then, as I suppose,
For elevene foot, or litel more or lesse,

For eleven feet, or little more or less,
My shadwe was at thilke tyme, as there,
My shadow was there at that same time,
Of swiche feet as my lengthe parted were
Of such feet as if my height were divided
In six feet equal of proporcioun.
Into six feet equal in size.

10 Therwith the mones exaltacioun,
Therewith the moon's exaltation—
I mene Libra, alwey gan ascende,
I mean Libra—steadily ascended
As we were entring at a thropes ende;
As we were entering at edge of a village;
For which oure Host, as he was wont to gye,
For which our Host, since he was accustomed to guide,
As in this caas, oure joly companye,
On this occasion, our jolly company,

15 Seyde in this wyse: "Lordings everichoon,
Said in this manner: "Gentlemen, every one,
Now lakketh us no tales mo than oon.
Now we lack no tales more than one.
Fulfild is my sentence and my decree;
Fulfilled is my plan and my decree;
I trowe that we han herd of ech degree.
I believe that we have heard from each social class;
Almost fulfild is al myn ordinaunce.
Almost fulfilled is all my governance.

20 I prey to God, so yeve him right good chaunce,
I pray to God, give right good luck to him,
That telleth this tale to us lustily.
Who tells this tale to us pleasingly.
"Sire preest," quod he, "artow a vicary?
"Sire priest," said he, "art thou a vicar?
Or art a person? Sey sooth, by thy fey!
Or art thou a parson? Tell the truth, by thy faith!
Be what thou be, ne breke thou nat oure pley;
Be whatever thou may be, break thou not our rules;

25 For every man, save thou, hath told his tale.
For every man, save thou, has told his tale.
Unbokele, and shewe us what is in thy male.
Unbuckle and show us what is in thy bag;
For trewely, me thinketh by thy chere,
For truly, it seems to me from your appearance
Thou sholdest knitte up wel a greet matere.
Thou shouldest well conclude a long discourse.
Telle us a fable anon, for cokkes bones!"
Tell us a fictional tale right now, for cock's bones!"

30 This Persone him answerde, al at ones,
This Parson answered, immediately,
"Thou getest fable noon y-told for me;
"Thou gettest no fiction told by me,
For Paul, that wryteth unto Timothee,
For Paul, who writes unto Timothy,

Repreveth hem that weyven soothfastnesse
Reproves them that abandon truthfulness
And tellen fables and swich wrecchednesse.
And tell fictional tales and such wretched things.
35 Why sholde I sowen draf out of my fest,
Why should I sow chaff out of my feast,
Whan I may sowen whete, if that me lest?
When I can sow wheat, if I so wish?
For which I seye, if that yow list to here
For which I say, if you want to hear
Moralitee and vertuous matere,
Morality and virtuous subject matter,
And thanne that ye wol yeve me audience,
And providing that you will give me your attention,
40 I wol ful fayn, at Cristes reverence,
I will very gladly, to Christ's reverence,
Do yow pleasaunce leefful, as I can.
Provide you with permissible pleasure, insofar as I can.
But trusteth wel, I am a Southren man:
But trust well, I am a Southern man;
I can nat geste—rum, ram, ruf—by lettre.
I can not recite 'rum, ram, ruf,' letter by letter,
Ne, God wot, rym holde I but litel bettre.
And, God knows, rime I consider but little better;
45 And therfore, if you list, I wol nat glose.
And therefore, if you wish—I will not deceive you—
I wol yow telle a mery tale in prose
I will yow tell a merry tale in prose
To knitte up al this feeste and make an ende.
To conclude all this festivity and make an end.
And Jesu, for his grace, wil me sende
And Jesus, for his grace, send me wit
To shewe yow the wey, in this viage,
To show you the way, in this journey,
50 Of thilke parfit glorious pilgrimage
Of that same perfect glorious pilgrimage
That highte Jerusalem celestial.
That is called Jerusalem celestial.
And, if ye vouchesauf, anon I shal
And if you agree, I shall right now
Biginne upon my tale, for whiche I preye
Begin my tale, for which I pray you
Telle youre avys, I can no bettre seye.
To tell your decision; I can say nothing better.
55 But nathelees, this meditacioun
"But nonetheless, this meditation
I putte it ay under correccioun
I put it ever subject to correction
Of clerkes, for I am nat textuel;
By clerks, for I am not learned in texts;
I take but the sentence, trusteth wel.
I take from them only the meaning, trust well.
Therfor I make protestacioun

Therefore I make this declaration
60 That I wol stonde to correccioun."
    That I will be subject to correction."
        Upon this word we han assented sone,
        Upon this word we have quickly assented,
    For, as us semed, it was for to done,
    For, as it seemed, it was the best to do—
    To enden in som vertuous sentence,
    To end in some virtuous subject matter,
    And for to yeve him space and audience,
    And to give him time and attention,
65 And bade oure Host he sholde to him seye
    And told our Host he should to him say
    That alle we to telle his tale him preye.
    That we all pray him to tell his tale.
        Oure Host hadde the wordes for us alle:
        Our Host had the words for us all;
    "Sire preest," quod he, "now fayre yow bifalle!
    "Sire priest," said he, "now may good fortune come to you!
    "Telleth," quod he, "youre meditacioun.
    Tell," said he, "your meditation.
70 But hasteth yow, the sonne wol adoun;
    But make haste; the sun is about to go down;
    Beth fructuous, and that in litel space,
    Be fruitful, and that in little time,
    And to do wel God sende yow his grace!"
    And to do well God send you his grace!
    Sey what yow list, and we wol gladly here."
    Say what you wish, and we will gladly hear."
    And with that word he seyde in this manere.
    And with that word he said in this manner.

Chaucer's Retraction

Here taketh the makere of this book his leve

Now praye I to hem alle that herkne this litel tretis or rede, that if ther be any thing in it that liketh hem, that therof they thanken oure Lord Jesu Crist, of whom proceedeth al wit and al goodnesse. And if ther be any thing that displese hem, I praye hem also that they arrette it to the defaute of myn unconning, and nat to my wil, that wolde ful fain have said bettre if I hadde had conning. For oure book saith, "Al that is writen is writen for oure doctrine," and that is myn entente. Wherfore I biseeke you mekely, for the mercy of God, that ye praye for me that Crist have mercy on me and foryive me my giltes, and namely of my translacions and enditinges of worldly vanitees, the whiche I revoke in my retraccions: as is the *Book of Troilus*; the Book also of *Fame*; the *Book of the Five and Twenty Ladies*; the *Book of the Duchesse*; the *Book of Saint Valentines Day of the Parlement of Briddes*; the *Tales of Canterbury*, thilke that sounen into sinne; the *Book of the Leon*; and many another book, if they were in my remembrance, and many a song and many a leccherous lay: that Crist for his grete mercy foryive me the sinne. But of the translacion of Boece

De Consolatione, and othere bookes of legendes of saintes, and omelies, and moralitee, and devocion, that thanke I oure Lord Jesu Crist and his blisful Moder and alle the saintes of hevene, biseeking hem that they from hennes forth unto my lives ende sende me grace to biwaile my giltes and to studye to the salvacion of my soule, and graunte me grace of verray penitence, confession, and satisfaccion to doon in this present lif, thurgh the benigne grace of him that is king of kinges and preest over alle preestes, that boughte us with the precious blood of his herte, so that I may been oon of hem at the day of doom that shulle be saved. *Qui cum patre et Spiritu Sancto vivit et regnas Deus per omnia saecula. Amen.*

Chaucer's Retraction

Here the author of this book takes his leave

Now I ask all those who hear or read this little treatise that, if there be anything in it that pleases them, they thank our Lord Jesus Christ, from whom all understanding and all goodness derive. And if there be anything that displeases them, I ask them also that they do not attribute it to my lack of skill, and neither to my ill will, since I would much rather have expressed myself better if I had had the skill to do so. For our book (the Bible) says: "All that is written is written for our instruction," and that is my intention. On account of which, I beseech you humbly, for the mercy of God, that you pray for me in order that Christ have mercy upon me and forgive me my sins, and especially my translations and compositions of worldly vanities, which I revoke in my retractions. *The Book of Troilus*; the *Book of Fame*; the *Book of the Twenty Five Ladies*; the *Book of the Duchesse*; the *Book of Saint Valentine's Day Concerning the Parliament of Birds*; the *Canterbury Tales*, those that tend towards sin; the *Book of the Lion*; and many other books, if only I could remember them, and many a song and many an erotic poem: pray that Christ, for his great mercy, forgive me the sin (of having written these). The translation of Boethius' *Consolation of Philosophy*; other books of the lives of saints; homilies; and matter concerned with morality and spiritual devotion: for these I thank our Lord Jesus Christ and his blessed Mother, and all the saints of heaven, beseeching them that from henceforward unto the end of my life they send me grace to weep for my sins and to work for the salvation of my soul. I pray also that they send me the grace of true penitence, confession, and of repayment for my sins in this life here, through the benign grace of him who is king of kings and priest over all priests, who redeemed us with the precious blood of his heart, so that I may be among them who are saved at the Day of Judgement. *Who lives with the Father and the Holy Spirit and you, God, who reign for all eternity. Amen.*

1386–1400

LYRICS AND OCCASIONAL VERSE

Troilus's Song

If no love is, O God, what feele I so?
If love does not exist, Oh God, then what am I feeling?
And if love is, what thing and which is he?
And if it does, then what is its nature?
If love be good, from whennes cometh my wo?
If love should be good, whence comes my pain?
If it be wikke, a wonder thinketh me,
If it be wicked, it amazes me,
5   Whan every torment and adversitee
Since each torment and adversity
That cometh of him may to me savory thinke,
That derives from it may seem delicious to me,
For ay thurste I, the more that ich drinke.
For I always thirst, the more I drink.

And if that at myn owene lust I brenne,
And if I burn in my own desire,
From whennes cometh my wailing and my plainte?
Whence comes my weeping and complaint?
10 If harm agree me, wherto plaine I thenne?
If harm agrees with me, why then should I complain?
I noot, ne why unwery that I fainte.
I don't know, nor why I faint without being weary.
O quikke deeth, O sweete harm so quainte,
Oh living death, oh sweet, strange pain,
How may of thee in me swich quantitee,
How may you exist in me in such quantity,
But if that I consente that it be?
Unless I should consent that it be so?

15 And if that I consente, I wrongfully
And if I should consent, then I wrongfully
Complaine: ywis, thus possed to and fro
Complain; indeed, I am tossed to and fro
All stereless within a boot am I
Within a rudderless boat
Amidde the see, bitwixen windes two,
On the sea, between two winds
That in contrarye stonden everemo.
That evermore stand opposed.
20 Allas, what is this wonder maladye?
Alas, what is this strange disease?
For hoot of cold, for cold of hoot I die.
I die of heat caused by cold, and of cold caused by heat.

Truth

Flee fro the prees and dwelle with soothfastnesse;
Flee from the crowd, and stay with truthfulness;
Suffise unto they thing, though it be smal;
Be content with your goods, even though they be little;
For hoord hath hate, and climbing tikelnesse;
For hoarding causes hatred, and ambitious climbing uncertainty.
Prees hath envye, and wele blent overal.
The ambitious crowd produces envy, and wealth blinds everywhere.
5   Savoure no more than thee bihoove shal;
Relish no more than befits you;
Rule wel thyself that other folk canst rede:
You, who know how to counsel others, govern yourself.
And Trouthe shal delivere, it is no drede.
And Truth/Fidelity shall certainly liberate you.

Tempest thee nought al crooked to redresse
Don't torment yourself to set right all that is wrong
In trust of hire that turneth as a bal;
In trust of her (Fortune) who turns as a ball;
10 Muche wele stant in litel bisinesse;
Much prosperity consists in little activity;
Be war therfore to spurne ayains an al.
Be therefore careful not to kick against a sharp tool.
Strive nat as dooth the crokke with the wal.
Don't strive as does the jug against the wall.
Daunte thyself that dauntest otheres deede:
Master yourself, you who master the deeds of others:
And Trouthe shal delivere, it is no drede.
And Truth/Fidelity shall certainly liberate you.

15 That thee is sent, receive in buxomnesse;
Accept in humility what is given to you;
The wrastling for the world axeth a fal;
Wrestling for this world is asking for a fall;
Here is noon hoom, here nis but wildernesse:
Here is no home, there is nothing here but wilderness.
Forth, pilgrim, forth! Forth, beest, out of thy stal!
Forth, pilgrim, forth! Forth, beast, from your stable!
Know thy countree, looke up, thank God of al.
Look up: know your true country, and thank God for everything.
20 Hold the heigh way and lat thy gost thee lede:
Keep to the main road, and let your spirit to lead you:
And Trouthe shal delivere, it is no drede.
And Truth/Fidelity shall certainly liberate you.

Envoy

Therfore, thou Vache, leve thyn olde wrecchednesse
Therefore, you Vache, give up your old sinfulness;
Unto the world; leve now to be thral.

Give up being a slave to the world.
Crye him mercy that of his heigh goodnesse
Beg Him for mercy, who, of His divine goodness
25   Made thee of nought, and in especial
Created you from nothing, and above all
Draw unto him, and pray in general,
Go towards Him, and pray more generally
For thee and eek for othere, hevenelich meede:
For heavenly reward both for yourself and for others:
And Trouthe shal delivere, it is no drede.
And Truth/Fidelity shall certainly liberate you.

To His Scribe Adam

Adam scrivain, if evere it thee bifalle
Adam Scribe, if you should ever happen
Boece or *Troilus* for to written newe,
To write a new copy of Boethius or Troilus,
Under thy longe lokkes thou moste have the scale,
May you have scurf under your long locks,
But after my making thou write more trewe,
Unless you copy my composing more accurately,
5   So ofte a day I moot thy werk renewe,
So many times a day I must redo your work,
It to correcte and eek to rubbe and scrape:
To correct it and also to erase and scrape away:
And al is thurgh thy negligence and rape.
And all is because of your carelessness and haste.

Complaint to His Purse

To you my purs, and to noon other wight,
To you my purse and to no other person,
Complaine I, for ye be my lady dere.
I complain, for you are my lady dear.
I am so sory, now that ye be light,
I am so sorry now that you are light / fickle,
For certes, but if ye make me hevy cheere,
For certainly, unless you show me a heavy/gloomy look,
5   Me were as life be laid upon my beere;
I'd just as soon be laid on my bier;
For which unto youre mercy thus I crye:
Because of which I beg you for mercy / favor:
Beeth hevy again, or elles moot I die.
Be heavy again or else I must die.

Now voucheth sauf this day er it be night
Now grant, this day before it is night,
That I of you the blisful soun may here,

That I may hear your blissful sound,
10   Or see youre colour, lik the sonne bright,
Or see your color, bright like the sun,
That of yelownesse hadde nevere peere.
Which never had an equal for yellowness.
Ye be my life, ye be myn hertes steere,
You are my life, you are my heart's rudder,
Queene of confort and of good compaignye:
Queen of comfort and of good company:
Beeth hevy, etc.

15   Ye purs, that been to me my lives light
You purse, who to me are the light of my life
And saviour, as in this world down here,
And savior, in this world down here,
Out of this towne helpe me thurgh your might,
Through your might help me get out of this town,
Sith that ye wol nat be my tresorere;
Since you do not want to be my treasurer;

For I am shave as neigh as any frere.
Because I'm shaved as close as any friar.
20   But yit I praye unto youre curteisye:
But still I pray to your courtesy:
Beeth hevy, etc.

Envoy to Henry IV

O conquerour of Brutus Albioun,
O conqueror of Brutus's Albion,
Which that by line and free eleccioun
Who by descent and free election
Been verray king, this song to you I sende:
Are true king, I send you this song:
25   And ye, that mowen alle oure harmes amende,
And you, who may make good all our troubles,
Have minde upon my supplicacioun.
Give heed to my supplication.